UNDERSTANDING
the
Arab-Israeli
Conflict

UNDERSTANDING
the
Arab-Israeli Conflict

WHAT THE HEADLINES HAVEN'T TOLD YOU

MICHAEL RYDELNIK

MOODY PUBLISHERS
CHICAGO

© 2004 by
MICHAEL RYDELNIK

All Scripture quotations, unless otherwise indicated, are taken from the *Holy Bible, New International Version®*. NIV®. Copyright © 1973, 1978, 1984 by International Bible Society. Used by permission of Zondervan Publishing House. All rights reserved.

Scripture quotations marked NASB are taken from the *New American Standard Bible®*, Copyright © The Lockman Foundation 1960, 1962, 1963, 1968, 1971, 1972, 1973, 1975, 1977, 1995. Used by permission.

Library of Congress Cataloging-in-Publication Data

Rydelnik, Michael, 1957-
    Understanding the Arab-Israeli conflict : what the headlines haven't told you / by Michael Rydelnik.
        p. cm.
    Includes bibliographical references.
    ISBN 0-8024-2640-9
    1. Palestine in Christianity. 2. Arab-Israeli conflict—Religious aspects—Christianity. I. Title.

BT93.8.R93 2004
956.04—dc22

2004002725

1 3 5 7 9 10 8 6 4 2

Printed in the United States of America

To my wife, Eva,
my beloved, my friend, my partner,
and my co-laborer in life and ministry,
and who, like the Lord,
"loves the gates of Zion more than all the dwellings of Jacob."
(Psalm 87:2)

Contents

Foreword

What comes to mind when you think of the Middle East? For many, that part of the world produces a kaleidoscope of images and impressions. Scenes from the Bible drift through our consciousness. Abraham. Moses. David. Jesus. But darker images also appear. Angry Palestinians hurling rocks and Molotov cocktails at heavily armed Israeli soldiers. Stunned Israelis carrying the wounded and dead from a bombed-out bus. To most Americans it seems so confusing. Can anyone make sense of the Arab-Israeli conflict?

Thankfully, the answer is yes. My friend and colleague, Dr. Michael Rydelnik, cuts through the confusion and clutter to provide a biblically accurate analysis of the conflict tearing apart God's Promised Land. This is more than just another book on the current Middle East crisis. Michael puts the current crisis in its proper historical and biblical context.

This book will take you on a journey through time. Starting with events that come from the headlines of the evening news, Michael walks the reader back through the history of the Jewish people. Along the way he also introduces you to the Palestinians, and to Islam, and helps you understand the complex relationship between the Israelis and the Palestinians—the two groups who have laid claim to the same land.

You will find this book to be both reliable and readable. Michael has spent years analyzing this often-complex subject. He knows the history. He knows the issues. He knows the Bible. And he has the ability to cut through all the hype and hysteria and identify the bottom-line problems that lie at the heart of the conflict. He writes as he teaches—with clarity and passion.

I challenge you to enter this book as an active student. Read carefully and prayerfully. Take time to underline and highlight key points. And when you are done, you will find yourself better able to make sense of the confusing—and often conflicting—news reports now coming from the Middle East.

JOSEPH M. STOWELL
PRESIDENT, MOODY BIBLE INSTITUTE

Acknowledgments

The book writing process has taught me the truth of Edward Abbey's words, "In order to write a book, it is necessary to sit down (or stand up) and write. Therein lies the difficulty." Therefore, I want to thank the following for their help in getting me to the place of sitting down to write: the administration and faculty of the Moody Bible Institute, which granted me a sabbatical, giving me the time to write; Greg Thornton, executive editor of Moody Publishers, who has always been encouraging, patient, and supportive in this project; James Vincent, general editor at Moody Publishers, whose skill and wisdom are evident throughout, and without whose prodding the book would have been finished at a much later date; and my students at the Moody Bible Institute, whose questions and ideas constantly teach me.

I am also grateful to patient friends who began to wonder, "Whatever became of Michael?" while they waited for me to complete this book.

Finally, a big thanks to my wife, Eva, who was more committed to my completing the book than I was and who also checked every endnote; and to my two sons: Zack, whose confidence in me is always an inspiration, even while he lives away at college; and Seth, whose cheerful optimism and sacrificial attitude about both computer time and "Dad" time made this book a reality.

Terms in the News

Occupied Territories   Refers to land taken from Jordan (the West Bank) and Egypt (Gaza) by Israel during the 1967 Six Day War. Palestinians contend this is their territory in its entirety, while Israel maintains that these areas were never internationally recognized as belonging to Jordan or Egypt so they are "disputed territories."

Settlements/Settlers   Refers to Israeli communities in the disputed territories developed after 1967 in areas where Jewish communities were evacuated in the 1948 Israeli War of Independence. Palestinians contend that these consist of illegal land acquisitions and population transfer, while Israelis argue that they are legal because the land is disputed and no Israeli has ever been forced to live in these areas.

Right of Return	Israelis contend that every Jewish person has a right to return to their ancient homeland, Israel, and therefore have passed "the law of return." Palestinians believe that the Arab refugees who left Israel during the War of Independence have a right to return to their previous homes.
The Green Line	The line that was the border between Israel and Jordan between 1949 and 1967. Since 1967, it has been considered the boundary between Israel proper and the disputed West Bank territories.
Resolution 242	United Nations Security Council resolution passed after the 1967 Six Day War that calls for "withdrawal from territories" as part of a negotiated peace treaty with new "secure and recognized boundaries." Palestinians contend that it requires the return of all the territories taken in the war, while Israel contends that it calls for adjustments to previous boundaries.
Terrorism	Violence against civilians intended to intimidate or coerce them and/or to influence the policy of a government. Palestinians have used various forms of terrorism in an effort to obtain further Israeli concessions. Palestinians claim this is only violent resistance.
Militants/Militancy	Terms that describe Islamic terrorists and terrorist acts. News media frequently use these amoral characterizations in an attempt to avoid judgment of motives.

Security Fence/ Separation Wall

The barrier that Israel is building in the West Bank, along the Green Line. Israel maintains that this is an "antiterrorist" fence, designed to restrict infiltration of terrorists from Palestinian areas. Palestinians contend that this is a land grab intended to establish a new border without negotiations.

Anti-Semitism

A nineteenth-century term coined to describe "hatred of the Jewish people" and does not apply to racism against any other people group, even those speaking "Semitic" languages.

Two-State Solution

The plan to solve the conflict by creating two separate states, one for Israel and one for the Palestinians.

Phased Strategy

Policy of the Palestine Liberation Organization, adopted in 1974, calling for the destruction of Israel through a graduated or "phased" strategy. Obtaining a Palestinian state in the West Bank and Gaza is viewed merely as a step towards the ultimate goal of a Palestinian state encompassing both Palestinian areas and Israel.

The Road Map

The peace plan proposed by "the Quartet" (United States, Russia, the European Union, and the United Nations) after the 2003 U.S. Iraq War, embracing a two-state solution through performance-based phases.

1
The Vanishing Peace

"Peace, peace," they say, when there is no peace.

—Jeremiah 8:11

Rioting erupted on the Temple Mount in Jerusalem on September 29, 2000. Soon the violence spread to the West Bank and the Gaza Strip and even into Israel proper. At the time, it was thought that these disturbances would be settled quickly and Israelis and Palestinians would make a rapid return to the peace table. That did not happen. Instead the fighting escalated from rioting to terrorism and, finally, all-out guerrilla war.

Today television news brings the carnage of terrorism into our homes on almost a daily basis, with images of the dead and the wounded being evacuated from bombed buses, pizzerias, cafes, and hotels. Often those scenes are followed by video of Israeli soldiers and armed Palestinians fighting on the streets of the Holy Land.

How did this outburst of violence develop when just seven years earlier a remarkable peace agreement had been reached?

On September 13, 1993, Yasser Arafat, chairman of the Palestine Liberation Organization (PLO), and Yitzhak Rabin, prime minister of Israel, signed a historic peace accord at the White House.

"Enough of blood and tears. Enough!" Rabin declared in his speech. Then, with a gentle prod from U.S. President Bill Clinton, he shook Arafat's hand. Arafat, who claimed to have sworn off terrorism and to have recognized the state of Israel, promised to lead his people in a democratic government at peace with Israel.

The historic Declaration of Principles, also known as the Oslo Peace Accord, provided for Palestinian autonomy on the West Bank and Gaza and set in motion a new plan for peace and security in Israel. Despite the ups and downs of the peace process, there was a growing expectation that peace would reign in this troubled region.

In July 2000 President Clinton had hosted then–Prime Minister Ehud Barak and PLO Chairman Arafat as they sought to hammer out a final status agreement between Israel and the Palestinian Authority. Now, just two months after those final status talks ended (without an agreement but the stated commitment to continue negotiations), violence erupted once again.

The Oslo accords are dead today, as are multitudes of Israelis and Palestinians. Pitched battles are being fought in the ancient Holy Land and all attempts at mediation seem to have failed. Meanwhile the surrounding states are edging closer to a regional war, and the danger of a potential world war looms. What exactly happened? Why had all attempts at mediation failed to restore the Israelis and Palestinians to the peace process?

Newspapers, journals, cable news networks, and Sunday morning talk shows endlessly discuss these questions but rarely give insight. These three opening chapters will attempt to clarify what has been dubbed the *Al-Aqsa Intifada,* or Intifada II, by looking behind the headlines to the reality of events and their actual causes.[1]

A Shattered Plan: Behind the Intifada

Israeli political leader Ariel Sharon visited the Temple Mount on September 28, surrounded by one thousand Israeli security agents. The next day riots erupted between Palestinians and Israeli troops. Many believe that this violence broke out as a spontaneous response to Sharon's walk on the Temple Mount. Yet the facts do not seem to bear this out. The situation was brewing for months and ready to erupt at any moment. A number of factors came together to set the violence in motion.

The Oslo Slowdown

The first element that led to Intifada II was the slowdown of the Oslo peace process. When the Israeli and Palestinian leaders signed the Oslo accords in 1993, they agreed to take gradual steps over time toward Palestinian autonomy in order for the parties to overcome the years of hostility. They needed to work together in order to become true partners. The Declaration of Principles called for a final status agreement to be made by May 4, 1999. As time passed, it became clear that the final status deadline would not be met.

The previous year, Israel had relinquished administration of 40 percent of the West Bank territory and all of the Gaza Strip to Palestinian Authority oversight. Security cooperation continued between the Israel Defense Forces and the Palestinian Preventative Security Police. Yet Israel was reluctant to proceed much further because of the Palestinian Authority's failure to carry out some of their Oslo commitments. In violation of Oslo, the Palestinian Authority had not revised the Palestinian National Charter, which called for the destruction of Israel, nor had it prevented incitement and hostile propaganda and was not active in systematically fighting terrorist organizations and infrastructure.

According to Dennis Ross, who was the chief U.S. negotiator under the first President Bush and President Clinton, the United States turned a blind eye to serious violations by the Palestinians. According to Ross, the Palestinians had 40,000 troops although Oslo only permitted 30,000, with weapons forbidden by the Oslo accords. Also, when the Palestinian Authority would arrest those engaged in terrorism against Israel, they would frequently release them shortly thereafter.[2]

A case in point was the response of Palestinian police after Israeli Prime Minister Benjamin Netanyahu in 1996 opened an exit to the Hasmonean Tunnel, which runs along the base of the Western Wall of the Temple Mount in Jerusalem. This opening would do no damage to any aspect of the Temple Mount and would merely allow tourists to exit the tunnel without retracing their steps. It would benefit Palestinian shopkeepers as the departing tourists would then pass and most likely frequent their shops. The opening of the tunnel had been negotiated by the previous Labor government and approved by the Palestinian Authority.

When Netanyahu came to office, he proceeded to open the tunnel. Yasser Arafat, leader of the Palestinian Authority, called for protest marches, declaring the tunnel opening a "big crime against our religion and holy places." Although no Muslim holy places were actually threatened by the tunnel opening, Arafat made this charge to incite Palestinian violence. Historian Efraim Karsh has noted the rioting offered Arafat several benefits and concluded, "The tunnel was but a handy pretext that could be disposed of once it had outlived its usefulness (the new exit has remained open since September 1996 to the benefit of tourists and local merchants), with the PA dropping the issue from its agenda after a few months."[3]

After Arafat's call for action, violence ensued for five days, with fifteen Israeli soldiers and sixty Palestinians killed. Most troubling was that Palestinian police, encouraged and authorized by Arafat, turned their weapons on the Israeli police and military which were trying to restore order.

Historian Itamar Rabinovich then described the significance of this action: "For many Israelis it was proof that the Palestinian Authority could not be trusted to be a genuine partner in protecting Israeli security, that Arafat gave his cooperation only so long as his expectations were met, *that if final-status negotiation were deadlocked violence could be expected*" (italics added).[4]

By 1999 most Palestinians were frustrated that a final status agreement, as envisaged by the Oslo accords, was not yet in place. There was a widespread belief among Palestinians that Israel would continue to drag its feet to avoid such an agreement. Israelis, on the other hand, felt compelled to slow the process to wait for Palestinian compliance with Oslo. Although the Israelis did continue to turn land and civil administration over to the Palestinians, they tended to take a more cautious view of their Oslo requirements. Israel showed considerable reluctance regarding the release of land to Palestinians. Also, restrictions of Palestinian commercial freedom continued, along with barriers to Palestinian fishermen spreading their nets in agreed-upon waters.

Nevertheless, by September 2000, the Palestinian Authority had 40 percent of the West Bank and ruled over 98 percent of Palestinians. In exchange for these substantial transfers, Israel had received the mere promise of continued peaceful negotiations. The United States and many Israelis overlooked Palestinian violations of Oslo because they were convinced that they were on the path to peace and they hoped that in time a final peace accord could and would come.

The Election of Ehud Barak

The second factor leading to the outbreak of hostilities was the 1999 election of Ehud Barak as prime minister of Israel. Barak had been the chief of staff of the Israel Defense Forces and was the most decorated soldier in Israeli history. Despite this background as a warrior, Barak was a protégé of Yitzhak Rabin, the assassinated prime minister who had been the

Israeli architect of Oslo. As leader of the left leaning Labor party, Barak was elected on a peace platform. He promised to negotiate and make hard concessions to bring about a final status agreement with the Palestinians. He also promised to resolve the Israeli occupation of southern Lebanon and to make peace with Syria.

Hopes were high in Israel for a final peace settlement for Israel with its Arab neighbors. Nevertheless, the actions taken by the Barak government led not to a peaceful, final status arrangement but an outbreak of violence in less than two years. The reason: Palestinians viewed his commitment to peace as a weakening of Israeli resolve which could be exploited.

Withdrawal from Lebanon

A third factor contributing to the outbreak of violence in September 2000 was the unilateral Israeli withdrawal from Lebanon in May of 2000. Israel had entered Lebanon in 1982 because of the Palestinian terror campaign waged against Israel from bases in Lebanon. Dubbed "Operation Peace for Galilee," the Israeli Defense Forces had sought to clean out the terrorists from that area. They then established a security zone in conjunction with their Christian Maronite allies. This was designed to keep Israeli civilian targets from being shelled by Palestinian terrorists in southern Lebanon. What followed was a long-term guerilla war against the Israel Defense Forces by the Hezbollah, a Lebanese-based Palestinian-Muslim terrorist group sponsored by Iran and Syria. The continuing casualties sustained by Israel made many of its citizens call for the government to get out of the morass of Lebanon. Israel had been assured that the Lebanese army would guarantee security along the border. Therefore, on May 24, 2000, Israel withdrew its military to the border as established by the United Nations.

Hezbollah then claimed that there was still more land that belonged to Lebanon, an area called Shebaa Farms, so its members continued to wage a guerilla terrorist war against Israel. The Lebanese army allowed Hezbollah to take up positions on the border with Israel and continue their attacks.

Rather than interpreting the Israeli withdrawal as a desire for peace, Hezbollah viewed it as a sign of weakness. They boasted that they had defeated the vaunted Israeli army. The Israeli withdrawal gave Palestinian terrorist groups and the Palestinian Authority itself confidence that they could achieve their aims more effectively with terror and violence than with negotiations and compromise. In August 2000 even prior to the outbreak of Temple Mount violence, journalist Khalil Osman wrote in *Crescent International,* the magazine of Global Islam, that Arafat

> has been coming under increasing pressure since the liberation of south Lebanon, which had the effect of a match thrown into the tinderbox of accumulated Palestinian fury. Hezbollah's example has given Palestinians a powerful and attractive contrast, an example worthy of being emulated. In Lebanon, the Islamic resistance's unwavering determination succeeded in bringing about total liberation with no strings attached.[5]

The Palestinians had come to believe that the Israelis comprised a weak and corrupt society that did not have the stomach for continual violence. Thus, terror and violence would be the chosen method of obtaining a Palestinian state.

The Failure of Camp David II

The fourth and most significant cause of the outbreak of hostilities was the breakdown of the peace process at the Camp David II meetings. Israeli Prime Minister Barak and U.S. President Clinton desperately wanted a final peace accord with Yasser Arafat and the Palestinians, each for different reasons. Barak believed that the state of war in which Israel had existed for more than fifty years was sapping the country's strength. Moreover, he believed that continued oversight of Palestinian areas would only serve to incite Palestinians and lead to violence. Therefore, he was committed to a final status agreement even if it required painful Israeli concessions.

Clinton had other reasons for wanting to conclude a final peace agreement between Israel and the Palestinians. Certainly foremost in his mind was that a final peace accord would stabilize the dangerously volatile Middle East. With the United States increasingly dependent on Middle Eastern oil and with dangers presented by dictators (e.g., Saddam Hussein) and extremist governments (e.g., Iran), it was in the U.S.'s strategic interest to foster peace between Israel and the Palestinians.

Additionally, Clinton was facing the end of his term. Potentially, his legacy as president would be chiefly the Monica Lewinsky scandal and his being only the second president ever impeached. Resolving the seemingly endless Arab-Israeli conflict and winning the expected Nobel Peace

Prize as a result would go a long way towards rehabilitating the Clinton presidency. The election of Barak on a peace platform gave President Clinton the opportunity to press for a final status peace conference at the Camp David presidential retreat. Significantly, he chose the location where President Carter had brought Israel's Menachem Begin and Egypt's Anwar el-Sadat together to negotiate a peace treaty between Israel and Egypt more than twenty years earlier.

It seemed that Palestinian leader Arafat would have also desired to reach a final settlement, since he would be negotiating with a moderate Israeli prime minister. He could have expected a far better negotiated settlement from the left-of-center Barak than the previous conservative Israeli Prime Minister Netanyahu. Moreover, since Arafat's ultimate goal was the establishment of a Palestinian state, it appeared that the time was right for reaching a final settlement. Nevertheless, the Palestinian leader was reluctant to come to Camp David and had to be pressured by President Clinton to accept the invitation.

President Clinton convened the conference on July 11, 2000, with Barak, Arafat, and their negotiating teams present. The conference extended beyond the original time allotted to fourteen days of marathon negotiations. Although no official record of the negotiations has been released, participants have leaked the substance of the discussion. Barak moved dramatically from his opening position to accepting most of President Clinton's bridging proposals.

By the end of the two weeks, Barak had agreed to recognize a Palestinian state within the Gaza Strip and almost 95 percent of the West Bank. Barak was willing to give up the Jewish settlements that were in the territory allotted to the Palestinian state. Israel would allow up to 100,000 Palestinian refugees to return to Israel proper for family reunification and would help remunerate other Palestinian refugees for land and homes that they had lost. Barak was also willing to share sovereignty in Jerusalem with the new Palestinian state. In return, he expected Arafat to recognize the end of the conflict with nothing further to negotiate. Although Barak's mentor (Rabin) had been assassinated for offering even less, Barak was willing to risk his life for the sake of peace.

Arafat's position was that Israel should allow all Palestinian refugees the right to return, not just to the new Palestinian state but to Israel proper. He also demanded that Israel withdraw completely to the 1967 borders[6] and transfer sovereignty of the Old City of Jerusalem to the Palestinians.

He tried to convince President Clinton that there was no historical Jewish link to Jerusalem.

Although Prime Minister Barak had moved dramatically from his opening positions, Chairman Arafat refused even to offer a counterproposal. Moreover, it was impossible for Barak to agree to the return of nearly four million Palestinian refugees to Israel proper. Their return would cause such a demographic shift that it would spell the end of the Jewish state. Further, Israelis would never again tolerate Arab control of Jewish holy sites and neighborhoods in the Old City of Jerusalem. When Old Jerusalem was under Arab rule between 1948 and 1967, Arab rulers forbade Jewish people from worshiping at the Western Wall (the outer wall of the ancient holy temple), considered the holiest site in Judaism. Also, Arab rulers had destroyed the Jewish neighborhoods of the Old City and desecrated the ancient Jewish cemetery on the Mount of Olives. Barak moved far but would not concede any further.

Arafat had several reasons for his intransigence. He believed that he had already conceded Israel's right to exist and therefore should not be expected to make any further compromises. Since he believed that Israel existed on land that was part of historic Palestine, he saw no reason to make any further adjustments to the border. Furthermore, Arafat had failed to prepare the Palestinian people for any compromise. He had so frequently promised the Palestinian people that the end result of Oslo would be a Palestinian state within the pre-1967 borders with Jerusalem as its capital that the Palestinians would view any concessions as a defeat. He also knew any shared sovereignty of Jerusalem with the Jewish state would be despised throughout the Muslim world. If Arafat would sign a final peace accord on terms other than his opening position, he risked assassination by Muslim extremists.

The result was that despite marathon negotiations, a final status agreement could not be reached. Furthermore, while not seeking to place blame, in his statements after the summit President Clinton clearly identified Yasser Arafat as the negotiator less willing to compromise. For example, President Clinton said, "Prime Minister Barak showed particular courage, vision, and an understanding of the historical importance of this moment. Chairman Arafat made it clear that he, too, remains committed to the path of peace." In explaining his commendation of Barak, President Clinton added, "I think it is fair to say that at this moment in time, maybe because they had been preparing for it longer, maybe because they had thought through it more, that the prime minister moved forward more from his initial position than Chairman Arafat, on . . . particularly surrounding the questions of Jerusalem." He summarized his praise for Barak by saying,

> My remarks should stand for themselves, because not so much as a criticism of Chairman Arafat, because this is really hard and never been done before, but in praise of Barak. He came there knowing that he was going to have to take bold steps, and he did it. And I think you should look at it more as a positive toward him than as a condemnation of the Palestinian side.[7]

A Prelude to Violence

Doubtless, these comments gave Israel a short-lived public relations bonanza in the eyes of the world, but they also served to embarrass Chairman Arafat publicly. Moreover, it appears that Arafat decided that he had achieved as much as possible through negotiations and that any further Israeli concessions would come as a result of Palestinian violence.

Nearly seven years after the historic Rabin-Arafat handshake at the White House, the stage was set for an outbreak in violence. Prior to going to Camp David, Prime Minister Barak had warned that failure there would likely lead to a violent confrontation. Amazingly, most of the world, including Israel, was then taken by surprise by the outbreak of hostilities that followed less than three months later.

2
Intifada II and the Search for Peace

[We must have] jihad . . . to eliminate Jews from Palestine.

—Ikrina Sabri
Grand mufti of Jerusalem

With one thousand Israeli police officers providing security, the leader of the right-wing opposition Likud party, Ariel Sharon, led a six-member delegation of Likud Knesset (the Israeli parliament) members on September 28, 2000, on an outing. Their destination: the Temple Mount, site of Islam's Dome of the Rock and Al-Aqsa Mosque sitting above, as well as Judaism's Wailing Wall and ancient holy temples (still buried beneath). While on the sacred site, Sharon did not enter any mosques nor did any members of his group or their police escorts. After a one-hour walkabout, they departed.

During their visit to the Temple Mount, there was some scuffling between some one thousand protesters and Israeli police, resulting in injuries to thirty Israeli policemen and four Palestinian protestors. It was not imaginable that within a few hours the entire framework for peace between Israel and the Palestinians would come crashing down.

The Violence Erupts

Within four hours of the visit, Yasser Arafat declared on Voice of Palestine radio that Sharon's visit was "a serious step against Muslim holy places" and demanded that Palestinians "move immediately to stop these aggressions and Israeli practices against holy Jerusalem." Other Palestinian leaders used radio broadcasts to accuse Sharon of defiling the mosques and Israel of desiring to take over the Muslim holy places. The next day, during Friday prayers, the mufti of Jerusalem called for a jihad "to eliminate the Jews from Palestine."

Soon hundreds of Palestinians began to throw large rocks down on Jewish worshipers praying, in preparation for the upcoming Rosh Hashanah holy day, at the Western Wall at the base of the mount. Other Palestinians began to riot and broke through the gate that leads to the Western Wall plaza. Israeli border guards responded by engaging the rioters and opening fire with rubber bullets, killing four Palestinians and wounding more than one hundred.

The following day a riot broke out near a Jewish settlement in the Gaza Strip. Palestinian gunmen and Israeli security forces engaged in a vicious gun battle. Tragically, a twelve-year-old boy, Muhammad al-Dura, was caught in the cross fire and died in his father's arms. The horrifying pictures were seen around the world as television broadcast footage of him being shot and killed, although it was unclear which side fired the bullets that killed the boy.[1] The image of the boy slumping into his father's arms inflamed Palestinians all over the West Bank and Gaza. It also sparked Israeli Arabs to riot in Israel proper, resulting in Israeli police killing thirteen Israeli Arabs. Additionally, Yasser Arafat released terrorists from Palestinian prisons, giving them carte blanche to participate in the new Intifada (uprising).

The Palestinian Authority (PA) claimed that this uprising was a spontaneous burst of anger from the populace, when in truth it was coordinated and promoted by Arafat's government. Beyond releasing its own imprisoned terrorists, the PA had coordinated the assembling of rock piles weeks in advance of the outburst of rage and used its media outlets to call Palestinians to take part in planned violence. The PA also used buses to transport protesters to violent demonstrations in different cities.

Acts of violence and even desecration escalated. Within a week, a small battalion of the Israel Defense Forces that had been guarding Joseph's Tomb in the West Bank town of Nablus withdrew. The Palestinian Authority assured the Israeli government that they would protect this sacred Jewish tomb of Joseph, revered as the traditional burial place of the patriarch who was carried home to Israel after the Exodus. Upon the army's departure, a Palestinian mob destroyed the holy place and its sacred Torah scrolls. Later, Hillel Lieberman, an Israeli of U.S. origin who had gone to protect the ancient Torah scrolls and holy books, was found murdered. That same day, three Israeli soldiers were abducted by Hezbollah as they patrolled the Lebanese border. They were later murdered. For six months, the United Nations withheld videotape of their abduction and denied the existence of the videotape. The UN turned the tape over, but only after they had blurred the faces of the terrorists to prevent Israel from identifying and capturing them.

On October 12, two unarmed Israeli reservists made a wrong turn and found themselves in Ramallah. They were seized, brought to the police station, and then a mob lynched them. A news crew videotaped one of the murderers exultantly raising his bloody hands to the frenzied crowd outside the police station. In the battle for public opinion, these brutal murders caused popular support to swing toward Israel. Israel then notified the Palestinian Authority of their intention to retaliate by destroying that Ramallah police station. They gave warning so that those present in the station could escape.

With the violence getting out of control, the Clinton Administration had dispatched Secretary of State Madeline Albright to Paris to broker a cease-fire. Although Arafat agreed to its terms, his administration continued to incite Palestinians to take up arms against Israel. For example, just two days after agreeing to a cease-fire on October 4, 2000, the PA broadcast called for a "day of rage" on October 6. The PA also used its TV broadcasts to incite the population. In an October 14, 2000, sermon from a Gaza mosque, Ahmad Abu Halabiya, member of the PA-appointed "Fatwa Council" and former acting rector of the Islamic University in Gaza, called upon Palestinians to kill Jews and Americans:

> Have no mercy on the Jews, no matter where they are, in any country. Fight them, wherever you are. Wherever you meet them, kill them. Wherever you are, kill those Jews and those Americans who are like them—and those who stand by them—they are all in one trench, against the Arabs and the Muslims, because they established Israel here, in the beating heart of the Arab world, in Palestine.[2]

At this point, just weeks after the outbreak of the riots, it became clear that the events in Israel were not just a temporary detour on the path to peace but rather a return to war.

The Violence Escalates

While the media consistently described the situation in Israel and the Palestinian territories as "a cycle of violence," thereby maintaining equivalence between the parties, the actions were not necessarily equal. Plainly, the Palestinians initiated violence and Israel retaliated. Were there not Palestinian violence, there would be no Israeli reprisals. Nevertheless, both Palestinians and the state of Israel did indeed use force—the Palestinians engaging in terrorism and Israelis in military reprisals.

Palestinian Violence

On the Palestinian side, what began as violent protests by young men with rocks and militants with gasoline bombs and automatic weapons escalated dramatically. Shortly after the beginning of Intifada II, Palestinian militants began to shoot mortars from the Palestinian village of Beit Jala at Gilo, a suburb of Jerusalem. By November of 2000, Palestinian terrorists began to leave bombs in Jewish neighborhoods, killing and injuring civilians, while causing damage to neighborhoods. Traveling on the highways of Israel became precarious as Palestinian snipers began to shoot drivers randomly.

One particularly tragic shooting was of Shelhevet Pass, a ten-month-old infant brutally murdered by a sniper while in her mother's arms. Other shooters would infiltrate Israeli city streets and open fire on pedestrians, killing and maiming all in their path. On January 17, 2002, a Palestinian shooter killed six and injured thirty when he opened fire at a Bat Mitzvah celebration. Not all the killings were random—Palestinian terrorists also assassinated right-wing Israeli Cabinet member Rehavam Ze'evi, the Israeli Minister of Tourism.

Yet the most horrific turn of events was the advent of a new terror technique: suicide bombing. Packing their bodies with bombs filled with bolts, nails, screws, and rat poison in order to cause maximum damage, these terrorists would blow themselves up in areas crowded with Israelis. During 2001 several gruesome attacks took place. On June 1 a homicidal bomber[3] killed twenty-one young Israelis and wounded more than one hundred others at the Dolphinarium, a beachside disco popular with Israeli teens. On August 9, a homicide bomber killed fifteen people and wounded 130 at a Sbarro Pizza restaurant in downtown Jerusalem. By December these terrorists coordinated their attacks, one killing eleven people and injuring 188 in downtown Jerusalem while another bomber killed fifteen and injured forty on a bus in Haifa in northern Israel. Before too long Israelis became terrified of going to celebrations or even to a local cafe for a cup of coffee.

Suicide murders escalated with the tragic Passover Massacre in early 2002. A suicide bomber entered a hotel crowded with Israelis for the Passover celebration. As they were about to begin the traditional Seder service on this holy day, the bomber detonated the explosives, killing twenty-eight Israelis, including a Holocaust survivor. Scores more were injured.

After nearly seventy suicide bombings, the Israeli cabinet, led by Prime Minister Ariel Sharon, determined to crush the terror that was crippling the nation with fear.

Israeli Retaliation

Following the March 29 Passover Massacre, Israeli troops moved into major Palestinian cities and refugee camps in cities like Nablus and Jenin. The battle in Jenin was fierce, and Israel destroyed ninety-five homes with bulldozers (after warning civilians to leave) to deal with booby-trapped buildings. Afterwards Palestinians claimed that a massacre of three thousand civilians took place, but journalists, human rights groups, and U.S. Secretary of State Colin Powell reported that there was no evidence of a massacre. Independent groups determined that about fifty Palestinians died, the majority armed combatants, compared to twenty-six Israeli deaths in the battle.

President Bush called on Israel to withdraw "without delay," but Israel persisted in its attempt to clear out the terrorist infrastructure. When Israeli troops stormed Arafat's Ramallah compound at the start of the operation, confining him to two rooms, they discovered a number of incriminating documents tying Arafat and the Palestinian Authority to encouraging, organizing, and funding terrorism.

This heightened push to quell Palestinian violence followed almost two years of responding to Palestinian terror with a variety of measures. The Israeli government had moved troops and tanks into areas of fighting and authorized the use of rubber bullets and tear gas on rioting crowds. Additionally, Israeli leaders authorized their troops to use deadly force when their troops' lives were endangered. At times, Israel used helicopter gunships to attack targets in a more precise way, such as the firing of missiles to destroy the Ramallah police station after the lynching of the two

Israeli reservists. With greater frequency, Israel would demolish PA jails and police stations in retaliation for terrorism, usually using bulldozers, tanks, or helicopter gunships but on occasion using F-16 jets.

Israel also established checkpoints throughout the disputed territories to keep Palestinians from traveling to organized violent protests. The terror attacks caused the Jewish nation to use more stringent checkpoints to attempt to block terrorists from making their way into Israel proper. This in turn led to Palestinian protests that they could not move freely, get to their jobs, or have their ambulances get to hospitals in sufficient time because of the checkpoints. Checking ambulances was crucial, because Israel discovered that ambulances were being used to smuggle terrorists, explosives, and weapons.[4] Some Palestinians have made spurious claims that several pregnant women died because Israeli troops at checkpoints kept them from getting to hospitals.

One of the more controversial Israeli responses to the terror was a policy of targeted killings. Initially, Israeli rules of engagement permitted the Israel Defense Forces to kill only terrorists who were actually enroute to carrying out a terror attack. On July 4, 2001, the Israeli security cabinet decided that the IDF could even act against terrorists that were not about to strike. Although human rights organizations labeled these actions "extra-judicial killings," Israel termed them "active self-defense" and justified them by citing laws of armed conflict which prohibit armed combatants to claim immunity or civilian status.

Israel repeatedly gave the PA lists of Palestinians wanted for terrorism and murder only to have the PA ignore their responsibility to arrest them. And when the PA did make arrests, they released those same terrorists shortly afterward; thus, PA prisons became, in effect, no more than revolving doors. Those who were not released were allowed to continue to guide terror operations from their cells.

Another Israeli response to terror was to confine Yasser Arafat to his Ramallah headquarters in December of 2001 after destroying his helicopters. By surrounding his compound with tanks, the IDF initially kept Arafat under virtual house arrest for five months. Arafat claimed that his confinement kept him from taking action against terror. Israel responded by citing his inability to control terror when he had freedom of movement for the previous fifteen months.

The IDF also entered Palestinian refugee camps in March of 2002 in an attempt to break the grip of the terror attacks. After two weeks, the Israeli troops withdrew, but the terror still increased. March became a month of terror with hundreds of Israelis killed and wounded, culminating in the Passover Massacre at the end of the month.

Only six months earlier American citizens had experienced the fear and anguish of terrorism on their own shores when Islamic extremists flew planes into the World Trade Center and the Pentagon. The terrorist attacks of September 11, 2001, created both empathy among Israelis, who watched the TV rebroadcasts in horror, and understanding among Americans of terrorism's terrible toll upon individuals. In President Bush's September 20 speech to the U.S. Congress, he declared war on all terrorism. He defined terrorists as those who actually plan and carry out their murderous acts or those who support and harbor terrorists. Subsequently, the U.S. attacked the Taliban in Afghanistan for supporting and harboring Osama bin Laden and his Al-Qaeda terrorist network. The Israelis maintain that they are the front line against terrorism, as they attempt to root out terrorism in PA-administered territories.

Peace Attempts

An International Peace Summit . . . and Hot Words

As the violence escalated, so did international efforts to halt it, particularly by the United States. At the very outset, President Clinton, Prime Minister Barak, Chairman Arafat, Egyptian President Hosni Mubarak, Jordan's King Abdullah II, UN Secretary General Kofi Annan, and European Union foreign policy chief Javier Solana gathered at a peace summit in Sharm el-Sheik, Egypt, on October 16–17, 2000.

At the conclusion of the summit, President Clinton announced that Barak and Arafat had agreed to a cease-fire. Furthermore, an international fact-finding commission led by former U.S. Senator George Mitchell would be formed to investigate the causes of the violence.

Nevertheless, the cease-fire collapsed almost immediately as Palestinian mobs with gunmen continued to confront Israeli troops. By October 22, Barak announced that Israel would take a "time-out" from the peace process, to which Arafat responded that there would be a Palestinian state with Jerusalem as its capital and if Barak did not like it, he could "go to hell!"[5]

At this point, the violence added terrorist attacks against Israeli civilians to confrontations between Palestinian mobs and Israeli troops. Three bombs exploded in three weeks during November, killing six and wounding dozens, the most severe being a roadside attack on a school bus in the Gaza Strip that killed two Israelis and wounded nine, including five children. On November 28, Barak announced that he would resign as prime minister and call for new elections.

With new elections scheduled for February 6, 2001, further peace negotiations between Palestinians and Israelis took place at the Egyptian sea resort of Taba. Negotiators said that they were making progress with the knowledge that the upcoming election loomed as a referendum on Barak's ability to make peace. Yet when Arafat gave a vitriolic speech calling Israel a fascist nation, Barak called off the discussions. Although the negotiators hoped to resume their meetings after the Israeli election, their hopes were frustrated by the defeat of Barak and the Labor party by the right-wing Likud's leader, Ariel Sharon.

Calls for Another Cease-Fire

The next effort in peacemaking was the issuing on May 21, 2001, of the Mitchell Report, which called for an immediate cease-fire, a cooling-off period, confidence building steps, and a return to political negotiations. Among the fifteen suggestions for building confidence, the Mitchell Report called upon Israel to cease settlement activity in the West Bank and Gaza Strip (though by no means equating building settlements with terrorism) and for the Palestinian Authority "to make clear through concrete action, to Israelis and Palestinians alike, that terror is reprehensible and unacceptable, and the Palestinian Authority is to make a total effort to prevent terrorist operations and to punish perpetrators acting in its jurisdiction."

Both sides officially accepted the Mitchell Report, and Ariel Sharon declared a unilateral Israeli cease-fire on that very day.

In the next twenty days after the Sharon cease-fire announcement, there were over three hundred attacks by Palestinian terrorists. The deadliest was the June 1 suicide bombing at the Dolphinarium disco that killed twenty-one teens. Despite the horror of this attack, Prime Minister Sharon refrained from any military reprisals.

More Calls for a Cease-Fire

In another attempt to bring peace, U.S. CIA director George Tenet announced on June 12, 2001, yet another cease-fire. It called for security cooperation and seven days of quiet, to be followed by an Israeli military pullback from Palestinian areas. The cease-fire went into effect at 3 P.M. on June 13, but within hours Palestinian gunmen shot and killed an Israeli woman near Ofra, an Israeli settlement. Later that day, Palestinians fired mortars on an Israeli army post in the Gaza Strip. The cease-fire never took hold, and for the next nine months there were no days without incident, let alone seven days of quiet. Finally, Prime Minister Sharon gave up on his demand for the seven days of quiet for which the Tenet plan called before a return to political negotiations. This concession on his part led to an increase in further terrorism.

On several occasions, President Bush dispatched a special negotiator, General Anthony Zinni. Each attempt to secure a cease-fire brought an increase in terrorist attacks, returning General Zinni to the United States without securing any agreements.

On December 16, 2001, after a wave of suicide terror attacks against Israeli civilians and under pressure from the international community, Yasser Arafat himself called for a cease-fire. For the next few weeks, relative but not complete quiet prevailed. The calm was broken on January 5, 2002, when Israel captured a Palestinian arms vessel, the *Karine A,* loaded with fifty tons of weapons, including plastic explosives, anti-tank missiles, and rockets. Despite Arafat's initial disavowal of association with the vessel, the evidence was overwhelming. Four days later, Palestinian militants attacked and killed Israeli soldiers in the Gaza Strip, ending the temporary cease-fire. Israel retaliated by destroying homes used by terrorists in the Rafah refugee camp and by carrying out a targeted killing of a leading Palestinian terrorist. So the violence again began to spiral out of control.

A Peace Proposal by Saudi Arabia

Saudi Arabian Crown Prince Abdullah offered yet another plan for peace at an Arab League Summit in March of 2002. He called for Israel to return to the pre-1967 borders and a complete right of return of all Palestinian refugees to Israel proper in exchange for peace and normalization of relations with the Arab world. While many acclaimed this as a significant breakthrough, it was simply a restatement of Arafat's demands at Camp David II. Nevertheless, Prime Minister Sharon said that he would begin direct negotiations based on the Saudi proposal.

The Saudis were unwilling themselves, however, stating that Israel's total acceptance of their proposal was required for any direct negotiations.

It appears that this was not a legitimate proposal for peace but rather an attempt by the Saudis to rehabilitate their image, which had been tarnished following the terrorist attacks on America in 2001. (Fifteen of the nineteen terrorists were Saudi nationals.) Nevertheless, both the U.S. and Israel remained willing to begin negotiations with the Saudi proposal as an opening position.

President Bush dispatched U.S. Secretary of State Colin Powell during Israel's April military action in the Palestinian refugee camps. Powell could not secure any agreement from either party. Arafat refused to denounce terrorism in Arabic, and Israel refused to withdraw immediately. Powell returned to the United States having failed to secure a cease-fire.

An American Call for a Palestinian State

President George W. Bush issued one of the most important statements on the Intifada two months later. Following twin terrorist bombings—one on June 18 that killed nineteen and injured seventy-four on a crowded bus in Jerusalem and a second on June 19 that killed seven at a Jerusalem bus stop—President Bush delayed a major policy statement for several days. Then in a remarkable departure, on June 24 President Bush called for the formation of a provisional Palestinian state to exist beside Israel. No U.S. president had ever made such a commitment. But President Bush also called for the Palestinian Authority to adopt a democratic constitution, hold elections, and establish a leadership not compromised by terror, obviously disqualifying Yasser Arafat.

President Bush had offered a state to the Palestinians but demanded that they reform their government and put an end to terror. Israeli Prime Minister Ariel Sharon, as well as most Israelis, welcomed the initiative, but most Palestinians rejected the offer.

The "Road Map" to Peace

In the ensuing year, the United States went to war to remove Saddam Hussein, the dictator of Iraq. With the completion of major combat operations in the second Gulf War, President Bush turned his attention back to the Israeli-Palestinian conflict. He offered Israel and the Palestinians a plan drafted by the so-called Quartet (the United States, the United Nations, the European Union, and Russia), called the "Road Map." It offered the establishment of a Palestinian state in short order, but it required a new Palestinian leadership to "declare an unequivocal end to violence and terrorism and . . . to arrest, disrupt, and restrain" terrorist groups.

Bowing to international pressure, on April 29, 2003, Yasser Arafat appointed Mahmoud Abbas to the newly formed position of Palestinian prime minister. Both Israelis and Palestinians gave verbal agreement to the Road Map, and Abbas set off to negotiate a cease-fire with terrorist groups. That achieved, Abbas unequivocally rejected carrying out the Road Map demand that the PA deal with terrorism in a decisive way. Just days after a June 4, 2003, summit held in Aqaba, Jordan, with President Bush, Prime Minister Sharon, and Prime Minister Abbas, four Israelis were killed by the terrorists who had supposedly agreed to a cease-fire.

After several weeks of relative quiet, Islamic terrorists sprang into action once again. On a nearly daily basis, Israelis were killed in terror attacks. On several occasions, terrorists were able to murder many Israelis. For example, during two bus attacks in Jerusalem just one month apart, two suicide terrorists killed a combined forty people, including several children, and wounded 236 others. Amazingly, all this occurred during an alleged cease-fire.

The PA's unwillingness to carry out the Road Map's requirement to deal with terror in a forceful way pushed Israel, with President Bush's approval, to pursue the leaders of the Hamas terrorist group. By September 6, 2003, Mahmoud Abbas resigned as PA Prime Minister. Undermined by Arafat and unable to rein in terrorists, he walked away from the seemingly impossible task, with the Road Map in ruins.

Understanding the Cease-Fire Failures

Why is it that every cease-fire attempt thus far has failed? It appears that the Palestinians believe that a cease-fire would not be in their interest but would only favor Israel. After three years of fighting (through year-end 2003), they want to see some tangible benefit to their uprising rather than a mere return to the situation as it was prior to the beginning of the violence.

Israel, on the other hand, refuses to have political negotiations under fire. With the Oslo agreement, the Palestinians had agreed to renounce terrorism and to achieve their objectives only with peaceful negotiations. Israel believes negotiating under fire would simply reward terrorism and threaten all future peace negotiations. They fear that Palestinians would resort to terror any time they did not succeed at negotiations—thus, the impasse.

Although it seems impossible to find a way to peace, it is possible to understand the causes and escalation of the violence. That is the purpose of the next chapter.

3
Understanding Intifada II

The Sharon visit did not cause the Al-Aksa Intifada.

—The Mitchell Commission report

Imagine watching a cable news show. The anchor man, hair in perfect order, is interviewing a representative of the government of Israel about a suicide bombing. The articulate spokesperson seems to make perfect sense in explaining the conflict as the product of Palestinian terrorism. The anchor, after thanking the Israeli for participating on the show, says, "Now we turn to a Palestinian Authority spokesperson for a Palestinian perspective on the violence." This person also seems to argue clearly and passionately that it is the Israeli government that provokes violence.

How can we understand all the arguments and counterarguments in the dispute? Is it possible to distinguish between truth and propaganda? This chapter will attempt to do so.

The Cause of Intifada II

Did Ariel Sharon's Temple Mount Visit Cause Intifada II?

To understand Intifada II, it's necessary to identify what caused it to erupt. As noted in chapter 1, it is far too simplistic to believe that Ariel Sharon's visit to the Temple Mount spurred a spontaneous violent response that spiraled out of control. In truth, Sharon's stroll, though ill advised, was not the cause of the violence. To begin with, the Israeli government cleared Sharon's visit in advance with Palestinian Preventative Security Service Chief Jibril Rajoub. Rajoub had assured the Israelis that if Sharon did not attempt to enter any mosque, his visit would pose no problem to the Palestinians.[1] The entire visit was videotaped by journalists, and the tape shows conclusively that Sharon made no effort to enter any mosque. After investigating the cause of the violence, the Mitchell Commission reported categorically, "The Sharon visit did not cause the Al-Aksa Intifada."

Why did Sharon want to go to the Temple Mount, thereby creating a pretense for violence, and why would the Israeli government permit him to go? The answer is that in reality, the Sharon Temple Mount visit was not directed at the Palestinians but rather was part of an internal political dispute within Israel. The then–Prime Minister Barak had offered partial sovereignty over the Temple Mount to the Palestinians the previous July. Ariel Sharon, as the opposition leader, wanted to show his disagreement with the Barak offer. He was being pressed on his right by the former prime minister and rival for party leadership, Benjamin Netanyahu. Sharon wanted to position himself not only as opposed to Barak's plan but also as sufficiently conservative to continue leading his party rather than let them turn to Netanyahu. The prime minister did not seek to dissuade Sharon's visit because he felt that appearing soft on Jerusalem would cause political problems for himself. Thus, the Israeli political leadership, with an amazing lack of foresight, viewed the Sharon Temple Mount visit entirely as an internal political matter and not a threat in any way to the Palestinians.[2]

So if the Sharon visit was only a pretense for violence, what was the actual cause of the outbreak of the Intifada?

The True Cause

In chapter 1, we traced the roots of the hostility to four factors: the Oslo slowdown, Barak's election, Israeli withdrawal from Lebanon, and the failure of Camp David II. These were all key contributing factors to a setting ripe for conflict. But the primary cause rested with the Palestinian Authority's strategy. It appears that the Palestinian Authority planned the violence as far back as the breakdown of the final status talks in July of 2000. The Palestinian Authority daily newspaper *Al-Ayyam* confirmed this when it reported in its December 6, 2000, edition:

Speaking at a symposium in Gaza, Palestinian Minister of Communications Imad el-Falouji confirmed the Palestinian Authority had begun preparations for the outbreak of the current intifada from the moment the Camp David talks concluded, this in accordance with instructions given by Chairman Arafat himself. Mr. Falouji went on to state that Arafat launched this intifada as a culminating state to the immutable Palestinian stance in the negotiations, and was not meant merely as a protest of Israeli opposition leader Ariel Sharon's visit to the Temple Mount.[3]

The minister said the Intifada "had been planned since Chairman Arafat's return from Camp David, when he turned the tables on the former U.S. president and rejected the American conditions."[4] In short, the PA and its leader planned the Intifada as an alternative to a peaceful settlement when Arafat saw that he could not achieve all his objectives through negotiations.

Two Other Theories of Why Intifada II Erupted

Although it should be clear that Sharon's visit to the Temple Mount did not cause the uprising, two other causes are often suggested. Each represents a flawed theory.

The first is *the Israeli "occupation" caused the Intifada.* Palestinians frequently claim that the Israeli occupation of the West Bank and the Gaza Strip incited the violence: The terror will stop if the Israelis end the occupation. Yet in July of 2000 that was exactly what Ehud Barak was trying to do. Some pundits have even said that Arafat could not take yes for an answer. If the occupation was the cause of the Intifada, then the occupation could have ended without violence had Arafat accepted the Clinton bridging proposals.

Another reason that it is doubtful that the occupation caused Palestinian terrorism is that there were thousands of Palestinian terrorist attacks between 1948–67, prior to any Israeli occupation. For example, in 1952, there were about three thousand incidents of cross-border violence,[5] extending from the malicious destruction of property to the brutal murder of civilians. During the five years ending in 1955, 503 Israelis were killed by Arab terrorists infiltrating from Jordan, 358 were killed in terrorist attacks from Egypt, and 61 were killed in terrorist attacks originating from Syria and Lebanon. It is wrong to blame terrorism on the occupation, since

Palestinian terrorism existed before the occupation—and even before the existence of Israel as a state.

Notice that the Israeli-Palestinian conflict and the formation of the Palestine Liberation Organization both predate the occupation. In 1947, when the UN partitioned Palestine into a Jewish state and a Palestinian one, the Arabs rejected the plan. Instead Jordan annexed the West Bank and Egypt took the Gaza Strip. They could easily have created a Palestinian state, but they refused. At that time, the Palestinian objection was not the occupation of the West Bank and Gaza (an Israeli occupation there did not exist) but rather the existence of the Jewish state. This remains the problem. Plainly, groups like Hamas and Islamic Jihad reject Israel completely. They do not seek a Palestinian state next to Israel but in place of Israel.

Yasser Arafat and the Palestinian Authority do claim to accept a two-state solution (Israel and the creation of a state of Palestine) but only on Arafat's terms. These include the right of return to Israel for all Palestinian refugees or their descendants. However, if Israel would allow millions of Palestinian refugees to come to Israel proper, it would result in the destruction of Israel as a Jewish state and the creation of one new state of Palestine consisting of the West Bank, the Gaza Strip, and Israel proper. Therefore, Arafat and the PA have the same goal as the other groups, the end of the state of Israel. In light of these factors, it is erroneous to blame the occupation for the current outbreak of violence.

The second theory is *the building of Israeli settlements on the West Bank caused the Intifada.* Since 1967, Israel has built approximately 150 communities there, with about 200,000 Israeli citizens. Frequently, Palestinians claim that these Israeli settlements are "illegal" and therefore have caused the violence. Yet nothing in the Oslo Peace Accord prohibited the settlements. The Mitchell Report did indeed call for a freeze on settlements but only as one of fifteen confidence building measures. Nevertheless, Senator Mitchell and fellow committee member Warren Rudman in a clarification letter stated explicitly: "We want to go further and make it clear that we do not in any way equate Palestinian terrorism with Israeli settlement activity, 'seemingly' or otherwise."[6]

The Palestinian objection to the settlements is based on the assumption that Israeli settlements are foreign elements in the West Bank and Gaza, which previously had been solely populated by Palestinian Arabs. Yet that territory was never part of a Palestinian state. In fact, Jewish settlement always existed in those areas, with ancient Jewish population centers driven out when the territories were captured by Jordan and Egypt in the Israeli War of Independence of 1948.

As to the legality of the settlements, various scholars have argued that they are in fact lawful. International legal scholar Stephen Schwebel maintains that a country, acting in self-defense, may seize and occupy territory.[7] Also, Eugene Rostow, former undersecretary of state for political affairs in the Johnson Administration, has affirmed that "the Jewish right of settlement in the area is equivalent in every way to the right of the local population to live there."[8]

Despite the legality of the Jewish settlements, Prime Minister Barak was willing to dismantle the vast majority of the settlements in exchange for a final peace agreement. In fact, the Israeli general who carried out the removal of the settlements as part of the Israel-Egypt peace treaty was current Prime Minister Ariel Sharon. If Arafat had been serious in his desire to make peace, it would have spelled the end of the vast majority of settlements.

Despite this, many Israelis believe that expansion of the settlements, although legal, is not in Israel's best interest. They support a complete freeze in settlements as a show of good faith and a desire to bring Palestinians to the negotiating table, as well as to end criticism by many in the world community. By year-end 2003, Prime Minister Sharon's government had built thirty-five new settlements since he came to office. Nevertheless, it is unfair to attribute the violence to the existence of Israeli settlements since Palestinians could have ended all settlement activity by agreeing to peace.

The Bottom Line

So what caused the violence? Simply put, the violence was a planned attempt to achieve political goals by force. As noted under "The True Cause" above, Yasser Arafat planned the Intifada after the final status talks did not yield a Palestinian state on all of Arafat's terms. Rather than negotiate a compromise, Arafat was determined to launch a war. He did this with the intended goals of turning world opinion to the Palestinian cause and driving Israel to even greater concessions in exchange for ending the violence.

It is for this reason that two American journalists, left-wing columnist Thomas Friedman and right-wing columnist George Will, have both labeled Intifada II, "Arafat's War."

The Israeli Use of Force

While agreeing that Israel did not cause the violence, some have argued that the Israeli use of disproportionate force in response has escalated the Palestinian violence. Media images of Palestinian teens hurling rocks at heavily armed Israeli troops gave the perception that Israel was Goliath to the Palestinian David. Furthermore, after eighteen months of Intifada II, Palestinian casualties outnumber Israeli ones by three to one.

Greater Force in Response to Greater Terrorism

Israelis have responded to the charge of excessive force by arguing that the initial violence was not as commonly portrayed. Along with rocks, Palestinians threw gasoline bombs and fired automatic weapons. Palestinians soon were carrying out terrorist activities such as armed ambushes, car bombings, and suicide killings, causing Israeli troops to respond with greater force. Palestinians then desired to extract as much world sympathy for their losses as possible, in order to internationalize the conflict and bring in outside forces to keep peace. This would have given a distinct advantage to Palestinian terrorists. Peacekeeping troops would not be able to stop terrorist attacks but would prohibit Israeli military responses. Therefore, the Israeli government continues to oppose the imposition of outside forces.

The strongest example of Israeli force was the Operation Defensive Shield military action that followed the Passover Massacre. This was the largest Israeli military operation in twenty years. Advancing into major West Bank cities, Israeli troops fought door-to-door to arrest or kill terrorists and destroy terrorist infrastructure. Although President Bush called for an Israeli withdrawal "without delay," the Israeli government persisted until completing the operation a month later. Even President Bush's own Republican political base opposed his demand, finding it difficult to condemn Israel's pursuit of terrorism in light of U.S. actions in Afghanistan. Israelis feel justified in their action, citing the dramatic decrease in Palestinian terrorism following the campaign.

Casualties on Both Sides

As is to be expected in an armed conflict, there continues to be casualties on both sides, unfortunately including civilians. Palestinian casualties remain higher because of the skill and effectiveness of Israeli troops. Battles are between Palestinian armed militias and the highly trained and supplied Israel Defense Forces. Nevertheless, one distinction remains: Palestinian terrorists intend to kill as many civilians as possible, whereas Israeli troops do their utmost, even endangering themselves, to limit civilian Palestinian casualties.

It is not possible to identify the aggressor in an armed conflict by assuming that the one with the fewer casualties is responsible. The U.S. military had dramatically fewer casualties than Iraq in the Gulf War; nevertheless, it is plain that the Iraqis were the aggressors. Even during World War II, the United States sustained 295,000 fatalities, compared to Japan's 1.8 million and Germany's 7 million, nearly half civilian. Plainly, the aggressors had far greater casualties. On this basis, the excessive and disproportionate force argument lacks merit.

The Players in the Conflict

Discussions of Intifada II not only revolve around the causes of the conflict and the Israeli use of force, but the alleged personal feud between Prime Minister Ariel Sharon and Palestinian Authority Chairman Yasser Arafat. This is a case of the media attempting to "personalize" the story. Sharon is one of the most hated men in the Arab world as Arafat is among Israelis and Jewish people. Both groups blame the other leader for the violence.

To understand the motives of each leader, we need to know the background and training of each man. We also need to know the backgrounds and philosophies of a third set of players: the terrorist groups that support the Palestinian cause.

Ariel Sharon

Ariel Sharon was a highly decorated and successful general who turned to politics. As defense minister in the 1982 war in Lebanon, Sharon allowed Israel's Christian Phalangist allies into Palestinian refugee camps where they carried out massacres. Upon hearing of the massacres, Sharon sent Israeli troops to stop the bloodshed. An Israeli investigation found that Sharon did not order or carry out the massacres, yet it declared him "indirectly responsible" for not anticipating the violence. As a result, he stepped out of the government for a short time and also became notorious among Palestinians. Although Sharon did not actually commit any atrocities, Palestinians have claimed that he was indeed directly responsible for them.

Sharon has been a leader in conservative Israeli politics and has been associated with the movement of settlers into the West Bank. He has moderated his positions in that today he does claim to want to see the establishment of a democratic Palestinian state.

Sharon has created a number of furors with some impolitic statements. For example, at one point he told an interviewer that he regretted that he allowed Yasser Arafat to escape when he was cornered in Lebanon in 1982. He has also said that negotiations with Palestinians will only succeed when there are sufficient Palestinian casualties to force the Palestinians to the table.

In spite of all this, it is unfair to characterize Intifada II as Sharon's war. Clearly, the violence was planned by the Palestinians following the collapse of peace talks, two months before Sharon took a walk on the Temple Mount. Also, the constantly increasing violence during Ehud Barak's tenure as prime minister led Barak to call for the new elections that brought Sharon to office. It is more accurate to say that Palestinian violence brought Sharon to office rather than Sharon brought the violence.

Yasser Arafat

Egyptian-born Yasser Arafat became chairman of the Palestine Liberation Organization in 1967. An avowed terrorist, he was the first person to address the United Nations with a revolver at his side. He masterminded the airline terrorism of the 1970s and gave the order to kill American diplomats. He oversaw terrorist acts against Israel,[9] such as the slaughter of eleven Israeli athletes at the 1972 Munich Olympics and twenty Israeli schoolchildren in 1974.

His later disavowal of terrorism and signing of the Oslo accords made him a partner in peace with Israel. However, Intifada II, the current uprising, marked the return of Arafat to violence and terrorism. Arafat claims that the violence is spontaneous and that terrorism is carried out by terrorist groups that he does not control. Yet when Israel captured the *Karine A* terror ship, they learned the captain and crew members were members of the Palestinian naval police. Moreover, the PA was paying for the illegal arms on the ship. Further, when Israel entered Arafat's Ramallah compound in April 2002, they discovered vast documentation of Arafat himself funding the terror operations against Israel.

Beyond these smoking guns is Arafat's tie to the most deadly of Palestinian terror groups operating during March 2000, the Al-Aqsa Martyrs Brigade. This group is part of the larger Fatah movement, an organization led directly by Arafat. Although he might claim that Hamas or Islamic Jihad are beyond his control (unlikely since PA funds go to these groups as well), he does exercise control over the Force 17 Presidential Guard, the Tanzim, and the Fatah-led Al-Aqsa Martyrs. (See "Palestinian Terror Groups" beginning on page 48 for more on these groups.)

Despite his association with terrorism, Arafat consistently claims to desire peace. In an opinion piece published in the *New York Times* entitled "The Palestinian Vision of Peace," he condemned terrorism and claimed that "Palestinians are ready to end the conflict."[10] However, only one week before the *Times* printed his vision of peace, Arafat gave a fiery speech in Arabic at a rally in Ramallah, vowing "We will make the lives of the infidels Hell!" calling for "Jihad, Jihad, Jihad" and "a million martyrs marching on Jerusalem."[11]

Clearly Arafat uses the word "martyrs" to refer to the suicidal terrorists who murder as many innocent civilians as possible. Moreover, Arafat habitually adjusts his message depending on the audience he is addressing and the language he is speaking.

For these reasons, President George Bush has said that Arafat has not earned his trust and the Israeli government has declared Arafat "irrelevant."

The Terrorist Organizations

A third player in the conflict is the group of terrorist organizations that support the creation of a Palestinian state and the demise of the nation of Israel. Their means to achieve those goals are acts of physical terror that take human life in the cause of jihad.

The chart on the next two pages lists alphabetically the ten terrorist groups currently active. Notice that the Palestinian Authority, a governmental authority, is actually considered a terrorist entity by many.

The Role of the Media

Indirectly, a fourth player has shaped Intifada II: the news media. From the very outset of the Palestinian uprising, the media has served to frame public opinion. First, television news networks repeatedly showed the

PALESTINIAN TERROR GROUPS

NAME	DESCRIPTION

Al-Aqsa Martyrs — An affiliation of West Bank terror groups under the authority of Arafat's Fatah movement. It is devoted to Palestinian nationalism rather than political Islam. It has been carrying out terrorist operations since the outbreak of Intifada II.

Fatah — Terrorist group founded in Kuwait and led by Yasser Arafat. It is the largest faction within the PLO and officially renounced terror as part of the Oslo Peace Accord. Fatah has actively participated in terror during Intifada II both in the disputed territories and Israel proper. The word "Fatah" is a reverse acronym for the Arabic "conquest by means of jihad."

Force 17 — Force 17 is security apparatus for Yasser Arafat and the Palestinian Authority. It has 3,500 members and has engaged in terror attacks against Israelis throughout Intifada II.

Hamas — Also known as Islamic Resistance Movement, Hamas formed in 1987 as the Palestinian outgrowth of the Muslim Brotherhood. It receives its funding from Arab countries and Palestinian expatriates. Committed to the destruction of Israel, Hamas carries out terror operations in Israel proper, the disputed territories, and Jordan as well as against Palestinians suspected of collaboration with Israel. Besides its terrorism, it also has an extensive social services division for Palestinian people.

Hezbollah — Also known as the Party of God, it is a radical Shiite Muslim group based in southern Lebanon and funded by Syria and Iran. Initially devoted to driving Israeli troops out of Lebanon, it now engages in terror for the destruction of Israel.

Palestine Islamic Jihad

A militant Islamic terrorist group committed to the destruction of Israel and the establishment of an Islamic Palestinian state. PIJ carries out terrorist actions in Israel proper and the disputed territories. It is also anti-American and opposed to moderate Arab governments.

Palestine Liberation Organization (PLO)

The umbrella organization of Palestinian terrorist groups established in 1964 and led by Yasser Arafat since 1967. The PLO's official rejection of terror and recognition of Israel led to the Oslo accords. Groups within the PLO continue to sponsor and carry out terror attacks against Israel.

Palestinian Authority

The autonomous government of the Palestinians established with the Oslo accords. The PA has not been officially designated a terrorist entity by the United States, but its sponsoring of terrorist groups has led Israel to treat it as such.

Popular Front for the Liberation of Palestine

A Marxist-Leninist terrorist group that is supported by Syria and Libya. It advocates Pan-Arab Marxist revolution, the destruction of Israel, and the establishment of a Palestinian Marxist Arab state. It suspended its participation with the PLO because of its opposition to the Oslo accords.

Tanzim

The armed wing of Fatah and has a twofold function. It is a paramilitary, informal, unofficial "Palestinian army" that engages the Israeli military and carries out terrorist attacks without officially breaking signed agreements with Israel. It is also a Fatah militia to rival radical Islamic groups which oppose Arafat's negotiations with Israel. Marwan Barghouti led the Tanzim in the West Bank until his arrest during the Israeli Operation Defensive Shield.

heartbreaking video of young Mohammad al-Dura being caught in a cross-fire resulting in his death in his father's arms, prompting sympathy for the Palestinian uprising. Then they played the graphic videos of the lynching of two unarmed Israeli reservists in a Palestinian police station, leading to support of Israel's defense against terrorism.

The first major cry of media bias emerged when newspapers across the country ran a photo of a teenager, blood dripping from his head, standing under the imposing figure of an Israeli policeman with a club in his hands. The caption read: "An Israeli policeman and a Palestinian on the Temple Mount." After the photo ran in the *New York Times*, the boy's father wrote to the *Times* with this surprising revelation:

> Regarding your picture on page A-5 of the Israeli soldier and the Palestinian on the Temple Mount—that Palestinian is actually my son, Tuvia Grossman, a Jewish student from Chicago. He, and two of his friends, were pulled from their taxicab while traveling in Jerusalem, by a mob of Palestinian Arabs, and were severely beaten and stabbed.
>
> That picture could not have been taken on the Temple Mount because there are no gas stations on the Temple Mount and certainly none with Hebrew lettering, like the one clearly seen behind the Israeli soldier attempting to protect my son from the mob.

Tuvia Grossman and Media Bias

The *Times'* correction only stated that the young man in the picture was "an American student in Israel," failing to identify him as a Jew beaten by an Arab mob. It then said that the picture was taken in the Old City of Jerusalem, when in fact it was taken in an Arab neighborhood of Jerusalem. Only after public outrage did the *Times* reprint the picture with the correct caption and a story about the near lynching of Tuvia Grossman, the young American Jewish student. He would have been killed were it not for the intervention by the Israeli police officer, who stood over him and guarded him with his club.

The picture of Tuvia Grossman has become a symbol of the media bias in reporting the events of this Intifada. It appears that the reporting of events consistently shows a media skewered in order to defend Palestinian violence. First and foremost, media bias is seen in its moral equivalency in depicting death: It portrays unintentional civilian deaths in military operations by the Israel Defense Forces as equally heinous to the deliberate murder of civilians by Palestinian terrorists. Also, moral equivalency is evident in numerous sympathetic human interest stories of suicide killers as opposed to their victims.

Missing Context, Biased Terms, Limited Understanding

A second major form of bias has been in the failure to provide context for news. For example, when reporting on Israeli reprisals, frequently the terrorist act that prompted the retaliation is absent in the report. Israelis frequently objected to media reports on Operation Defensive Shield without mentioning the month of terror, culminating in the Passover Massacre, that preceded it.

Another evidence of bias is in the very terminology that the news outlets use to describe events. For example, calling members of terrorist groups "militants" as opposed to "terrorists" distorts the events which are being reported and legitimizes terrorism. Also, characterizing Yasser Arafat as "leader of the Palestinian people" while calling Ariel Sharon the "right-wing leader" of Israel distorts that Sharon is the duly elected prime minister.

Most egregious is the news media's failure to understand the history of the Arab-Israeli conflict. Thus reporters and analysts cannot accurately weigh both sides' claims and counterclaims. Apparently, the more effective the propaganda, the more gullible reporters become.

In addition, the need to report stories before the facts become clear leads to distortion of reality. For example, newspapers, particularly in Europe, reported that an Israeli massacre of Palestinians took place in Jenin during Operation Defensive Shield, when in fact, there was no massacre at all—as accurately reported in one headline in the *Washington Post,* "Jenin Camp Is a Scene of Devastation but Yields No Evidence of Massacre."[12] At the same time U.S. Secretary of State Colin Powell told Congress he had no evidence of an Israeli massacre at the Jenin refugee camp.[13] "There is simply no evidence of a massacre," reported Peter Bouckaert, a senior researcher of the Human Rights Watch.[14] Only a handful of international media got the facts right.[15]

Joshua Muravchik, a scholar at the Washington Institute for Near East Policy, calls the trend to report information as "facts" before evaluating the information "systematic" and warns:

The quality of the information provided by the two sides in this conflict is highly asymmetrical. By this I mean simply that the Palestinians repeatedly lie. It starts with Arafat and goes down to his many deputies. It seems even to reach to doctors in Palestinian hospitals and to many subjects of apparently man-in-the-street interviews.[16]

It is the media's skewered perspectives and lack of context that demands a deeper look at the events that dominate the news and threaten the world's peace. Newspaper readers and television viewers cannot understand the Intifada and the Arab-Israeli conflict unless they read behind the headlines and hear beyond the rhetoric to get the actual facts. The rest of this book will give the historical background, political insight, and biblical information helpful to understand the ongoing Arab-Israeli conflict.

4

The Land of Israel:
From Roman to British Rule

Palestine sits in sackcloth and ashes.

—Mark Twain
The Innocents Abroad

To Christians, Israel is "the land where Jesus walked" two thousand years
ago. But two millennia before the birth of Jesus, the Jewish people lived
in the land that would become today's Israel. The descendants of Abraham, Isaac, and Jacob—who was renamed Israel—governed themselves
both before and after the Assyrian and Babylonian captivities.

After the Romans began their domination of the land, Jewish people
twice fought for their independence, but both revolts failed. The first (A.D.
66–73) saw the destruction of Jerusalem and the second Jewish temple
in A.D. 70. The second (A.D. 132–35) also ended in failure, with the Romans banishing Jews from Jerusalem, renaming the city *Aelia Capitolina,*
and building a pagan temple on the site where the Jewish temple had
stood.

Those two wars brought massive Jewish casualties, both military and
civilian, and further scattered many Jewish people around the world. But
what of the land of Israel? What happened to it between the Jewish revolts and the modern period? This chapter will survey the history of the
land during this period.

Roman Rule (A.D. 135–313)

After the Romans defeated the Jewish rebels in the second Jewish revolt, they attempted to sever the Jewish connection with the land of Israel. In addition to renaming Jerusalem and banning Jewish people from that city, they also renamed Judea *Syria Palestina*, after the ancient Philistines who had inhabited the coastland of Israel. Nevertheless, there was a rapid recovery of the Jewish population.

As a result of the Roman ban on Jews living in Jerusalem, Galilee became the center of Jewish life. The Sanhedrin (the assembly of Jewish leaders) reconvened in Tiberias. A *nasi* (prince) was appointed to lead the Jewish people both in the land of Israel and in the Diaspora. Despite initial economic hardship, the Jewish community in Galilee was reinforced by returning exiles.

By the third century, the Romans began to ignore their ban on Jerusalem, so Jewish people returned to their holy city. Archeological remains of synagogues in sites at Capernaum, Korazin, Bar'am, and Gamla, as well as others, have demonstrated a continuing and vital Jewish presence throughout the land. During this period, Rabbinic law was codified in the Mishnah under Judah Ha-Nasi (Judah the Prince). By the beginning of the fourth century, there was a significant Jewish population and economic growth.[1]

Byzantine Rule (313–636)

Byzantine rule began as a continuation of Roman control when Emperor Constantine left Rome and established his capital in Byzantium (renamed Constantinople). When Constantine converted to Christianity and made it the religion of the Byzantine Empire, the majority of the population of the land of Israel also became Christian. Constantine's mother, Helena, identified alleged holy sites and churches were built in Jerusalem, Bethlehem, and Galilee. Also, monasteries were established around the country. Constantine and later his son Constantius enacted restrictive legislation, including prohibiting Jews from owning non-Jewish slaves, proselytizing non-Jews, and marrying Christian women.

Nevertheless, a significant population of Jewish people remained in the land. Julian the Apostate's (360–63) ascension to the throne brought new opportunities for Jewish people. Julian wanted to restore Jewish Jerusalem and even offered to rebuild the holy temple. But Julian's reign was short, and after his death the government undertook even greater official persecution of the Jews than had existed before Julian. In the late fourth century, the Theodosian Code was established, making its anti-Jewish laws part of the area's jurisprudence.

In 614, the Jewish population supported the Persian invasion of the land. The Persians showed their appreciation of the Jewish aid by giving them the administration of Jerusalem. However, this lasted for a mere three years. When the Byzantines recaptured Jerusalem, they expelled the Jewish populace from their holy city once again. Nonetheless, the entire Byzantine period saw a significant Jewish presence in the land, so much so that the Talmud of the land of Israel was completed and codified in Galilee by the fifth century.

Arab Rule (636–1099)

The Islamic conquest of the land of Israel began a period of thirteen hundred years of continued foreign rule by various empires and governments. The Arabs, who began their conquest from Arabia, were the first of these rulers. The Arab caliphs ruled the land of Israel for four hundred years, first from Damascus, then Baghdad, and finally Egypt. (See Appendix I for key dates in Islamic history.) For the first three centuries, the Omayyad Dynasty, based in Damascus, governed as military rulers and did not establish an Arab population in the land of Israel.

By the third century of the Muslim era, Syrians, Mesopotamians, and Persians began to profess Islam, primarily because of the social advantages that conversion obtained. These multiethnic converts then moved to the land of Israel and began to spread Islam and the Arabic language to the local population. Although the local population in Palestine became known as Arabs, this was more of a linguistic identification than an ethnic one.

Initially, with the Muslim conquest, Jewish life in the land of Israel improved. Muslims granted Jewish people a measure of protection as a people of the Book. Additionally, Jewish people were required to pay special taxes. In exchange, Muslims leaders gave Jewish people security for their property and their lives, as well as freedom of religion.

However, by the eighth century, restrictions against Jews were introduced, which included heavy taxes, abridgement of rights, change in legal status, and limitations of religious observances. Jewish people moved to towns and became artisans, while scribes known as Masoretes worked on the biblical text in Tiberias. There was also a considerable Jewish population in Jerusalem, consisting of Rabbinic scholars and Karaites, a sect that did not recognize rabbinic authority. By the tenth century, 300,000 Jewish people lived in the land of Israel. Muslim authorities continued to persecute the Jewish community, leading to a decline in size in the eleventh century, with a loss of organizational and religious cohesiveness.

The Crusader Period (1099–1291)

Following an appeal by Pope Urban II to recover the Holy Land from the Muslims, Crusaders captured Jerusalem in July of 1099 and massacred the non-Christian population. As Jewish people attempted to defend their quarter, they were either burnt to death or sold into slavery. The Jewish population dropped dramatically: When Benjamin of Tudela, a Jewish traveler, arrived in Jerusalem in 1167, he found only one thousand Jewish families in the land.

The Crusaders extended their rule throughout the country through bloody military battles and occasionally through treaties. The Crusaders established the Latin kingdom of Jerusalem but governed only as a military ruling minority located primarily in cities and castles and not in outlying villages or rural areas.

As the Crusaders settled in the Holy Land, pilgrims arrived from Europe. Increasingly, Jewish people sought to return to their land. When Saladin, a Kurdish officer from Iraq who had become the sultan of Egypt, defeated the Crusaders (1187), he restored Muslim fortunes in the Holy Land. Ultimately, he repelled the third Crusade and reached an accord with Richard I of England that allowed the Christians to have a presence in the land with a network of fortified castles.

Saladin called for Jews the world over to settle in the land of Israel and granted them a measure of freedom. This led to significant Jewish population growth in the land, primarily in the city of Acre. At the same time, Jerusalem's Jewish population continued its decline. Crusader rule came to a complete end in 1291 when they were defeated by the Mamluks, a Muslim military class that had come to power in Egypt.

Mamluk Rule (1291–1516)

The Mamluks feared Crusaders returning by sea, so they destroyed the seaports of Jaffa and Akko, which hampered trade with Europe. Before too long, the land of Israel became a desolate province, governed from Damascus. The cities became ruins, Jerusalem was deserted, and the small Jewish community lived in abject poverty. The few people that remained in the land also experienced plagues, locust invasions, and earthquakes. By the end of the Middle Ages, as Mamluk rule came to an end, the Holy Land had become a devastated and dismal place, a far cry from the land of milk and honey described in the Bible.

Ottoman Rule (1517–1917)

Ottoman Turks defeated the Mamluks so that by 1517 their empire included Egypt, Syria, Iraq, western Arabia, and the land of Israel. The Turks adopted a tolerant attitude toward the Jews, leading to a Jewish return to the land. Jewish people, having been expelled from Spain, settled throughout the country, but especially in Jerusalem, Hebron, Tiberias, and Safad. With approximately 10,000 Jews, Safad became a center of Jewish mysticism.

At the outset, the Ottoman Empire was characterized by more efficient administration. Governing from Istanbul, the Turks attached the land of Israel to the province of Damascus and divided it into four districts. After the death of Ottoman Sultan Suleyman the Magnificent (Suleyman I, 1566), the land began to languish once again. The Ottomans viewed Palestine merely as a source of revenue and imposed oppressive taxes. Once again, Jewish people took flight, so that there were only about seven thousand living there by the end of the seventeenth century. By the end of the eighteenth century the land was owned by absentee landlords living in Damascus, Beirut, and Cairo, who leased it to destitute tenant farmers, who were heavily taxed. To avoid paying a tree tax that the Ottomans imposed, many of the trees were cut down, shaving the land of its forests. The agriculturally rich land became swampy in the north and desert in the south.

By 1800, the total population of Palestine was less than 300,000, of which 25,000 were Christian and 5,000 Jewish. In the nineteenth century, Europe began to take an interest in the land once again. British, French, and American scholars established schools of biblical archeology. The opening of the Suez Canal accelerated the land's usefulness as a crossroads for commerce. Merchant ships began to travel between Palestine and Europe, postal and telegraphic connections were established, and a road was built between Jerusalem and Jaffa. In 1840, the Jewish population had doubled, and by 1856 there were 17,000 Jews in the land.

By the middle of the nineteenth century, enough Jews had returned to cause overcrowding in the old city of Jerusalem. As a result, in 1860, Jews built the first neighborhood outside the city walls. In the next twenty years, seven more neighborhoods were established outside the walls forming the beginnings of the new city of Jerusalem. By 1880, 25,000 Jews lived in the land, and the city of Jerusalem had a Jewish majority, consisting almost entirely of ultra-orthodox Jews. Most lived on charity and spent their days studying ancient texts and praying. As the Ottoman Empire weakened in the nineteenth century, Europe developed a growing attention to the ancient land of Israel.

Conditions in the Nineteenth Century

The nineteenth century saw the beginning of Jewish interest in a large-scale return to the land. Many were shocked at the plight of their ancient homeland. In what condition was the land?

First, *Palestine was a land in waste.* "Its canal and irrigation systems were destroyed and the wondrous fertility of which the Bible spoke vanished into desert and desolation. . . . Under the Ottoman empire of the Turks, the policy of defoliation continued; the hillsides were denuded of trees and the valleys robbed of their topsoil."[2] Pilgrim after pilgrim described the land as ruined, dilapidated, and barren.[3] According to Peters, an 1827 German encyclopedia described Palestine as "desolate and roamed through by Arab bands of robbers."[4]

Second, *Palestine had become a depopulated area.* Not only was the land devoid of trees, plants, and agriculture, it also had few people. The British consul in Palestine reported in 1857 that "the country is in a considerable degree empty of inhabitants and therefore its greatest need is that of a body of population."[5] Writing of his 1867 visit to the Holy Land, Mark Twain described the depopulated nature of the Jezreel valley: "There is not a solitary village throughout its whole extent—not for thirty miles in either direction. There are two or three small clusters of Bedouin tents, but not a single permanent habitation. One may ride ten miles hereabouts and not see ten human beings."[6]

Twain described the land in tragic tones in *The Innocents Abroad.* He concluded his section on Palestine with these melancholy observations:

> Palestine sits in sackcloth and ashes. Over it broods the spell of a
> curse that has withered its fields and fettered its energies. . . . Nazareth

is forlorn; about the ford of Jordan where the hosts of Israel entered the Promised Land with songs of rejoicing, one finds only a squalid camp of fantastic Bedouins of the desert; Jericho the accursed lies a moldering ruin today, even as Joshua's miracle left it more than three thousand years ago; Bethlehem and Bethany, in their poverty and their humiliation, have nothing about them now to remind one that they once knew the high honor of the Saviour's presence; the hallowed spot where the shepherds watched their flocks by night, and where the angels sang, "Peace on earth, good will to men," is untenanted by any living creature and unblessed by any feature that is pleasant to the eye. Renowned Jerusalem itself, the stateliest name in history, has lost all its ancient grandeur and became a pauper village. . . . The noted Sea of Galilee, where Roman fleets once rode at anchor and the disciples of the Saviour sailed in their ships, was long ago deserted by the devotees of war and commerce, and its borders are a silent wilderness; Capernaum is a shapeless ruin; Magdala is the home of beggared Arabs; Bethsaida and Chorazin have vanished from the earth, and the "desert places" round about them, where thousands of men once listened to the Saviour's voice and ate the miraculous bread, sleep in the hush of a solitude that is inhabited only by birds of prey and skulking foxes.

    Palestine is desolate and unlovely. . . . Palestine is no more of this workday world. It is sacred to poetry and tradition—it is dreamland.[7]

After years of neglect and isolation, a land that once sustained millions, Palestine by 1882 had shrunk to 260,000 Arabs and 25,000 Jews.[8]

    A third characteristic of the land was that it was *an ethnic melting pot*. Although the predominant population was considered Arab, that was more of a linguistic definition than an ethnic one. After the Arab conquest, various people groups entered the land and became part of the population. In *From Time Immemorial,* Joan Peters wrote, "Among the peoples who have been counted as 'indigenous Palestinian Arabs' are Balkans, Greeks, Syrians, Latins, Egyptians, Turks, Armenians, Italians, Persians, Kurds, Germans, Afghans, Circassians, Bosnians, Sudanese, Samaritans, Algerians, Motawila, and Tartars."[9] She cited the *Encyclopaedia Britannica* (1911 edition) as describing the population of Palestine as composed of a widely differing group of inhabitants with no less than fifty languages. For this reason, the encyclopedia stated, "It is no easy task to write concisely . . . on the ethnology of Palestine."[10]

    Thus, an official British historical analysis published in 1920 stated that the people living west of the Jordan "are not Arabs, but only Arabic speaking," and are of "mixed race."[11]

A fourth characteristic of nineteenth-century Palestine was that *it consisted of a migratory population.* For centuries, the Muslim inhabitants of Palestine consisted of immigrants and peasants who had originated in other lands. Throughout the nineteenth century, Muslims from Egypt and Turkey, Algerians from Damascus, Kurds, and Berbers all settled in Palestine.[12] The immigrants would be exploited by oppressive landowners or corrupt Turkish government officials, and they in turn would prey upon the oppressed Jewish population. It has been deduced that 25 percent of the Muslim population present in 1882 had arrived only after 1831.[13]

By the close of the nineteenth century, Palestine had not had an indigenous government since the fall of the Jewish commonwealth in A.D. 73. Instead, it had been ruled for two thousand years by foreign, imperial governments. The land was barren, inhabited by a migratory, mixed population. More than anything, it needed people who would once again cultivate and build it. The time appeared ripe for the Jewish people to return to their ancient homeland.

5
The Return to Zion

My heart is in the East, and I in the depths of the West.
My food has no taste. How can it be sweet?
How can I fulfil my pledges and my vows,
When Zion is in the power of Edom, and I in the fetters of Arabia?
It will be nothing to me to leave all the goodness of Spain.
So rich will it be to see the dust of the ruined sanctuary.

—Judah Halevy
Jewish poet (from *Odes to Zion*)

The enduring link between the Jewish people and the land of Israel could not be obliterated by exile and dispersion. During the first exile in Babylon, the psalmist wrote, "If I forget you, O Jerusalem, may my right hand forget its skill. May my tongue cling to the roof of my mouth if I do not remember you, if I do not consider Jerusalem my highest joy" (Psalm 137:5–6). More than a thousand years later, medieval Jewish poet Judah Halevy wrote *Odes to Zion* and reminded the world that though he lived in the West, his heart was in the East.

Clearly the Jewish people refused to forget their ancestral homeland. During the long years of Diaspora, oppression, and persecution at the hands of the Gentiles, the Jewish longing to return to the land of Israel was expressed with prayers and pilgrimages and the promise that Messiah would one day regather all the Jewish people to Zion.

This spiritual longing to return was given realism and practicality with the onset of modern times and the rebirth of Jewish nationalism. This chapter tells the story of how longing became reality with the Jewish return to Zion.

The Meaning of Zionism

Before launching into the story of the regathering, we must understand one very important term: *Zionism*. The word and belief have been maligned as racist and redefined as extremist. What does Zionism actually mean?

Some Definitions

Simply put, Zionism, a term coined by Nathan Birnbaum in 1890, is Jewish nationalism.

According to the *Encyclopaedia Britannica*, Zionism is the "Jewish nationalist movement that has had as its goal the creation and support of a Jewish national state in Palestine, the ancient homeland of the Jews (Hebrew: *Eretz Yisra'el*, 'the Land of Israel')."[1] Originating in eastern and central Europe in the latter part of the nineteenth century, in many ways the movement continues the ancient nationalist attachment of the Jews and of the Jewish religion to the land of Israel, where one of the hills of Jerusalem was called Zion. Hence, the term "Zionism."

At the first Zionist congress, it was declared that "Zionism seeks to secure for the Jewish people a publicly recognized, legally secured home in Palestine." I would propose a more modern definition of Zionism: the belief that the Jewish people rightfully have an autonomous state in their ancient homeland.

Misconception About Zionism

These three definitions clarify three serious misconceptions about Zionism. First, it is erroneously alleged that Zionism is a colonial movement and not a national one. Zionism was never about colonizing. Colonialism refers to the oppression and exploitation of an indigenous population. Zionist settlers strove to be farmers and laborers, to sustain their lives by their own work. As Emir Feisal wrote in 1919 to Harvard professor and future Supreme Court Justice Felix Frankfurter,

> The Arabs, especially the educated among us, look with deepest sympathy on the Zionist movement. . . . We will wish the Jews a hearty welcome home. . . . We are working together for a reformed and revised Near East and our two movements complete one another. The Jewish movement is nationalist and not imperialist.[2]

Zionism is primarily a national liberation movement that contends that Jewish people, like people of any other nation, are entitled to a homeland.

A second misconception is that Zionism is imperialistic and seeks to conquer Arab territory. If that were true, the people of Israel would have never returned the Sinai Peninsula to Egypt in exchange for peace in 1979, or offered the return of the Golan Heights to Syria in exchange for a full peace agreement. Nor would they have offered all of Gaza and 97 percent of the West Bank to the Palestinians in exchange for a final peace agreement. Israeli governments have consistently been willing to give the tangible asset of land in exchange for mere promises of peace.

Yet a third error about Zionism is that it is racist and hateful of Arabs. The United Nations, led by the Union of Soviet Socialist Republics and the Arab states, passed a resolution in 1975 (repealed in 1991) claiming that Zionism is "a form of racism and racial discrimination."[3] Israel's democratic society is evident in its one million Arab citizens who have more freedom than Arabs in any other Arab country. The Zionist state of Israel has been scrupulous in protecting the religious, civil, and political rights of all Christians and Muslims in the state. To identify Jewish self-determination exclusively as racist is in reality anti-Semitic. American civil rights attorney Alan Dershowitz rebuked those in the international community who have termed Zionism racist, arguing, "A world that closed its doors to Jews who sought escape from Hitler's ovens lacks the moral standing to complain about Israel's giving preference to Jews."[4]

With this proper understanding of Zionism, we can now return to the story of the Jewish quest to return to Zion.

The Precursors to Zionism

Treatment in Europe and Russia

In the mid- to late nineteenth century, the dispersed Jewish community figured prominently in the rise of Zionism. In central and western Europe, Jewish people had been emancipated. After centuries of persecution, oppression, and violence in Christian Europe, by 1871 Jewish people had been granted citizenship in the emerging democracies of the West. Even European monarchies were influenced by this liberalizing trend, thereby enabling Jewish people to break with the restrictions and limitations of the ghetto. As a result, Jewish people began to assimilate into the dominant European cultures around them.

In eastern Europe, conditions for the Jewish people remained depressed, however. And in Russia they tried to cope with anti-Semitic peasants, grinding poverty, and the czarist government's oppressive policies. The government forced Jewish people to live within a prescribed area within Russia (called the Pale of Settlement), and mandated that Jewish boys be conscripted into the czarist military at age ten for twenty-five-year terms. Jewish communities regularly encountered the violence of *pogroms*, government-sponsored riots against the Jews. Jewish people were assaulted, raped, and murdered in brutal fashion.

Thus, in the East, the harsh conditions were destroying the Jewish people themselves; in the West, freedom and emancipation were destroying Jewish identity and culture. It was in this context that the idea of a return to Zion germinated.

Calls from Orthodox Jews

Two Orthodox rabbis from distinctly different backgrounds each rejected the traditional doctrine that Jewish people were not to force a return to the land then called Palestine. The first was Judah Alkalai (1798–1878), a Sephardic (Mediterranean) rabbi from Semlin, a town near Belgrade. The false blood libel charge[5] against the Jews of Damascus in 1840 convinced Alkalai that the only hope for the Jewish people was a return to a politically independent land of Israel. He reasoned that a Jewish presence in the land was a necessary precondition to redemption by the Messiah. Since it appeared in Scripture that Messiah would come to the Jews in Zion, by logical extension Alkalai argued that Jews must be present in Zion when Messiah came.

Alkalai called for diplomacy by Jewish notables to achieve this end, as well as financial backing, agricultural settlements by Jewish people, and a national organization to represent Jewish claims. He even called for the revival of Hebrew as a secular language (as opposed to its status at the time as solely a holy language of prayer and study).

Shortly thereafter, another Orthodox rabbi, Zvi Hirsch Kalischer (1795–1874), from an Ashkenazic (European) background, began to promote similar ideas, without any knowledge of Alkalai's works. Writing from Posen, Poland, Kalischer argued that messianic redemption must begin by natural means. His point was that the Messiah would not bring a Jewish return to the land of Israel; rather a Jewish return would precipitate the coming of the Messiah.

Kalischer's plan was almost identical to Alkalai's, calling for the immediate agricultural settlement of the land of Israel. Although visionary in their approaches, both Alkalai and Kalischer were virtually ignored by the Jewish world.

Calls from Secular Jews

Besides these proposals from religious Jewry, secular Jews also put forward prescient ideas of return to the land. Moses Hess (1812–75), a former close associate of Karl Marx, became upset with the parlor anti-Semitism of Paris. He read Kalischer and began to investigate nationalism. In 1862, Hess wrote *Rome and Jerusalem,* a tract that used Italian patriot Giuseppe Mazzini and Italian nationalism as the model for the Jewish people. With his Jewish identity reawakened after twenty years of dormancy, Hess called for a return to the land of Israel because he believed assimilation would not succeed in overcoming hatred of the Jews. His book called for wealthy Jews to finance Jewish agricultural settlements, while prominent Jews were to engage in diplomacy to achieve international recognition of the Jewish return. The impact of this book was negligible. Two hundred copies of *Rome and Jerusalem* sold in five years.

Yet another secular Jewish voice was Leon Pinsker (1821–91), an assimilated Jewish physician from Odessa. He was shocked by the pogroms of 1881 and became convinced that Judeophobia was indestructible as long as Jews were guests throughout the world. Therefore, he wrote *Auto-Emancipation,* calling Jews to emancipate themselves by becoming a proper nation with their own territory. His plan called for a National Jewish Congress to organize these aspirations and for wealthy European Jews to fund agricultural settlements in the land. Although repudiated by most Jewish people, Pinsker became a leader of the fledgling Lovers of Zion movement originating in Russia.

Other Calls and the First Settlements

The *Hovevei Zion* (Lovers of Zion) were societies in eastern Europe that believed that a return to the land of Israel was the only hope for Jewish people to survive in a world filled with anti-Jewish hatred. In 1882, seven thousand society members succeeded in establishing the earliest agricultural settlements in Ottoman (Turkish) controlled Palestine. In the same year, an organization called BILU[6] also began to establish agricultural settlements. With Russian persecution increasing between 1881 and 1903, many Russian Jews sought to escape by immigrating to the United States.

But a small minority, some 25,000 people, instead settled in the land of Israel. This first immigration wave, known in Hebrew as an *aliyah* (literally *ascent*), was difficult and did not see much agricultural success. The settlers would not even have been able to stay were it not for the philanthropy of Baron Edmonde de Rothschild of France, who became known throughout the settlements as "our well-known benefactor." Another struggle facing these *Chalutzim* (Hebrew-pioneers) was that as secular Jewish immigrants (called the new *Yishuv* or new settlers), they encountered conflict with religious Jewish people already living in the land (called the old Yishuv or old settlers).

Despite these difficulties, one remarkable accomplishment of the first *aliyah* was the resurgence of Hebrew as a modern spoken language. Eliezer Ben-Yehuda, the father of modern Hebrew, developed the first modern Hebrew dictionary and would not permit his son to speak any language other than Hebrew. This radical approach kept the boy from speaking at all until four years of age, but ultimately, the lad became the first native Hebrew speaker in the land of Israel. Before long, all the new Yishuv were speaking Hebrew. They, in turn, organized new schools, where children began to study secular subjects in Hebrew.

Despite the hardships of these first settlers, in the midst of the first *aliyah*, events arose that made Zionism and its aspirations known around the world. These revolve around an urbane assimilated Jew: Theodore Herzl.

Theodore Herzl and the Birth of Zionism

Theodore Herzl (1860–1904), coming from a wealthy, "enlightened" Budapest Jewish family, had his bar mitzvah in a Reform temple. He received his doctor of laws degree at age twenty-four and always envisioned making a name for himself in German letters. By age thirty-one, Herzl reached the apogee of his professional and financial ambitions when he became the Paris correspondent of the leading Viennese newspaper *Neue Freie Press*. Herzl was successful, cosmopolitan, and above all, assimilated and withdrawn from any Jewish identity.

Herzl's life took a radical turn in 1894 when he covered the treason trial of the French Jewish Captain Alfred Dreyfus. Charged with selling French military secrets to the Germans, Dreyfus was framed, convicted, and sent to Devils Island. When it became apparent that Dreyfus was innocent, the French military, motivated by anti-Semitism and a desire to save face, refused to exonerate him. During his trial, crowds roamed the streets of Paris, crying, "Death to the Jews!"

That this could occur in liberal France, the seat of Jewish emancipation and freedom, devastated and transformed Herzl. He wrote *The Jewish State* (1896) which called for the return of the Jewish people to their historic homeland as the only solution to anti-Semitism.

The World Zionist Organization and Herzl's Diplomacy

Herzl formed the World Zionist Organization (by this time the Hovevei Zion groups had almost entirely disintegrated) to represent Jewish interests for a state. Herzl also convened the World Zionist Congress in Basel, Switzerland, in 1897. There he wrote in his journal, "In Basel, I founded the Jewish state!" He anticipated that within fifty years a revived Jewish state would exist in what was then known as Palestine.

Relying on his powerful and persuasive personality, Herzl undertook diplomatic efforts with world leaders to obtain a charter for Jewish settlement in the land of Israel. He obtained audiences with the sultan of the Ottoman Empire, Kaiser Wilhelm of Germany; Vyacheslav Von Plehve, the interior minister of the czar; and Joseph Chamberlain, the British colonial secretary, as well as other British officials. Regularly he reminded Zionist congresses of the ultimate goal of obtaining a charter for the Jewish people in the land of Israel. At one point, he considered a British proposal to grant the Zionists a charter in Uganda, but the British offer was never serious and the World Zionists overwhelmingly rejected it. Zionism was forever tied to the land of Israel.

Herzl's Impact

Theodore Herzl put Zionism on the map. Viewed as a king by the masses of eastern European Jewry, hated as an assimilationist by Orthodox rabbis, suspected as a threat by Western secularized Jewish leaders, Herzl became the embodiment of the return to Zion. Chaim Weizmann, who became the leader of the Zionist movement shortly after Herzl's death and also the first president of the state of Israel, captured the impact of Herzl's book, and also of his personality, when he wrote,

> It was an utterance which came like a bolt from the blue. . . . Fundamentally, *The Jewish State* contained not a single new idea for us. . . .

Not the ideas, but the personality which stood behind them appealed to us. Here was daring, clarity, and energy. The very fact that the Westerner came to us unencumbered by our own preconceptions had its appeal. We were right in our instinctive appreciation that what had emerged from *Judenstaat* was less a concept than a historic personality.[7]

The Second *Aliyah*

Herzl's efforts reinvigorated the first *aliyah* but it took an onslaught of anti-Semitism to motivate a second wave of immigration. State-sponsored attacks against Jews took place on April 6–7, 1903, in the capital of Moldova, under czarist rule. Mobs in Kishinev murdered forty-nine Jews, injured five hundred, and destroyed seven hundred homes; six hundred businesses were looted. Another pogrom on October 19–20, 1905, left nineteen Jews dead and fifty-six injured. These terrifying attacks impelled many Jews to flee Russian rule for the United States. But some chose to go to Israel, causing the second *aliyah* (1905–14). Future Israeli leaders David Ben-Gurion (Israel's first prime minister) and Yitzchak Ben Zvi (Israel's second president) came to the land of Israel during this time.

Another significant immigrant was A. D. Gordon, who entered from the Ukraine, under czarist rule. A lifelong bureaucrat, Gordon arrived in the land at age forty-seven and articulated a philosophy of labor that influenced other Jewish settlers. Called *Avodah Ivrit* ("Hebrew labor"), his philosophy called upon Jews to work the soil themselves rather than employing others. His goal was to restore the land to usefulness through Jewish sweat and tears.

The immigrants of the second *aliyah* did the backbreaking work of draining swamps in the Galilee and irrigating and reforesting the barren areas of Judah. Embracing socialist ideals, the pioneers formed *kibbutzim* (communal settlements) based on strict equality and communal property. These settlements, purchased at exorbitant prices from Arab landowners, became the key to Jewish expansion, unity, and defense.

Another 40,000 Jewish people arrived during this period. With Hebrew firmly rooted as the language of the settlers, Hebrew newspapers and periodicals began to flourish. The future for Zionist growth was hopeful despite Turkish reluctance to support the new movement. But World War I would bring drastic change to the Middle East generally and to the Zionist enterprise specifically.

The Balfour Declaration

World War I disrupted the return of Jews to the land, since the Ottoman Turks were suspicious of the Jewish settlers. The Turks made life difficult for them, and many left the country. Additionally, food shortages produced starvation, causing the death of some of the old yishuv while 12,000 settlers fled the area. When the situation was bleakest for the Zionists, British interests in the region would dramatically change their fortune.

Governing Authority for Britain

The British long wanted control of Palestine to provide a buffer zone to protect the Suez Canal in Egypt. In 1916, they made the secret Sykes-Picot agreement with France, delineating what the spheres of influence in the Middle East would be after the war. From this agreement, it appeared that Palestine would be divided between the two empires. But Great Britain's stronger desire was to exclude France completely from Palestine, so they continued to seek other ways to gain complete control of the Holy Land.

As the fighting persisted, Great Britain issued the Balfour Declaration on November 2, 1917, as a means of gaining governing authority in all of Palestine. This private letter from Arthur Balfour, British foreign secretary to Lord Rothschild, affirmed the policy of the British government as approved by the cabinet, stating,

> His Majesty's Government views with favour the establishment in Palestine of a national home for the Jewish people, and will use their best endeavours to facilitate the achievement of this object, it being clearly understood that nothing shall be done which may prejudice the civil and religious rights of existing non-Jewish communities in Palestine or the rights and political status enjoyed by Jews in another country.[8]

Self-Determination for the Jews

The British issued the Balfour Declaration for a variety of reasons. First, they believed in national self-determination. By creating a Jewish national home for Jewish people in Palestine, for the first time in nearly two thousand years Jewish people would determine their own destiny and not be beholden to the graciousness of host countries for their survival.

Also, the British felt a sense of gratitude to Chaim Weizmann, a scientist and leader of the Zionist movement. His development of synthetic acetone for the British war effort and then his effective lobbying of Arthur Balfour led to their recognition of Jewish claims to the land.[9]

Additionally, the British were motivated by political self-interest. They hoped that American Jewish support for the Balfour Declaration would influence the United States to enter the war on the British side. However, their estimate of Jewish influence at the State Department was greatly mistaken.

Finally, some British leaders were influenced by their own faith in the Scriptures. While certainly hoping to alleviate the suffering of the Jewish people, particularly those in Russia, more important to governmental leaders like Prime Minister Lloyd George and Foreign Secretary Balfour was their understanding of the biblical promises God made to the Jewish patriarchs Abraham, Isaac, and Jacob, as well as the prophecies concerning a Jewish return to Zion.[10] In fact, many others in Great Britain and around the world saw the regathering as the beginnings of prophecy being fulfilled. As Jewish people returned to their ancient homeland they found support among Bible believers such as William Blackstone and even D. L. Moody. As Barbara W. Tuchman points out, "For Balfour, the motive was Biblical rather than imperial."[11]

Prelude to a National Home in Palestine

British forces, under T. E. Lawrence (the famed Lawrence of Arabia) in the south and General Allenby in Jerusalem, conquered Palestine and sought recognition of the empire's authority there. After the war, the Balfour Declaration was accepted by the League of Nations; on September 23, 1922, the League formalized the British Mandate for Palestine—granting temporary authority until the people of Palestine could become self-governing. The intent was to create a Jewish national home in Palestine, and the League of Nations incorporated the very words of the Balfour Declaration into the commission to the British. (See Map 1.)

Now the Zionist movement had international recognition of its aims, and the British permission to govern Palestine was sanctioned only if Britain would facilitate them.

Map 1
GREAT BRITAIN'S DIVISION
OF THE MANDATED AREA

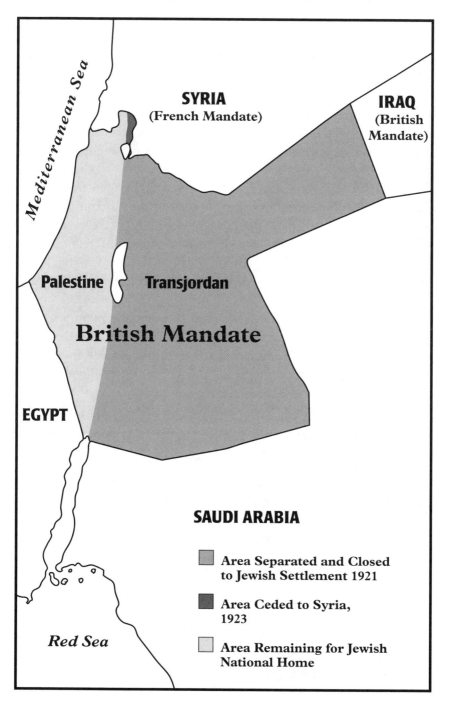

Mediterranean Sea

SYRIA
(French Mandate)

IRAQ
(British
Mandate)

Palestine **Transjordan**

British Mandate

EGYPT

SAUDI ARABIA

Area Separated and Closed
to Jewish Settlement 1921

Area Ceded to Syria,
1923

Area Remaining for Jewish
National Home

Red Sea

The Mandate Years

The Zionist movement now had sanction for a Jewish homeland. The British Mandate led almost immediately to a third *aliyah*. These immigrants were still fleeing Russia, but now, instead of czarist persecution, communist oppression motivated them. More than 40,000 Jewish people arrived between 1919–23, with many moving to new cities, such as Tel Aviv, rather than to agricultural settlements.

Arabs Express Opposition

The Arabs strongly opposed Jewish immigration. They claimed that the British had made counterpromises of political independence in the McMahon-Hussein correspondence. This letter, written in 1915, from Sir Henry McMahon, British high commissioner of Egypt, to Hussein Ibn Ali, Sherif of Mecca, promised British support for the restoration of the caliphate if the Arabs would support the British war effort against Turkey. McMahon did not mention Palestine by name but specifically excluded it from Arab control when he wrote that the "portions of Syria lying to the west of the districts of Damascus, Horns, Hama and Aleppo cannot be said to be purely Arab, and should be excluded from the limits demanded."[12] This awkward description was used in an effort to be more precise than in using the word "Palestine," an area that was southern Syria under the Turks and included both sides of the Jordan River when the mandate began.

Winston Churchill clearly understood that exception when in 1922, speaking as colonial secretary, he argued that "the whole of Palestine west of the Jordan was thus excluded from Sir Henry McMahon's pledge."[13] McMahon himself made this clear in a 1937 letter to the *London Times*, writing, "It was not intended by me in giving this pledge to King Hussein to include Palestine in the area in which Arab independence was promised."[14]

Arabs Act Against Immigrants

The Arabs also used violence to express their opposition to Jewish immigration. As early as 1919, Arab agitator Haj Amin el-Husseini provoked riots against Jewish settlers. He also began to demand that Great Britain place restrictions on Jewish immigration to Palestine while refusing any negotiations with Jewish people.

In an attempt to appease the Arabs, Churchill, the colonial secretary, issued a white paper (a statement of British policy) in 1922 diminishing the promises of the Balfour Declaration but recognizing that Jewish people were "in Palestine as of right and not on sufferance."[15] Nevertheless, he did restrict Jewish immigration to the "economic absorptive capacity" of the country.

Churchill named Haj Amin el-Husseini, the agitator of the violence, mufti of Jerusalem. He also lopped off the entire eastern half of Palestine, beyond the Jordan River, and created a new Arab kingdom of Transjordan, decreasing the area for Jewish immigration dramatically. Fifteen years later, however, the 1937 Peel Commission, appointed by the British government, would report that "the field in which the Jewish national home was to be established was understood, at the time of the Balfour Declaration, to be the whole of historic Palestine, including Transjordan."[16] But Churchill's action now allotted 80 percent of the proposed Jewish national home to become an Arab kingdom—and to be off-limits to Jewish immigration.

Still Jewish people continued to immigrate to Palestine. The fourth *aliyah* (1924–28) brought about 70,000 more, mostly shopkeepers and artisans from Poland, where they had experienced significant economic persecution. Under the mandate, the Jewish national home was taking shape as Jews, by this time, had formed a self-governing national council and an underground self-defense organization.

As more Jewish people arrived, Arab violence escalated. In August 1929, the mufti charged that the Jews desired to take over the Al-Aqsa mosque on the Temple Mount. Riots broke out around the country, and the British authorities made little effort to restrain the Arab rioters. After six days, 135 Jews were killed and nearly 350 wounded. The ancient Jewish community of Hebron had sixty-seven of its citizens murdered, and the rest were forced to abandon their homes and flee to Jerusalem.

The British established the Shaw Commission of Inquiry to investigate the causes of the violence. They decided that the Arab masses rioted because they feared economic displacement by Jewish immigrants. They called for a slowing and then an eventual halt to all Jewish land purchases.

As a result of the Shaw Report, the British government issued the Passfield White Paper of 1930, essentially ending all Jewish immigration and repudiating the Balfour Declaration. So great was the protest in Parliament and the League of Nations that Prime Minister Ramsey MacDonald had to offer a letter of interpretation to Chaim Weizmann, leader of the Zionists, annulling the previous white paper. Recognizing that the mandate was contingent on creating a Jewish national home in Palestine, MacDonald read his letter in Parliament and published it as a formal statement of governmental policy, thereby averting a political crisis and the loss of the mandate for Palestine.

The Mandate as World War Approaches

If the decade immediately after the establishment of the mandate was tumultuous, it would pale when compared to the turbulence that would follow in the years leading up to World War II.

To begin with, in 1933 Adolf Hitler became chancellor of Germany and unleashed a torrent of anti-Semitic laws that would isolate Jewish people from the rest of Germany. This prompted a fifth *aliyah,* primarily composed of German Jews fleeing Hitler. Approximately 225,000 Jewish people arrived, and many more would have come had the British not decided to limit their numbers.

This decision ultimately doomed to Hitler's death camps those who could not enter Palestine. However, those who did immigrate tended to be industrialists and professionals, thereby adding a third dimension to the developing Israeli culture. Previous immigrants had established agricultural communities, and some had become middle-class artisans and shopkeepers. Now, highly cultured German Jews brought capital and developed industry.

From 1931–39, major industry increased by 150 percent and electricity for industry 600 percent;[17] Haifa Bay was developed to facilitate trade. Physicians, lawyers, and other professionals also arrived, leading to the development of the arts among the Yishuv with the creation of museums, theaters, and opera houses.

An Arab Revolt

As the number of Yishuv grew, Arab violence exploded. Led by the mufti and his Arab Higher Committee, an Arab revolt from 1936–39 spread terrorism throughout Palestine. In the first month alone, attacking Arabs had killed eighty-nine Jews and wounded more than three hundred. Meanwhile, Arabs sought to paralyze the Palestinian economy by carrying out a general strike.

The Jewish response to the Arab revolt was to mobilize a defense for the new settlers. British Captain Orde Wingate, a committed evangelical Christian and friend of the Jewish community, began to train the Haganah (the Jewish Defense group) in counterterrorism. Organizing "Special Night Squads" and training them in surprise tactics, rapid mobility, and night fighting, Wingate made his Jewish fighters effective at resisting and even preempting Arab attacks. The mandatory government transferred Wingate and even prohibited his return to the country, but he left his legacy on the troops who would later develop the Israel Defense Forces based on the techniques he taught.

At the same time, a small number of the Yishuv sought to answer terror with terror. The Irgun, an armed underground militia of the maximalist Revisionist Zionist movement, rejected the principle of self-defense and began launching attacks against hostile Arab neighborhoods and British forces. Although these actions were condemned by the Jewish Agency, violence increased dramatically. In 1938, 486 Arab civilians, 292 Jews, and sixty-nine British were killed in the escalating conflict.

Recommendation of the Peel Commission

The British response to the Arab revolt was to form yet another investigatory commission, this one led by Lord Earl Peel. The Peel Commission found that Arab claims of displacement were at best minimal and most likely untrue. It also faulted British administration for tolerating Arab agitation and violence. Nevertheless, it found that the Arabs, whose conditions were greatly improved since the return of the Jewish people, remained firmly opposed to the Zionist settlement of Palestine.

The Peel Commission concluded, for the first time, that the only ultimate solution would be to partition the country into a Jewish state and an Arab one.

The Jewish community, led by the Jewish Agency, accepted Peel's findings, but the Arabs rejected it outright. The British government also determined that Peel's findings and proposals were unacceptable, so they further limited Jewish immigration and sponsored yet another commission (the Woodhead Commission of 1938) that would reject Peel.

As World War II approached, the situation in Palestine under the mandate had changed dramatically. The Jews had created a modern economy and saw the establishment of modern cities. The Hebrew University of Jerusalem had become a world-class academic institution. Between the two world wars, the Jewish population of Palestine increased by 375,000, while the Arab population increased by 380,000. Even though the British consistently attempted to appease the Arabs by restricting Jewish immigration, they permitted unrestricted Arab immigration from neighboring states. As conditions improved for the Yishuv, they also improved for the Arab population. Arab infant mortality declined, health conditions improved, and per capita income for Arabs doubled. But the looming war would devastate the Jews of Europe and transform the situation in Palestine.

The White Paper of 1939
And World War II

By 1939, it was clear that war between Great Britain and Germany was inevitable. The British government concluded that they needed to develop allies throughout the Arab world. They also assumed that the Zionists would support the British against the Nazis regardless of British policy in Palestine. Additionally, with the collapse of the League of Nations, the British determined that they no longer needed to maintain their commitment to create a Jewish national home, the very basis for their mandate in Palestine. So they issued what became known as the White Paper of 1939, in essence repudiating the Balfour Declaration in its entirety.

The white paper declared that Palestine would become an Arab state in ten years. To achieve this end, Jewish immigration would be limited to 15,000 for five years (75,000 total) and then cease altogether. At the same time, extensive restrictions were to be placed on Jewish land purchases, so that Jews could buy property without restriction in only 5 percent of Palestine. Finally, it called for an end to the idea of a Jewish national home in Palestine altogether.

This decision could not have come at a worse time for the Jewish people, damning them to their fate under Hitler with no homeland for their refuge and virtually no countries accepting Jewish people. The rare exceptions were Sweden, accepting approximately 8,000 Danish Jews smuggled from Denmark, and Great Britain, accepting the *"Kinder* Transport" of 7,500 children without their parents. The Evianne Conference (1938), in which the nations of the world closed their doors to Jews seeking refuge, had determined the fate of most European Jewry.[18]

The Jews of Palestine rallied under the formula set forth by David Ben-Gurion, leader of the Yishuv and chairman of the Jewish Agency: "We must assist the British in the war as if there were no White Paper, and we must resist the White Paper as if there were no war." Resist the White Paper they did with demonstrations, illegal immigration, and even attacks by some Jews against British rail and telephone lines as well as governmental property. World Zionists, meeting in the Biltmore Hotel in New York City in 1942, adopted the Biltmore program, which called for not just a Jewish national home but an autonomous Jewish state in Palestine.

To assist the British, the Jews of Palestine persistently offered to establish a Jewish brigade in the British Army. The British were reluctant to allow this because they feared that the force would ultimately fight the British after the war. But in 1940 the first armed Jewish unit was formed, and in 1944 the British finally allowed, at the behest of Winston Churchill, the creation of a Jewish brigade which saw action in Italy.

The Arabs of Palestine refused to support the British but did not resist them either. Their leadership fled, with the mufti settling in Germany, where he became a strong supporter of Hitler. Without the agitation of the mufti, the local Arab residents even abandoned terror against their Jewish neighbors. Jewish militants in Palestine turned their attention to opposing the British rather than defending themselves from the Arabs.

Meanwhile in Europe, the Nazi blitzkrieg brought nine million Jews under their control. Pursuing Hitler's genocidal order, the Nazis carried out the "final solution," hoping to kill every Jewish man, woman, and child. They nearly succeeded, and in so doing they destroyed a more than thousand-year-old European Jewish culture. For the most part, the governments of the world stood by passively, doing as little as possible to stop the genocide.[19] When the shooting stopped and the crematoria closed, six million Jews were dead; two-thirds of European Jewry had perished, and the survivors were homeless. These Jewish refugees longed for a place they could call home, a state of their own. They wanted to go to *Eretz Yisrael,* "the land of Israel," and start anew.

6

The Birth of Israel

The State of Israel . . . will be based on the principles
of liberty, justice and peace, as envisioned by the
Prophets of Israel.

—From Israel's Declaration of Independence

Near the midpoint of the twentieth century, Jewish leaders declared their
ancient homeland, known as Palestine since A.D. 135, to be the modern
state of Israel. Their Declaration of Independence focused on their right
to sovereign rule and hope for peace in the land:

> It is the natural right of the Jewish people, like any other people, to
> control their own destiny in their sovereign state. Accordingly we, the
> members of the People's Council of the Jewish people in Eretz-Israel
> [the land of Israel] and of the Zionist movement, are here assembled on
> the day of the termination of the British mandate over Eretz-Israel, and,
> by virtue of our natural and historic right and [of the resolution of the
> General Assembly of the] United Nations, we hereby declare the estab-
> lishment of a Jewish State in Eretz-Israel, to be known as the State of
> Israel.
>
> The State of Israel will be open for Jewish immigration and the in-
> gathering of the exiles. It will foster the development of the country for
> the benefit of all its inhabitants. It will be based on the principles of
> freedom, justice and peace, as envisioned by the Prophets of Israel. . . .
>
> Placing our trust in the Almighty [lit. Rock of Israel], we affix our
> signatures to this proclamation at this session of the Provisional Council

of State, on the soil of the homeland, in the city of Tel-Aviv, on this
Sabbath Eve, the fifth day of Iyar, 5708 (May 14, 1948).[1]

With those words, David Ben-Gurion called the state of Israel into
existence. After almost two thousand years of exile and against great odds,
the nation was reborn. As seen in the previous chapter, it was not as commonly described, a nation reborn in a day. Jewish people had begun their
return in 1881 and worked diligently to reclaim their land by draining
swamps, irrigating the desert, building cities, and planting trees. In 1945,
after the Nazi Holocaust, the greatest catastrophe the Jewish people and
the world had ever known, the creation of a Jewish state in Palestine still
seemed most unlikely. Yet the rebirth of Israel was imminent, as we shall
see.

The Resistance Against the British

Immediately after World War II, the Jews of Palestine expected the
British to abandon the anti-Zionist position of the White Paper of 1939
and support Jewish immigration once again. They believed this because
they had supported the British war effort and the Arabs had sympathized
with the Nazis. Moreover, Clement Atlee and Ernest Bevin, the new prime
minister and foreign secretary, respectively, had been elected on the Labour
ticket, a party that in the past had generally supported Zionist aims. In
reality, the exact opposite happened.

Foreign Secretary Bevin was particularly hostile to Jewish immigration
and made comments construed as anti-Semitic by some, even complaining that the Jews were trying to "rush to the head of queue" ahead of the
others who had suffered at the hands of the Nazis. President Truman appealed to the British to allow 100,000 Jewish displaced persons into Palestine, purely on humanitarian grounds.

A Rejected Report and an Illegal Immigration

Atlee and Bevin refused but agreed to a joint Anglo-American inquiry
commission. When the Anglo-American committee's report called for the
British to allow 100,000 Jewish refugees to immigrate, Atlee and Bevin still
refused. This exacerbated the confrontation between the British and the
Yishuv, leading to increased violence.

The British-Jewish conflict followed this cycle: The British continued to limit immigration so Jews resorted to *Aliyah Bet*[2] (illegal immigration). The British, in turn, would capture illegal immigrants and confine them in internment camps, derisively called "Bevingrad" by the Zionists. Jewish militants would then attack the internment camps, freeing the prisoners. So the British set up internment camps on the Isle of Cyprus, essentially placing those who survived Hitler's concentration camps into British captivity.

The British military also arrested Jewish Agency leaders; the Jewish Agency's defense force, Haganah; and other Jewish militants. Then the Zionists would attack British military and governmental installations in response.

Jewish Militant Action

Besides the Haganah, the military arm of the Jewish Agency, other Jewish militant groups had arisen. The *Irgun Ze'vai Leumi* ("National Military Organization"; usually called the Irgun or IZL) had been founded in 1931 by Revisionist Zionists who wanted a Jewish state on both sides of the Jordan River; Menachem Begin now led the Irgun. A third group was the *Lohamei Herut Yisrael* ("Fighters for the Freedom of Israel"; also known as the Lehi or the Stern Gang) which broke from the Irgun to pursue an even more extreme agenda.

On July 22, 1946, the Irgun blew up the British military and governmental headquarters at the King David Hotel in Jerusalem. The blast killed ninety-one, including fifteen Jewish civilians. Although the British received warning phone calls in advance of the bombing, according to Begin, they refused to evacuate the building, saying, "We don't take orders from Jews." The Jewish Agency condemned the bombing and disassociated the Haganah from actions with the Irgun. Nevertheless, violence spiraled out of control.

A British Black Eye

Illegal immigration continued unabated. On July 11, 1947, the illegal immigrant ship *Exodus 1947* set sail from France for Palestine. One week later, the British intercepted it. Rather than intern the refugees, Bevin decided to return them to France in prison ships, in order to discourage further illegal immigration. The passengers refused to disembark, and the French refused to support the British action. Then the British brought the refugees to Hamburg, in the British controlled sector of Germany, where the Holocaust survivors were forcibly removed. With Movietone news cameras filming these events, the British won this immigration battle but lost in the court of international opinion. The suffering of these Holocaust survivors at British hands caused much of the world to support Jewish immigration to Palestine and to oppose the continuation of the British Mandate.

Since the British had begun executing captured young Zionist fighters, Jewish leaders sought to free those in prison. On May 4, 1947, Jewish militants carried out a daring attack against the allegedly impregnable British fortress prison in Acre. Jewish fighters fought their way in and out, securing the release of all 251 inmates, 120 Jews and 131 Arabs.

The situation in Palestine had become a disaster for the British. Despite a large military presence—upwards of 100,000 troops—they could not stop Jewish paramilitary groups. The British public, appalled at the attacks against their soldiers, began to pressure the government to withdraw from Palestine. Recognizing that their mandate had spun out of control, the British decided to submit the question of Palestine to the newly formed United Nations.

The Partition Plan

The Majority Report: Partition Palestine

What to do about Palestine became one of the first questions the United Nations would take up. In April 1947, the international body immediately formed the United Nations Special Committee on Palestine, or UNSCOP, an investigating commission consisting of eleven "neutral" nations. The Jewish Agency of Palestine fully cooperated with UNSCOP, while the Palestine Arab Higher Committee boycotted the investigation and defied UNSCOP, leaving the newly formed Arab League to represent their interests. On August 31, 1947, UNSCOP presented its findings and recommendations to the General Assembly.

The majority report[3] proposed ending the British Mandate, partitioning Palestine into a Jewish state and an Arab state with an economic union between the two, and making Jerusalem an international city governed by the UN. A minority report recommended an independent federal state. Under the majority plan, the Jewish state would encompass the coastal plain, western Galilee, and the barren Negev Desert. The Arab state would have western Galilee, the central part of the country on the West Bank of the Jordan, and the Gaza Strip. (See Map 2.)

Response to the Partition Plan

Although the borders of the new Jewish state would be completely indefensible from Arab attack and the exclusion of cities like Jerusalem and Hebron from the state was extremely painful, the Jewish Agency accepted the proposal. At the same time, the Palestine Arab Higher Committee and the Arab League rejected it. The British accepted the end of the mandate but claimed neutrality on the outcome for Palestine. The United States, under the leadership of Harry Truman, accepted the partition plan despite the State Department's opposition to it.

The partition plan was placed before the United Nations General Assembly on November 29, 1947, and was approved by the necessary two-thirds majority vote.[4] Rejoicing erupted in the Jewish communities of Palestine and around the world, while Arab states bitterly denounced the decision and warned that they would wage war rather than accept partition. In fact, Arab irregulars in Palestine immediately began to wage a terror war against their Jewish neighbors in an effort to obstruct the UN's decision. Between December 1947 and May 1948, a virtual civil war raged throughout Palestine, while the British prepared to abandon the mandate after thirty years of contradictory government.

There were claims and counterclaims of atrocities. The Irgun and the Stern Gang were charged with horrific atrocities in the Arab village of Deir Yassin; Arabs murdered a convoy of Jewish medical personnel on the road to Hadassah Hospital in Jerusalem. In the midst of the bombings and firefights, the United States and the United Nations began to fear that partition would lead to a massacre of the Jewish people in Palestine, and there was some talk of a UN trusteeship instead. Nevertheless, President Truman and the Zionists remained resolute in their determination, and the British Mandate ended on May 14, 1948.

The Proclamation of the State of Israel

A Provisional Government, an Historic Declaration

The Jewish community in Palestine was not completely united in declaring statehood. The Mapam (liberal) party wanted to secure a truce

Map 2
THE U.N. PARTITION PLAN

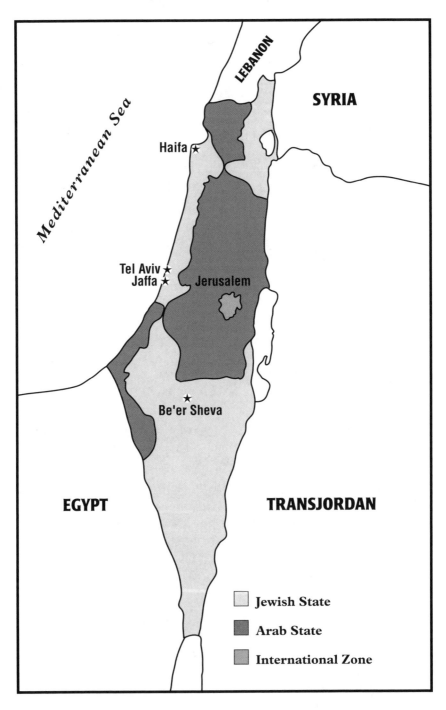

LEBANON

SYRIA

Mediterranean Sea

Haifa ★

Tel Aviv ★
Jaffa ★

Jerusalem

★
Be'er Sheva

EGYPT

TRANSJORDAN

Jewish State

Arab State

International Zone

before any proclamation of independence, while the right-wing Revisionist movement opposed statehood because they wanted a state in all of Palestine and not part of it. But in a rare case of political unity, David Ben-Gurion, leader of the Jewish Agency in Israel, and Chaim Weizmann, head of the World Zionist Organization, argued for declaring an independent Jewish state. This was absolutely essential to ensure the practical realities of governance. With British departure, the Jewish leadership had taken over the civil administration of the country. The utility companies needed to function; the police needed to maintain civil order. Anarchy was unacceptable. So a provisional council of government was formed with Ben-Gurion at its head. The Arab leadership, relying on other Arab states to come to their aid, failed to organize as the Jews had done.

Thus on May 14, 1948, in the Tel Aviv Museum, standing under the portrait of Theodore Herzl, David Ben-Gurion solemnly read Israel's Declaration of Independence. Citing the historic Jewish ties to the land, the Balfour Declaration, the UN Partition resolution, Jewish suffering during the Holocaust, and Zionist sacrifices for the land, Ben-Gurion declared, "By virtue of our natural and historic right and the strength of the United Nations General Assembly [resolution], we hereby declare the establishment of a Jewish state in Eretz-Israel, to be known as the state of Israel."

The declaration also opened the doors of immigration to all Jews, promised equal rights to all the citizens of the state, including the Arabs, and called for peace with the Arab states.[5]

International Recognition

Within minutes of the declaration, President Truman directed the U.S. representative to the UN to recognize the fledgling state. The Union of Soviet Socialist Republics followed with recognition shortly thereafter. Amazingly, recognition of the Jewish state was one of the rare areas of agreement between these super powers already engaged in a cold war. The United States supported Israel on principle while the Soviets wanted the British out of Palestine and hoped to establish a base to serve communist interests there. Israel's lively democracy and Western orientation, however, would soon convince the Soviets that Israel would not provide them with an entry to the Middle East, and the Soviets would adopt the Arab states as their clients there.

The United Nations itself tacitly recognized Israel by making no attempt to establish a successor regime to the British Mandate. There were no resolutions condemning the declaration nor any questioning the legality of it. Although Israel was not to join the UN for four years, it immediately became a recognized state. Such recognition was not forthcoming from the Arab states, most of which still do not recognize Israel. Instead they assembled to attack the newborn Jewish state, hoping to turn the state into a stillbirth.

The 1948 War of Independence

Within a day of the declaration of independence, five Arab armies attacked, launching a war of genocide on the nascent state of Israel. (See Map 3.) In reality, undeclared war had begun when the UN voted to partition Palestine, with Arab irregulars and Jewish paramilitary groups fighting for control of key cities and territories that would give a military advantage. (See "Response to the Partition Plan." above.) During the time for the partition vote to the declaration of independence, the British prohibited the Yishuv from importing weapons legally or forming a legitimate army. As a result, the surrounding Arab states were able to prepare for war openly, while the Yishuv were limited to forbidden smuggled arms.

The Arabs' Advantages

When the five Arab nations launched their assault on the newly declared Jewish state, Ben-Gurion declared that the war pitted 700,000 Jews against 27 million Arabs—one against forty. The military odds were serious but not quite so daunting: The Arab armies' assembled strength was 80,000 troops, compared with Israel's 60,000 trained soldiers. Israel's greater weakness was that only 19,000 Jewish soldiers were fully armed and prepared for war.

In addition, the Arab forces had the advantage of greater numbers, superior terrain, control of the skies (Israel's air force basically did not yet exist), and better equipment with tanks, artillery, and other weaponry.[6]

The first attack came when the Egyptian army bombed Tel Aviv, targeting the innocent civilian population. In response, the entire Jewish community mobilized for war, and in some Jewish settlements, men and women stopped Arab tanks with gasoline bombs, small arms, and even rakes and pitchforks.

Map 3
THE 1948 ARAB INVASION

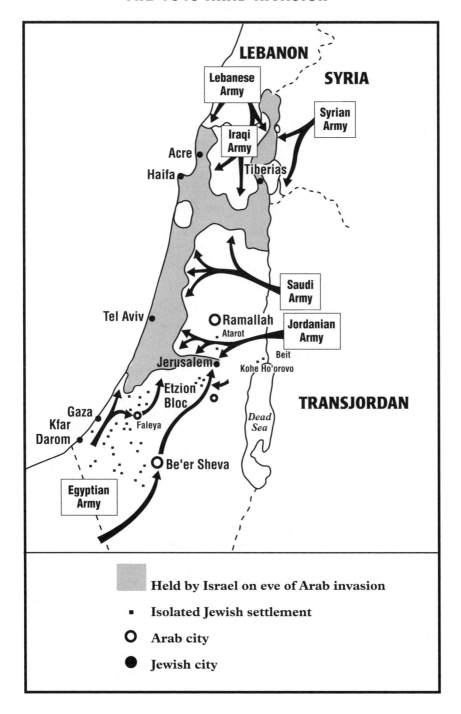

LEBANON

SYRIA

Lebanese Army

Syrian Army

Iraqi Army

Acre

Haifa

Tiberias

Tel Aviv

Saudi Army

O Ramallah

Atarot

Jordanian Army

Jerusalem

Beit Kohe Ho'orovo

Etzion Bloc

TRANSJORDAN

Gaza

Kfar Darom

Faleya

Dead Sea

O Be'er Sheva

Egyptian Army

Held by Israel on eve of Arab invasion

■ Isolated Jewish settlement

O Arab city

● Jewish city

Israel's Advantage

Israel's primary advantage was that of motivation. The new nation had no choice but to win or face genocide. Just three years after the Nazis almost succeeded in a complete destruction of European Jewry, Azzam Pasha, secretary general of the Arab League, promised, "This will be a war of extermination and a momentous massacre, which will be spoken of like the Mongolian massacres and the Crusades."[7] Besides bombing civilian areas, Arab troops massacred Jewish civilians, even after they had surrendered. In the village of Kfar Etzion, Arab Legion troops marched surrendering Jewish villagers into the center of the compound and "proceeded to mow them down," killing 120 Jews, twenty-one of them women. As a rule, "Jews taken prisoner during convoy battles were generally put to death and often mutilated by their captors."[8]

With Arab armies promising to drive the Jews into the sea, the threat was real. Thus the Jewish resistance to invasion was fierce and effective.

Three Phases of War

After the period of undeclared guerilla operations, the war was fought in three phases. The first, from May 15 to June 11, was a holding action against the Arab invasion. In the south, the Egyptian army was restrained by several kibbutzim, particularly Yad Mordechai, a kibbutz founded to remember Mordechai Anielewicz, the leader of the Warsaw Ghetto uprising. In the north, Syrian and Iraqi troops were able to come to the gates of the first kibbutz, Degania, but were held back by Haganah officer Moshe Dayan and a combination of troops and kibbutzniks (residents of the local kibbutz). Their primary source of success was a loud but largely ineffective World War I vintage artillery piece called a Davidka. The explosion was thunderous, frightening, and halting to the Arab troops. In the central part of the state, the invading Arab Legion from Jordan succeeded in securing the West Bank and the Old City of Jerusalem.

An Arab siege of Jerusalem almost cost the loss of the New City as well. The Israelis were able to break the stranglehold by bypassing the normal route to Jerusalem through building a "Burma Road" to resupply the city.

During the cease-fire that followed (June 11–July 8), the Israelis began to receive rifles, ammunition, artillery, and old war planes even as the Arab armies resupplied. Despite the strictly enforced U. S. arms embargo, in a strange quirk of history, Czechoslovakia, a Soviet client state, sold World War II military equipment to Israel with the approval of the USSR. While finding weapons for the army, the Israeli government also sought to unify the Israel Defense Forces into one army under civilian control. The new government outlawed all paramilitary and militia forces, leading to the momentous "Altalena" incident.

On June 20, an Irgun arms ship named the Altalena arrived off the coast of Tel Aviv. Although the Irgun had officially been incorporated into the new Israeli army, their leader, Menachem Begin, would not turn these arms over to the government but wanted them to remain with Irgun troops. Prime Minister Ben-Gurion adamantly opposed private armies and sent troops that actually fired upon the Irgun ship. The battle left fourteen Irgun members dead and sixty-nine wounded and killed two IDF soldiers. Begin believed that a civil war would destroy the new state so he succumbed to pressure and disbanded the Irgun. At the same time, Ben-Gurion dissolved the Palmach, the strike force of the left-wing Labor parties. Although these soldiers were completely loyal to the government, Ben-Gurion decreed that they would have to be consolidated into the Israel Defense Forces. There would be no private armies in Israel.

The second phase of the war, from July 8–18, was Israel's ten-day offensive to drive out the invading armies. With guns, ammunition, and artillery, the Jewish army was able to shatter the Egyptian invaders along the southern coast, repel the Jordanian Arab Legion into the West Bank, and drive the Lebanese army back to the northern border and take the city of Nazareth. Nevertheless, Egyptian troops remained in the Negev Desert, in striking distance of Jerusalem.

The third phase of the war lasted about two weeks (December 22, 1948–January 8, 1949). Finally, the IDF drove the Egyptians back to the Sinai and out of the Negev.

The Arab states' lack of organization, as well as their self-interest and failed leadership, had brought a shocking defeat. Moreover, Israeli desperation, determination, and daring had surprised the world. Against great odds and without any outside military support, Israel had survived the invasion and, when the armistice lines were set, had even extended the borders of the state. (See 1949 armistice lines in Map 4.) In the words of Ralph Bunche, the UN peace negotiator, Israel was "a vibrant reality."

Map 4
THE 1949 RHODES
ARMISTICE AGREEMENT

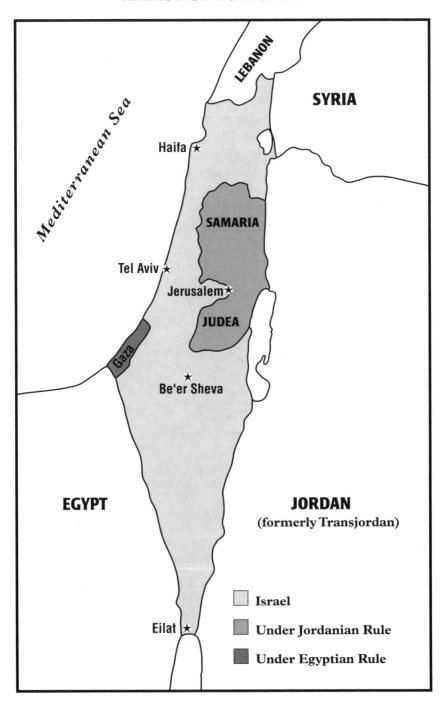

LEBANON

SYRIA

Mediterranean Sea

Haifa ★

SAMARIA

Tel Aviv ★

Jerusalem ★

JUDEA

Gaza

★
Be'er Sheva

EGYPT

JORDAN
(formerly Transjordan)

□ Israel

▨ Under Jordanian Rule

■ Under Egyptian Rule

Eilat ★

Results of the War

Ongoing War . . . and the Loss of Jerusalem

When the war ended, Israel fully expected to sign a peace agreement with her neighbors. Little did the state's leaders know that one of the outcomes of the war would be a seemingly interminable state of war with the Arab states, which would only be interrupted by short periods of all-out war.

A second result was the crushing loss of the Old City of Jerusalem. For many generations, Jewish people had been the majority population in the ancient walled city. It also contained Judaism's holiest site, the Western Wall, the only remaining part of the ancient holy temple. Jews had gathered there to pray for two millennia, and now they were cut off from their sacred place.

Although the Jordanian government had promised complete access to all holy sites, they did not fulfill their commitment. Instead, Jews were not able to enter the Old City to pray at the Wall. Other Jewish holy places were also desecrated—even the grave markers from the ancient Jewish cemetery on the Mount of Olives were torn up and used for Jordanian latrines.

The Refugee Problem

One of the most difficult consequences of the war was the creation of the Arab refugee problem. Even before all-out war began, Arab leaders began to flee the country. Then the Arab governments decided to report allegations of Jewish massacres in order to incite the anger of the Arab populace. This actually had an opposite effect: The reports led thousands upon thousands to flee. In a number of cases, Israeli troops, for military reasons, evacuated areas of their Arab residents, compounding the problem but by no means creating it.

Once the war was over, Ben-Gurion was unequivocal in forbidding the return of these refugees. At a June 16 cabinet meeting he said, "As for the return of the Arabs, not only do I not accept the opinion of encouraging their return . . . War is war . . . and those who declared war upon us will have to bear the consequences after they have been defeated."[9] Although the refugee problem is a tangled web (which will be addressed more thoroughly in chapters 11 and 12), it is untrue that Israel intended to increase the Jewish majority in the state by deliberately expelling the refugees. In fact, in places like Haifa and Tiberias, Jewish leaders attempted to persuade the Arab residents to remain and become full citizens of the democratic state.[10] For a variety of reasons, these pleas were rejected and one of the great obstacles to Arab-Israeli peace was born.

Casualties of War

One of the most painful consequences of the war was the price in Jewish lives. So soon after the Holocaust, almost 6,400 more Jews were killed, accounting for nearly 1 percent of the entire Jewish population of the new state. Five times as many were wounded. The difference was that these Israeli Jews fought back to create their own state. Rather than accept the fate of another genocide of the Jewish people, the Israelis defended themselves and their new country, making the declaration of the state of Israel a reality.

A Seat in the United Nations

Just two years after the Rhodes Armistice agreements were signed, Israel was granted membership in the United Nations. At that time, this was considered a meaningful evidence of national sovereignty. Historian Howard M. Sachar wrote,

> As the Israeli flag was ceremoniously hoisted in the plaza of the General Assembly building, Shertok, Eban, and other participants, together with the Jewish world at large, asked themselves whether only four years had passed since the Star of David had been identified primarily as the seal of doom worn by concentration camp inmates. The rise to independence of history's most cruelly ravaged people transcended the experience, even the powers of description, of case-hardened journalists and social scientists alike. It appeared as if a new law of nature had been born.[11]

As amazing as the reborn state was, growing into a viable modern country, despite being surrounded by sworn enemies, would be a significant task.

7
Growing Pains

In Israel, in order to be a realist you must believe in
miracles.

—David Ben-Gurion, First Prime Minister of Israel

In the Jewish world, the very existence of Israel is generally considered
miraculous. Many marvel that the nation could be reborn, like a phoenix
rising from the ashes of the Holocaust. Beyond that, the growth of the
nation into a modern democracy, boasting a strong economy, a potent military, and leadership in agriculture, science, and medicine, would indeed
make realists believe in miracles. This chapter will examine that miracle:
the amazing growth and survival of the Jewish state, despite economic
challenges, hostile neighbors, and international isolation.

The Ingathering of the Exiles

Almost immediately after the birth of the state of Israel, the new Israeli
Knesset, or parliament, enacted the "law of return." This gave any Jewish
person, or any person with a Jewish parent or grandparent, the right to
come to Israel and be granted immediate citizenship. And return they did.

Immigrants from European and Arab Countries

As soon as the state was declared, Jews from the internment camps
in Cyprus and the displaced persons camps of Europe began to flood the

new country. Many of them, having survived Hitler's death camps, picked up rifles (after brief military training) to fight for the survival of their homeland against the Arab invasion. Within three years, more than 300,000 Holocaust survivors had made their way to Israel.

But it was not only the Jews from Europe who came. As partition and war approached, Syrian Foreign Minister Faris el-Khouri warned, "Unless the Palestine problem is settled, we shall have difficulty in protecting and safeguarding the Jews in the Arab world."[1] This threat became a reality as more than one thousand Jews were murdered in anti-Jewish riots in Iraq, Libya, Egypt, Syria, and Yemen—Arab countries where Jews had lived for hundreds or even thousands of years. As a result, Sephardic Jews, who lived in Iraq, Iran, Yemen, and the Mediterranean world, fled to Israel in the state's first years of existence.

The anti-Jewish rioting that took place in Iraq, for example, both before and after the establishment of the modern state of Israel, led to the end of that 2,700-year-old Jewish community. The Iraqi government announced that it would allow Jews to leave if they surrendered their citizenship and gave up their assets. Israel organized Operation Ezra and Nehemiah, bringing 120,000 Jews from Iraq to Israel by 1951.

Anti-Jewish riots in Yemen, likewise, forced the emigration of virtually the entire ancient Yemenite Jewish community. Between 1949 and 1950, more than 50,000 came to Israel via Operation Magic Carpet. These Yemeni Jews, riding on planes for the first time, saw themselves as being borne "on eagle's wings" to the land of their fathers. Jews also fled from Egypt, Syria, Morocco, Algiers, Tunisia, Lebanon, and Libya. By 1951, approximately 400,000 Jews had fled Arab lands, gaining their Israeli citizenship but losing their property, businesses, and assets to the Arab governments in the lands they left. Within another decade, nearly 200,000 more Jews would flee from Arab lands, making a grand total of nearly 600,000 Jewish refugees from Arab countries immigrating to Israel.

In its first three years alone, Israel absorbed approximately 700,000 immigrants from both Europe and the Arab world, putting tremendous economic pressure on the new country. Most of the arrivals were penniless and needed the government to provide housing, medical care, and job training. Additionally, they all needed to learn to speak modern Hebrew, so the government established a special accelerated language school (called an *ulpan*) to quicken their transition to Israeli life. Before too long, Israel had tripled in size. The challenges of immigration in the early years of the state caused David Ben-Gurion to say,

The trebling of the population in this small and impoverished country, flowing with milk and honey but not with sufficient water, rich in rocks and sand dunes but poor in natural resources and vital raw materials, has been no easy task: Indeed, practical men, with their eyes fixed upon things as they are, regarded it as an empty and insubstantial utopian dream.[2]

An Influx from Eastern Europe and the USSR

The ingathering of the exiles continued into the 1960s with 215,000 immigrants from Eastern Europe. During the early 1970s, more than 100,000 Jews had arrived from Poland, Czechoslovakia, and the USSR. During the 1980s, Israel brought thousands of starving Ethiopian Jews to the land in Operation Moses. The largest increase came in the 1990s, when approximately one million Jews fled the former Soviet Union after its dissolution.

Even today, with terrorism driving tourists away and keeping *aliyah* low, Jewish people from Iran, Argentina, and France, where anti-Semitism is on the rise, are still making their way to the safety of the Jewish state. The population of Israel now stands at just under six million, with approximately five million Jewish citizens and one million Arab citizens. But gathering and sustaining this growing population was not enough. Defending the nation from military threats and terrorism has taken up much of the efforts and finances of the government of Israel.

The Wars of Israel: The Sinai Campaign of 1956

After the 1948–49 War of Independence, the Arab nations rebuffed any permanent peace settlement, refusing to recognize Israel and maintaining a permanent state of war with the Jewish state. At this time, Israel's primary threat did not come from Arab armies but from *fedayeen*. These fedayeen (literally "those who sacrifice themselves") were terrorists, armed and trained by Egypt, who would strike Israel from both Egypt and Jordan, attacking Israeli communities and kibbutzim, generally children's quarters first. In the six years after the armistice, Israel sustained 435 attacks from Egypt, in which 101 Israelis were killed and 364 were wounded.

Additionally, the Egyptians blockaded the Straits of Tiran, an international waterway and Israel's only supply route with Asia. The blockade not only proved harmful to Israel's economy, but was an act of war by international standards.

Israel was looking for an opportunity to deal a decisive blow that would stop the terrorism and open the Straits of Tiran. It arrived when Gamal Abdel Nasser, the president of Egypt, nationalized the Suez Canal, threatening British and French interests there.

New Allies: The British and the French

Both the British and the French were enraged by Nasser's decision and wanted a pretext for a military incursion to take the canal back. Their governments approached Israel with a plan for Israel to attack in the Sinai and land paratroopers near the canal. Britain and France would then call for both sides to withdraw from the canal zone with the expectation that Egypt would refuse. Then the British and the French would have their pretext to send troops to "defend" their interests in the canal zone.

Israel readily agreed to the plan, in part because of its close alliance with the French (Israel's primary military supplier and chief ally since 1949) but also because of the opportunity to open the Straits of Tiran and deal a blow to terrorism at the same time. Moreover, the two European allies promised to provide air support for the Israeli attack. Most importantly, Israel hoped for political cover from U. S. condemnation, since the U.S. government had not proven friendly to Israel.

Israel mobilized 100,000 troops in just three days and attacked Egypt on October 29, 1956. On the Israeli side, everything went as planned, although the British and French air support failed to materialize. Israeli paratroopers approached the Suez Canal, the British and French gave the ultimatum that both sides withdraw from the canal, and the Egyptians refused. France and Great Britain then vetoed a U.S.-sponsored Security Council resolution calling for an immediate Israeli withdrawal. With additional time, Israel conquered virtually the entire Sinai Peninsula and freed the Straits of Tiran within one hundred hours of the outbreak of hostilities. When the Soviet Union threatened to intervene, the British abruptly halted operations. As a result, France and Britain failed to achieve their objective of taking the Suez Canal.

Response by the United States

U. S. President Dwight Eisenhower was furious with his British and French allies as well as with Israel. He demanded that Israel withdraw from the Sinai, having warned the Soviets that any aggression toward France and Great Britain would be considered a threat to the United States. Strategically missing was any statement of how the United States would perceive Soviet actions against Israel. Therefore, David Ben-Gurion, after initially balking at the idea of withdrawal, agreed to do so.

In exchange, the United States assured the freedom of navigation of all nations in the Straits of Tiran, including Israel, and sponsored a UN resolution providing for a UN peacekeeping force in the Sinai to guard against terrorist incursions. Although Israel had hoped to barter a peace treaty in exchange for withdrawal, the nation's smaller objectives were met. Ships could pass through the Straits of Tiran to Israel's southern port of Eilat, and terrorism was somewhat curbed by UN peacekeepers. This state of affairs was to last for the next ten years.

The Wars of Israel:
The Six Day War of 1967

The ten years that followed the Sinai Campaign were relatively quiet, but they were not totally peaceful. Israeli farmers in the Galilee were subject to Syrian shelling from the Golan Heights. Also, Egyptian-trained *fedayeen* continued their terror attacks from Jordan. In 1965, the Palestine Liberation Organization (PLO) was formed. This was a terrorist organization with the avowed purpose of destroying Israel. From the time of its formation until April 1967, the PLO completed more than one hundred terrorist operations against Israel.

But tensions rose even more dramatically in the spring of 1967. Heavy Syrian bombardment of the Galilee from the Golan Heights in March and April of 1967 provoked a retaliatory Israeli air strike on April 7, 1967. In the dogfight that ensued, Israel shot down six Soviet-supplied Syrian MiG jets. Shortly thereafter, the Soviets warned the Syrians of an Israeli troop concentration in the north. Israel vehemently denied any military buildup and repeatedly invited the Soviet ambassador to tour the region and personally observe that there were no military preparations or troops concentrating in northern Israel. However, the Soviets refused to take up the offer. Their false information set in motion the events that led to war.

Following the Soviet instigation, Syria called for Egyptian military support based on their mutual defense pact. In May, Egyptian troops mustered in the Sinai while Syrian troops assembled on the Golan Heights. Egyptian President Nasser ordered the UN Emergency Force out of the Sinai

Desert. On May 22, the Egyptians once again blockaded Israeli shipping in the Straits of Tiran.

Harsh Threats, Failed Diplomacy

By the end of May, the threat against Israel was increasing as speeches, broadcast all over the Arab world, promised that the Arab nations were about to launch a genocidal war of annihilation against the Zionists. Cairo was plastered with posters of "Arab soldiers shooting, crushing, strangling, and dismembering bearded, hook-nosed Jews."[3] Nasser and other Arab leaders were daily broadcasting increasingly bombastic speeches threatening Israel's destruction. On May 25, Nasser told the Egyptian parliament, "The problem presently . . . is not whether the port of Eilat should be blockaded or how to blockade it—but how totally to exterminate the State of Israel for all time."[4] On May 28 he told the press, "We will not accept any possibility of coexistence with Israel."[5] Other Arab leaders made similar declarations, including the PLO's Ahmad Shuqayri, who promised to "drive the Jews into the sea," and that "there will be no survivors."[6] On May 30, King Hussein of Jordan signed a mutual defense pact with Egypt, adding yet another country to the armies surrounding Israel.

These threats of genocide were not taken lightly by Israel, having learned from European Jewry's error of failing to take Hitler's threats seriously.

With war looming, world diplomacy had sprung into action. However, despite UN Security Council discussions and private consultations with world powers, nothing happened to quiet the situation. The United States tried to assemble an international flotilla to break the blockade, while pressuring Israel not to take military measures against the illegal and provocative closure of the Straits of Tiran. Yet this came to naught. Traditional allies of Israel, like France, motivated by the need for Arab oil, now curried favor with the Arabs and failed to keep their promises of maintaining open navigation in the Straits.

Meanwhile Israel was in a national crisis, fearing for its very existence. With indefensible borders so dangerous that the country was only eleven miles wide at its center, Israel was now "ringed by an Arab force of some 250,000 troops, over 2,000 tanks and some 700 front line fighter and bomber aircraft,"[7] according to war historian Chaim Herzog. In response to this crisis, on June 1, war hero Moshe Dayan was sworn in as Israeli defense minister.

Despite U.S. pressure on Israel not to launch a preemptive strike, the Israeli government and military did not believe it could withstand a first-strike assault by the combined Arab forces and still survive. Furthermore, Israeli forces had been on alert for three weeks now, and it was not economically feasible for the country to continue its mobilization indefinitely. Although U.S. President Lyndon Johnson warned Israel "not to go it alone," the Israeli leadership believed they had no other way to go.

The First Strike

On June 5, Israel launched a preemptive strike. While most Egyptian pilots were eating breakfast, the Israeli air force began a surprise attack against the Egyptian air bases. Within two hours, the entire Egyptian air force, consisting of more than three hundred planes, was destroyed. A ground war ensued in the Sinai Peninsula, with the most vicious tank battles since World War II. Within four days, the entire Sinai, up to the Suez Canal, was in Israeli hands.

Before the onset of hostilities, Israel had sent secret messages to Jordan's King Hussein, imploring him to stay out of the war. Nevertheless, when Jordanian radar picked up the Israeli planes returning from the initial assault on the Egyptian air bases and being falsely informed by the Egyptians that the planes were theirs, King Hussein believed that an Egyptian air assault against Israel had begun. Therefore he ordered the Jordanian army to shell West Jerusalem. Since Jordan had initiated the hostilities with Israel, the Israeli air force proceeded to destroy the Jordanian air force (as well as half of the Syrian air force) and then launched a ground assault.

Within three days, the Israel Defense Forces captured the West Bank and the Old City of Jerusalem. The significance of capturing the Western Wall, the most sacred shrine in Judaism, cannot be understated. Jews around the world celebrated, knowing that they would have access to pray at the last vestige of the ancient holy temple.

While the vast majority of Israeli troops were engaged in the south with Egypt and in the central region with Jordan, a small force of Israeli soldiers held the Syrians at bay in the north. However, with the main Israeli force succeeding at its objectives, the troops were redeployed to the Syrian border. There Israeli troops fought uphill into the Golan Heights, taking severe losses, but intent on securing the high ground so that Israeli farmers would no longer be subject to bombing from Syrian emplacements on those hills. By June 10, despite many casualties, the Golan Heights was secured, and Israel and her Arab neighbors accepted a cease-fire. Israeli troops had conquered the Sinai Peninsula, the Golan Heights, and the west bank of the Jordan, including the Old City of Jerusalem. (See Map 5.)

Results of the Six Day War

Lost Lives, Ongoing Conflict

The outcomes of the war shocked the world. Despite being outgunned and outmanned, the Israel Defense Forces had won a stunning victory, though at great cost. Israel lost approximately 800 citizens—equivalent in per capita terms to 80,000 Americans. Another 2,563 were wounded. Arab losses were even more severe. Egypt lost more than 10,000 men with many more wounded; Syrian losses were placed at about 450 dead and 1,800 wounded. The Jordanians lost 700 men and over 6,000 were wounded or missing. The Israeli victory was so lopsided that it led to a tragic humiliation of the Arab nations and a dangerous overconfidence in Israel.

Another result of the war was the perpetuation of the conflict. Israel mistakenly believed that the Arabs would now negotiate a peace in return for returned land. But in August 1967, the Arab leaders met in Khartoum, Sudan, and issued three significant "nos": No peace with Israel, no negotiations with Israel, and no recognition of Israel. The state of war would continue.

A Controversial UN Resolution

As a further consequence of the war, the UN passed Resolution 242. Intended to be the basis for a peace agreement, it became the source of much controversy. The resolution called for "termination of all claims or states of belligerency" and recognition of the right of "every State in the area . . . to live in peace within secure and recognized boundaries free from threats or acts of force," and it required the freedom of navigation in international waterways, a direct response to the provocative actions of Egypt in the Straits of Tiran. It also called for the "withdrawal of Israeli armed forces from territories occupied in the recent conflict."

The last phrase has been the most disputed. While the Arab states and their supporters have contended that this requires Israel to return to the pre-1967 borders, this was not the intention of the original framers of

Map 5
BOUNDARIES OF CEASEFIRE
AT CLOSE OF THE SIX DAYS WAR

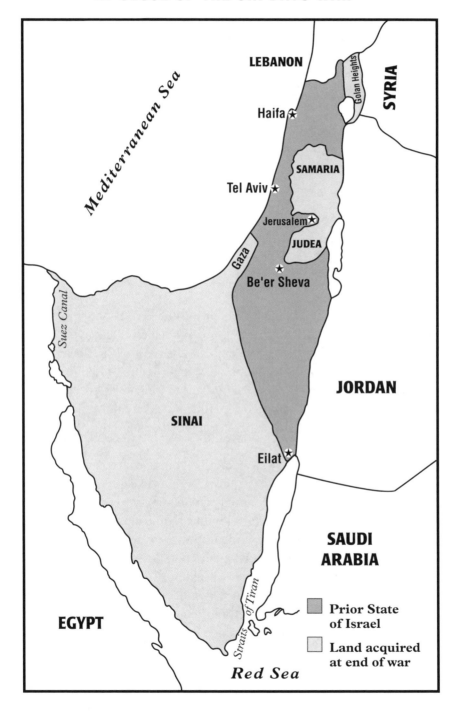

LEBANON

Golan Heights

SYRIA

Mediterranean Sea

Haifa ★

SAMARIA

Tel Aviv ★

Jerusalem ★

JUDEA

Gaza

Be'er Sheva ★

Suez Canal

JORDAN

SINAI

Eilat ★

SAUDI
ARABIA

Straits of Tiran

EGYPT

■ Prior State
of Israel

□ Land acquired
at end of war

Red Sea

the resolution. The British and U. S. ambassadors, who drafted the resolution, deliberately excluded the word *"all* territories" or even *"the* territories." Then U.S. Ambassador Arthur Goldberg clarified the intent of the resolution: "The notable omissions—which were not accidental—in regard to withdrawal are the words 'the' or 'all' and 'the June 5, 1967 lines.' . . . The resolution speaks of withdrawal from occupied territories without defining the extent of withdrawal."[8] Lord Caradon, the British ambassador, the second architect of the resolution, explained, "It would have been wrong to demand that Israel return to its positions of June 4, 1967, because those positions were undesirable and artificial."[9] Although all Israeli governments have been willing to give up almost all of the territories seized in the war in exchange for peace, none were willing to give up 100 percent because of the perceived danger to the country if it did so. Yet the willingness to restore territory is evident in Israel's return of the Sinai in 1982 in exchange for a 1979 peace agreement.

Refugees and Israeli Occupation

Another outcome of the Six Day War was the expansion of the Palestinian refugee problem. An estimated 325,000 Palestinians living in the West Bank fled to what they considered another part of their own country, Jordan, to escape being caught in the war's crossfire. Additionally, the Israeli military also moved a few Palestinians to Jordan for "security" reasons. Some of these were allowed to return, while others were resettled elsewhere. Nevertheless, the refugee problem that started with the War of Independence had expanded.

Yet another result of the war was the beginning of the Israeli occupation of the West Bank and Gaza. Many UN refugee camps now were in the area of Israeli governmental administration as were various Arab cities, towns, and villages. Israel's military administration allowed for moderate self-rule. Amazingly, under an occupying power, the refugees experienced improved life expectancy, decreased infant mortality, the creation of Arab universities, and a free press.[10] Notwithstanding, Israel was still considered an oppressive foreign ruler by the Palestinian population. Also, as part of the occupation, Israel developed settlements with Israeli citizens in the West Bank and the Gaza Strip, which became a flashpoint in the dispute, particularly as they expanded in the late 1970s and 1980s.

Terrorism and the PLO

The final result of the Six Day War was the rise of Palestinian terrorism. In 1965, just prior to the war, various Palestinian terrorist groups formed a centralized terrorist organization, the Palestine Liberation Organization (PLO), sworn to destroy the state of Israel. After the Six Day War, PLO operatives became innovators in terrorist methods. Most notable was their use of hijacking, along with taking hostages and murdering schoolchildren and invalids in cold blood. The nadir of their terrorism was the ruthless attack on Israeli athletes at the 1972 Munich Olympics in which eleven Israeli Olympians were killed.

Despite the horrors of terrorism, Israel refused to negotiate with terrorists or to recognize the PLO as an organization. One dramatic example of Israel's resistance to terrorism took place in 1976, when four terrorists hijacked an Air France jet and forced it to land at the Entebbe Airport in Uganda. After releasing the crew and all non-Jewish passengers, the terrorists demanded the release of fifty-three Palestinian terrorists or they threatened to kill the remaining 105 Jewish hostages. Israeli Prime Minister Yitzhak Rabin authorized a dramatic rescue operation, which included disguising a commando as Idi Amin, the Ugandan dictator who was complicit in the terrorist operation. In a spectacular one-hour operation, coincidentally on the date of the United States Bicentennial celebration, the Israeli commandos succeeded in rescuing 102 of the hostages while losing three hostages and the leader of the operation.[11] The sensational success of the Entebbe rescue reinforced Israel's reputation of resistance to terrorism and remarkable daring in its defense forces.

The PLO not only threatened Israel and Jews around the world, it also menaced Jordan, its host country. PLO leader Yasser Arafat set up a state within Jordan, functioning as a "thugocracy" and setting up a protection racket. In September of 1970, when it became apparent that Arafat was attempting to take over Jordan, King Hussein went to war against the PLO. This prompted the Syrians to intervene against Jordanian troops. Ultimately, the Jordanian army routed the PLO, killed thousands of Palestinians, and drove out the terrorist group only to have them relocate their terrorist forces in Lebanon. Palestinians came to call this "Black September" and even established a terrorist faction by that name. Meanwhile, Israeli support of King Hussein (at President Richard Nixon's urging, Israel offered air cover to Jordan) led to improved relations between Jordan and Israel but did not lead to a peace treaty.

The Six Day War shocked the Middle East and the world. Today, much of the conflict, but by no means all, revolves around the aftereffects of that war. In an amazingly prescient statement made just after the Egyptians expelled the UN Emergency Force from the Sinai Desert, the UN force's leader, Gen. Indar Jit Rikhye, predicted, "I think you're going to have a major Middle East war and I think we will still be sorting it out fifty years from now."[12]

The Wars of Israel:
The 1973 Yom Kippur War

On October 6, 1973, all Israel was observing Yom Kippur (the Day of Atonement), the most solemn and sacred day of the Jewish calendar, when Egypt and Syria launched a coordinated surprise attack against Israel. The skeleton Israeli forces on duty in both the Golan Heights and the Sinai Desert were simply overwhelmed: 180 Israeli tanks faced 1,400 Syrian tanks in the Golan Heights; 500 Israeli soldiers with three tanks faced 600,000 Egyptian soldiers with 2,000 tanks and 550 aircraft in the Sinai Desert along the Suez Canal.

Within the first few days of fighting, Israeli forces were driven out of the Golan Heights, while in the south Israeli troops retreated from the Suez Canal and into the Sinai Peninsula. Facing near destruction and with the USSR rearming the Arab attackers, Israel appealed to the United States for assistance in rearming.

Striking Back

Within a week of the outbreak of hostilities, the United States began a massive airlift of weaponry to Israel. These weapons, along with the mobilization of the Israel Defense Forces and the remarkable gallantry of Israeli troops, checked the Arab onslaught and ultimately turned the tide of war. In the Sinai, Israeli General Ariel Sharon engineered a dramatic surprise crossing of the Suez Canal by Israeli troops, successfully surrounding the Egyptian Third Army, and opening the way for the IDF to march to Cairo unopposed, had Israel wished to do so. In the north, at great cost, the Israelis retook the Golan Heights and actually were in striking distance of Damascus. What appeared to be a sure defeat was once again turned into an Israeli victory.

After the war, some interesting facts came to light. First, the Egyptian and Syrian assault was not a complete surprise. On October 5, one day before the war, Israeli Prime Minister Golda Meir had been notified by Israeli intelligence of an impending attack. But the U.S. Secretary of State Henry Kissinger pressured Israel not to mobilize troops or launch a preemptive strike, warning that doing so would risk fighting the war without U.S. support.

Also coming to light was that Israel considered using its "Samson option"—the use of nuclear weapons. So grave was Israel's military situation that Defense Minister Moshe Dayan raised the nuclear option to the prime minister. Mrs. Meir refused but allowed for the Jericho missiles to be armed with the full knowledge of U.S. intelligence. It was then that she appealed to the United States for rearmament, and Israel received the massive airlift. The U.S. made sure to provide conventional weapons to keep Israel from using its nonconventional option.[13]

The War's Impact

The Yom Kippur War dramatically changed the situation in Israel. First, Israeli losses included 2,688 dead, nearly 350 percent more than in the Six Day War. No family in Israel was untouched, leading to a national grief that lasted for years.

Second, the war pierced the veneer of Israeli invincibility. Israel won the war decisively, yet the victory was not assured until some time into the fighting. Israelis realized once again that they need only lose one war to bring the end of their state.

Third, the war also led to the Arabs unleashing the oil weapon. The ensuing Arab oil embargo put pressure on the international community to abandon support of Israel or face the loss of oil supplies. As a result, Israel was further isolated from the world community.

Yet another outcome was the postwar commission report that faulted Israeli intelligence and political leadership, leading to the collapse of Golda Meir's government. By 1977, Menachem Begin and the more conservative Likud party defeated the Israeli Labor party, breaking Labor's stranglehold on the prime ministry that had existed since the inception of the state.

Finally, the Yom Kippur War brought a measure of self-respect to the Arab states, particularly Egypt. Although Egypt ultimately lost the war, the initial successes and the heavy casualties inflicted upon Israel led Egyptian President Anwar el-Sadat to be sufficiently confident to visit Israel and sign the Camp David peace treaty with Israel in 1979. While this treaty brought much joy and hope to Israel, it would not provide peace with all of her neighbors.[14]

Menachem Begin and the 1982 Lebanon War

Destroying a Reactor in Iraq

In Israel, Prime Minister Menachem Begin (1977–82) was a staunch supporter of settlements in the disputed territories, using his leadership to fund new settlements and refusing to call the area captured in the Six Day War "the West Bank"; he insisted on using its biblical names, Judea and Samaria. Begin's tough approach to Israeli security led in 1981 to his authorizing the bombing of the Iraqi nuclear reactor. Israeli intelligence had determined that Saddam Hussein was planning to develop nuclear weapons, so Begin's cabinet authorized the plant's destruction before it actually became "hot."

In a daring and deceptive assault, the Israeli air force decimated the nuclear reactor, thereby incurring the wrath of the UN and even U.S. President Ronald Reagan. Israelis across the entire political spectrum celebrated the defeat of this dangerous threat. Ten years later, during the first Gulf War, even the United States came to appreciate the Israeli action, recognizing how dangerous it would have been for the U.S.-led coalition, had Saddam Hussein succeeded in obtaining nuclear weaponry.

Attacking Terrorists in Lebanon

Despite Begin's successes in both peace (signing the Camp David brokered peace treaty with Egypt) and war (the destruction of the Iraqi nuclear reactor), the most controversial aspect of his tenure as prime minister was his 1982 war with Lebanon. The war was provoked by the PLO's continuous bombing of northern Israel, forcing Israelis in cities like Naharyah and Kiryat Shmonah to spend weeks at a time in bomb shelters.

Begin's government determined to take action. The PLO had come to Lebanon after King Hussein had expelled them from Jordan, bringing terror to the previously peaceful Lebanese and oppressing both the Muslim and Christian populations there. With Yasser Arafat virtually taking over the entire country, Lebanon descended to civil war. Besides the disruption of Lebanon, Arafat also established a terrorist army that used

Lebanon to attack Israel. When the PLO assassinated Shlomo Argov, Is-raeli Ambassador to Great Britain, Begin authorized his defense minister, Ariel Sharon, to launch Operation Peace for Galilee on June 4, 1982.

Allying with Christian Phalangists, Christian and Muslim Shia Lebanese alike welcomed the Israeli army as liberators. However, as the PLO terrorist army withdrew to the cover of civilian population centers in Beirut, the IDF came under greater criticism because of the potential for civilian casualties in the war. Nevertheless, the IDF was able to secure a cease-fire that required the expulsion of Yasser Arafat and the PLO from Lebanon.

Initially Israel was able to secure a peace treaty with Lebanon's Presi-dent Amin Gemayal, who had recently replaced his assassinated brother. But with Lebanon's descent into civil war, Syrian troops occupied the coun-try and forced Gemayal to renege on the treaty within a year.

The Sabra and Shatila Massacres

A terrible consequence of the Lebanese war was the revenge massacres carried out by Christian Phalangist militia in Sabra and Shatila, two Pales-tinian refugee camps in the Beirut area. From September 16 to 17, 1982, Lebanese Christian Phalangist militia killed between 460 (Lebanese po-lice estimate) to as many as 800 refugees (Israeli intelligence estimate) after the IDF allowed the Phalangists to enter the camps to root out ter-rorists. By the time the Israeli army intervened and stopped the carnage, thirty-five women and children were among the victims.

The Israeli populace was shocked and grieved by the actions of their allies and blamed the military leadership for allowing the massacre to take place. More than 300,000 Israelis gathered to protest the actions of the army while, surprisingly, the Arab world had little reaction. The Israeli government formed the Kahan Commission of Inquiry, which found that Israel was *indirectly* responsible for not anticipating the possibility of vengeful violence by the Phalangist militia. As a result, Defense Minister Ariel Sharon and IDF Chief of Staff Raful Eitan were forced to resign. The Phalangists, who were the actual perpetrators of the massacres, were vir-tually ignored in the condemnation that followed.

The allegation that Sharon, currently the Israeli prime minister, au-thorized the massacres at the Sabra and Shatila refugee camps has be-come doctrine in the Arab world and much of the media. However, the Kahan Commission found that he was only guilty of not anticipating the actions of the Phalangists; it concluded he was unaware of the planned attacks.

A Resignation and a Withdrawal

With the Lebanese war being increasingly opposed by the Lebanese population and the Israeli citizenry, Israel withdrew to a security zone in south Lebanon. On September 15, 1983, Menachem Begin resigned as prime minister, withdrew from public life, and became a recluse until his death in 1993. Although he gave no explanation, Begin most likely resigned because of the difficulties of the war, the high number of Israeli casualties, and his grief over the loss of his wife, who died just months before the resignation. Israel remained in the security zone facing a steady stream of violence from the militant Islamic terrorist group Hezbollah.

Public outcry by the Israeli people over the mounting casualties in the security zone led Ehud Barak in May 2000 to withdraw unilaterally from the Lebanese security zone. This probably encouraged Palestinians to believe that they could achieve their goals via terrorism and contributed to the outbreak of Palestinian violence on September 30, 2000.

The First Intifada

During the first forty years of Israel's existence as an independent state (1948 until 1987), approximately three generations of Palestinians were raised in the squalor of refugee camps. Since 1967, many Palestinians had lived under Israeli administration in the disputed territories. The frustration of these young people and the incitement of the PLO leadership led to increased violent interaction between Palestinians and the Israelis. Finally, on December 6, 1987, an Israeli shopper in Gaza was stabbed to death by a Palestinian. The next day, an Israeli truck driver in Gaza lost control of his vehicle and smashed into an oncoming car, killing four passengers, all residents of a Palestinian refugee camp in Gaza. Rumors raged that the Israelis had killed the Palestinians deliberately, setting off rioting throughout the territories. The first Palestinian *Intifada* (uprising) had begun.

Initially organized by left-wing Palestinian residents of the disputed territories, the Intifada included Palestinian teenagers engaged in tire burning, stone throwing, and assaults with gasoline bombs on Israeli troops. Besides these attacks, Palestinians also used hand grenades, guns, and other explosives. But for much of the world, the images that were shown on television news were that of youths throwing rocks at troops. Israeli soldiers frequently commented that they would spend hours under assault by Palestinians without responding, but TV cameras only recorded IDF troops responding with force (when their safety was at risk), suggesting military brutality. This pattern of selective media reporting continued during Intifada II (see chapter 3, pp. 47–52.)

Within the first months of the Intifada, Yasser Arafat and the PLO leadership in Tunisia had co-opted the supervision of the uprising. Before long the PLO was calling for "Days of Rage," directing attacks against Jewish targets. Additionally, Palestinians employed by the Israeli Civil Administration in the territories became targets for "collaborating" with Israel. Surprisingly, Palestinian death squads killed more Palestinians in the uprising than did Israeli troops.

As a result of the propaganda war that was part of the Intifada, the image of Israel was further tarnished in the world community. Additionally, Yasser Arafat's disingenuous renunciation of violence in 1988 led the United States to recognize the PLO and enter into formal diplomatic discussions with the terrorist group. By 1990 it became clear that the PLO was still engaged in terrorist activities, causing the first President George Bush to cut recognition and discussions with the PLO.

The Intifada did not come to an abrupt conclusion but fizzled out when Arafat and the PLO supported Saddam Hussein in the first Gulf War. Cheering images of Palestinians celebrating Hussein's unprovoked Scud missile attacks against Israel were broadcast, while Israel showed restraint in the face of these attacks. As a result, for a short while world opinion turned in favor of Israel. By the end of the Gulf War, Arafat had lost all credibility in the Western world, as well as with the Arab states, so the uprising dwindled to a quiet end.

The Oslo Accords

The United States used its victory in the Gulf War to put pressure on Israel to come to a peaceful settlement with the Palestinians. Agreeing to Israeli demands that the Palestinians be represented by local leadership rather than the PLO, the United States brought the Israelis and the Palestinians together at the Madrid Peace Talks in 1991. The Palestinian delegation had no choice but to come. The Soviet Union had fallen, leaving the United States as the last remaining world power. With their loss of credibility and without a sponsor, the Palestinians agreed to meet with Israel in face-to-face negotiations. Throughout the Madrid Conference, the PLO leadership guided the Palestinian delegation behind the scenes. But this was not to be the major breakthrough for peace for which Israel had hoped. That was to come through a back channel in Oslo, Norway.

After the Madrid conference, other secret negotiations between Israeli and Palestinian academics in Oslo broke new ground for an agreement between Israel and the PLO. Israeli Prime Minister Yitzhak Rabin embraced the Oslo accords despite his reservations about Arafat and the PLO. His reason was that during the Intifada, Hamas, a radical Islamic terror group that was even more extreme than the PLO, had gained popularity in the territories. Fearing that Hamas would sabotage all efforts at peace, Rabin agreed to mutual recognition with the PLO. Arafat had assured the Israelis that he would be more aggressive in clamping down on Islamic terror.

This led to the formal Declaration of Principles between Israel and the PLO, yet another political recovery by Yasser Arafat, and the establishment of the Palestinian Authority to govern the Palestinian territories autonomously. The description of the signing of the agreement and the handshake between Rabin and Arafat is where this book opened. Arafat did not prove true to his word, however, breaking the Oslo Peace Accord by inciting the Palestinians, allowing terrorist acts to continue, and in some cases, sponsoring terrorism. Today Israelis and the Palestinians are engaged in their most violent war yet with the hope of peace seeming to be merely a pipe dream.

Israel has grown up as a nation despite the ravages of war. There is no human explanation for it. As David Ben-Gurion said, "In Israel, in order to be a realist you must believe in miracles." And the only way to understand that miracle is by examining what the Scriptures have to say about God's promises to Israel. That is what the next chapter will do.

8
Israel in the Center
of History and Prophecy

All things are mortal but the Jew; all other forces
pass, but he remains. What is the secret of his
immortality?

—Mark Twain

How is it that one small group of people has had such an immense impact
on society? The Jewish people comprise only one-fifth of 1 percent of the
world's population, yet have won 22 percent of all the Nobel prizes award-
ed.[1] The entire world recognizes the achievements of Jewish notables such
as Jonas Salk, who developed the polio vaccine; Albert Einstein, whose
theory of relativity catapulted the world into the atomic age; and Sigmund
Freud, who is the father of psychotherapy. People ask why the small state
of Israel, which is about the size of the state of New Jersey, seems to have
such a large role in world events, with news reports about it on a daily
basis.

Certainly Jewish people have had and will continue to have a profound
influence on the world because of God's choice of Israel to be His people. By examining God's Word, it is possible to understand what is hap-
pening in the news today and what will take place in the future. The best
place to start doing that is by looking at the past—when God called Israel to be His chosen people.

Israel's Past

The unconditional covenants that God made with Israel in the past are foundational for understanding Israel's importance in the prophetic future. These covenants with Israel govern our understanding of the Jewish people and form the backbone of biblical prophecy.

The Abrahamic Covenant

Genesis 12:1–3 records God's call of Abraham out of Ur of the Chaldees (Babylon) and the specific promises He made to him. These promises were confirmed and clarified in later passages of Genesis (13:14–17; 15:1–7; 17:1–21). Additionally, they were reconfirmed to Abraham's son Isaac (26:3–4) and grandson Jacob (28:13–15), clarifying which line of Abraham would receive God's promises.

The promises God made to Abraham fell into three categories: personal, national, and universal.[2] Particularly notable is the *national* promise: Abraham's descendants would multiply and be "as numerous as the stars in the sky and as the sand on the seashore" (Genesis 22:17) and that God would give Abraham and his people the land of Canaan as their "everlasting possession" (17:8), with its boundaries extending from the river of Egypt in the west to the Euphrates River in the east and the land of the Hittites in the north (15:18–21).

This is interesting in light of all the contemporary questions about ownership of the land of Israel today. Regardless of the political disputes, God has granted the title deed of the land of Israel to the Jewish people. At present, this land promise has not been fulfilled in its entirety. (This promise of land is discussed further in chapter 10.)

The national promises also gave Israel a unique position as God's barometer of blessing: Those nations that would bless Israel would be blessed and those that cursed Israel would be cursed (12:3; 27:29). This principle applied during Abraham's life (12:10–20; 14:12–20; 26:1–11) and throughout the history of the Jewish people (Deuteronomy 14:1–2; 30:7). Significantly, this will be the principle that guides God's judgment of the Gentile nations when Jesus returns. The sheep and the goats will be divided on the basis of their treatment of Jesus' physical brethren, the Jewish people. That is why He will say, "Whatever you did for one of the least of these brothers of mine, you did for me" (Matthew 25:40).

Regarding the *universal* aspects of the Abrahamic covenant—that God promised to bless the whole world through Abraham's descendants, or "seed" (Genesis 22:18)—the ultimate fulfillment of this promise occurred through the ministry of Jesus the Messiah of Israel. Through His death and resurrection, Messiah Jesus provided atonement for the whole world (Galatians 3:16).

The Other Covenants

The Land Covenant. Later biblical covenants expanded three particular aspects of the Abrahamic covenant, namely its promises of the land, the seed, and the blessing. For example, the land promise was expanded into the land covenant[3] found in Deuteronomy 28–30. This promise assured that the people of Israel would experience physical and material blessing from God if they would obey His Law. It also assured Israel that God would discipline the nation for persistent disobedience and idolatry by driving the people out of the land and into exile. God also promised to restore the Jewish people to their land after much suffering. Both their suffering and restoration are said to occur "in the latter days" (Deuteronomy 4:30; 31:29 NASB).

The Davidic Covenant. God's promise of seed for Abraham was further expanded in the Davidic covenant. This covenant is foundational for the messianic hope of the Hebrew Bible and the basis of the New Testament expectation of a future kingdom. When David wanted to build a house for God (a temple), instead God promised David that *He* would build a house for David (2 Samuel 7:8–16). God affirmed that He would give David an eternal dynasty and kingdom with an eternal ruler to sit on David's throne (verse 16). That ruler was to be one of David's sons (his seed) who was also to have a Father/Son relationship with God (verses 12–16).

In the course of the historical narrative of 1 Kings, it appears that this promise would be fulfilled through David's son Solomon. In fact, since Solomon even believed that he was the potential fulfillment, he built the temple. But the Lord warned Solomon that the promise would be fulfilled through him only if he would "follow my decrees, carry out my regulations and keep all my commands" (1 Kings 6:12). The author of 1 Kings quickly points out how miserably Solomon failed to obey God with his marriages to foreign women who turned his heart away from God (1 Kings 11:1–4). In fact, no Davidic king succeeded in obeying God completely but all—even the good ones—ended with failure.

Thus, the book of 2 Kings ends with the hope and expectation that God would one day send an eternal ruler who would build the true temple of God and sit on the throne of David. The prophet Zechariah foretold that this future King would come to unite the office of priest and king and build the temple of the Lord (Zechariah 6:9–15).

The hope and longing for this Son of David consumed the prophets, from Isaiah to Amos,[4] and found its fulfillment in the birth of Jesus. The angel Gabriel announced His birth, saying, "The Lord God will give him the throne of his father David, and he will reign over the house of Jacob forever; his kingdom will never end" (Luke 1:32–33). Jesus was the Promised One, the Son of David and the Son of God. He announced the coming of God's kingdom, and He will return to rule from the literal throne of David in Jerusalem and establish the kingdom of God on earth.

The New Covenant. The blessing component of the Abrahamic covenant was amplified by the new covenant. The name "new covenant" comes from Jeremiah 31:31–34, but it had already been promised by Moses (Deuteronomy 30:1–14) and would be affirmed in other prophets (Ezekiel 36:26–27). The newness of this covenant is derived from its distinction from the old covenant, the laws given by God on Mount Sinai. In Jeremiah 31:32 God promised that the new covenant would be unlike the old covenant He gave Israel after the nation left Egypt. This old covenant is an obvious reference to the Sinai covenant, not the Abrahamic covenant or any other covenant. Hebrews 8:13 confirms this when it states that the old covenant (the Sinai covenant) has been made obsolete by the establishment of the new covenant.

The new covenant was promised to Israel and Judah and ratified through the death of Jesus the Messiah (Matthew 26:27–28). The new covenant was indeed inaugurated with Israel through the righteous remnant of Jewish people who believe in Jesus as Messiah. Today, the church, composed of Jewish and Gentile followers of Jesus, shares those spiritual blessings through its relationship with the Messiah Jesus. However, only when Messiah returns and begins His kingdom will He establish the new covenant in its fullest sense. In that day, when everyone knows the Lord, all people will fully experience this universal aspect of the Abrahamic covenant.

Since God keeps His promises, these covenants from Israel's past remain significant for her present and future. The land aspect of the Abrahamic covenant reaffirms that the title deed to the land of Israel belongs to the Jewish people, and the covenant assures that there will be a future kingdom that will include all the land God promised—something which throughout her long history, Israel has never possessed. The Davidic covenant assures that Jesus the Messiah, the Son of David, will return and establish His kingdom on earth. He will rule from David's throne as the righteous King of Israel and sovereign of the world. Finally, the new covenant guarantees that there will be a time when all Israel will turn to her Messiah. Then Israel and all the nations of the world will know the Lord.

These covenants certainly give hope for the future, but what of Israel today? To Israel's present we now turn.

Israel's Present

Since these covenants are all from Israel's past, some people have improperly taken them away from Israel and applied them to the church today. It is true that the vast majority of Jewish people have failed to recognize Jesus as their Messiah. This rejection has motivated some sincere followers of Christ to adopt the erroneous opinion that Israel's promises have transferred to the church. Their approach seems to take a rather shortsighted view of the faithfulness of God.

One of the essential principles of the Abrahamic covenant is that it is unconditional and eternal. Abraham did not need to do anything to receive or maintain this covenant. Furthermore, when God reaffirmed His covenant with Abraham, He solemnized His divine oath with the offering of sacrifices (Genesis 15:8–17). In ancient times, when two parties wanted to bind themselves to a covenant, they would lay the severed parts of a sacrificial animal on the ground, and both parties would walk in their midst. This signified that both were in agreement and bound by the covenant. When God solemnized His oath to Abraham, He deliberately excluded Abraham from the process. Instead, God caused Abraham to fall into a deep sleep and God alone passed through the animal parts. This demonstrated that God was solely responsible for this covenant—it did not depend on Abraham or his descendants but on God alone. In light of the unconditional nature of the Abrahamic covenant, there are several truths about the Jewish people today that must be maintained.

Israel as God's Chosen People

God has retained Israel as His chosen people. This is not only an Old Testament concept; the New Testament agrees with it as well. Paul wrote that despite Israel's disbelief in Jesus, "God did not reject his people, whom he foreknew" (Romans 11:2). Moreover, although most Jewish people have rejected the good news of Jesus, the people of Israel remain God's beloved chosen people "on account of the patriarchs" (11:28)—a clear reference to the Abrahamic covenant. Paul categorically states that God's gifts and call to Israel are irrevocable (11:29).

Remaining God's chosen people does not mean that Jewish people have forgiveness and a personal relationship with God apart from faith in their Messiah Jesus. Jewish people, as all people, must trust in Jesus. Regardless, the Lord's words in Deuteronomy 14:2 remain true as ever: "Out of all the peoples on the face of the earth, the LORD has chosen you to be his treasured possession." God did this not because of any merit found in the Jewish people. God told Israel that He chose them "because the LORD loved you and kept the oath he swore to your forefathers" (7:8).

Since God is faithful to His promises and loyal in His love, the Jewish people are still the chosen people.

A Preserved and Protected People

God is active today preserving and protecting the Jewish people. Through the prophet Jeremiah, the Lord assures that it will be impossible ever to destroy the Jewish people. In fact, in order to put an end to the Jewish people, it would be necessary to stop the sun, moon, and stars from shining and also to measure all the heavens and the foundations of the earth. God declares that only if these impossible acts could be accomplished will "the descendants of Israel . . . cease to be a nation before me" or "will I reject all the descendants of Israel" (Jeremiah 31:35–37). Plainly, the Lord will preserve His people. That is why the prophet Zechariah says of the people of Israel that whoever touches them "touches the apple of [God's] eye" (Zechariah 2:8).

Throughout history there have been those who have sought Israel's destruction—from Haman to Hitler to Saddam Hussein—but they have never succeeded. In 1981, I attended the World Gathering of Holocaust Survivors in Jerusalem, as a second generation participant. There I heard Menachem Begin, the late prime minister of Israel, declare before those Holocaust survivors and their children that Hitler's attempt to annihilate the Jewish people ought not to cause them to doubt God's existence but rather to believe in Him. Begin said that apart from God's providential intervention, there was no way Hitler could have failed. The prime min-

ister recognized that God was true to His promise to preserve and ultimately to protect His chosen people.

Frederick the Great was said to have asked his chaplain for one clear
and compelling evidence for the existence of God. The chaplain replied:
"The amazing Jew, your Majesty."

The preservation of the Jewish people, despite a history of hatred
and persecution, has led historian Paul Johnson to call the Jews "the most
tenacious people in history." It is far better to say that the Jewish people
are protected by the tenacious God of history, who is faithful to His promises and relentless in preserving His people. For this reason, no weapon
formed against Israel will ever prosper (Isaiah 54:17).

A Remnant Being Saved

God is presently saving a remnant of Israel. Paul asserted, in Romans
11:1–5, that God did not reject the Jewish people, and as proof he offered the doctrine of the remnant. His point was that God has always
worked through a faithful remnant both during the Old Testament and the
present age. Even though the vast majority of the Jewish people have rejected Jesus as the Messiah, God in His faithfulness has preserved a remnant within Israel, chosen by grace, who would believe. So Paul wrote, "So
too, at the present time there is a remnant chosen by grace" (verse 5).

Throughout the entire church age there has always been a remnant
of Jewish people who have sincerely believed in Jesus as their Messiah and
Lord. Since 1967, a significant number of Jewish people have come to
believe in Jesus and still maintain their unique role as the Jewish remnant. There are approximately 250,000 messianic Jews worldwide participating in hundreds of messianic congregations and in many evangelical
churches. This movement is especially evident in North America, Europe, South America, the former Soviet Union, and Israel.

Paul anticipated a day when the remnant would become the whole.
He wrote in Romans 11:25–26 that at Jesus' return, when the full number of Gentiles have come in, Israel as a whole will turn to Jesus in faith
as their Messiah, "and so all Israel will be saved." Perhaps the Spirit of God's
unique move among the Jewish people today is a precursor to the far
greater movement that will take place yet in the future.

Restored to the Land

God is restoring the Jewish people to the land of Israel. Since their exile around the world nearly two millennia ago, Jewish people have daily prayed that they would be restored to the land of Israel. The Hebrew prophets foretold a day when God would draw His people back to their promised land. Throughout church history, Christians for the most part could not conceive of a literal fulfillment of this promise, so they interpreted it figuratively. However, some believers in the nineteenth century did indeed take the promise of a return literally and therefore began to anticipate a Jewish return to the land of Israel.

In previous chapters, this book has described the nineteenth century "Lovers of Zion," who believed that a return to the land of Israel was the only hope for Jewish people to survive in a world filled with anti-Jewish hatred. Chapter 5 recounted the story of Theodore Herzl and the rise of Zionism, which led to the immigration waves known as *aliyot* and the issuing of the Balfour Declaration (1917) that advocated a Jewish national home in Palestine. Chapter 6 told the story of the ingathering of the exiles after the birth of the state of Israel.

The State of Israel: A Fulfillment of Bible Prophecy

Bible believers frequently ask how the unprecedented reborn state of Israel fits with Bible prophecy. For several reasons, it appears that the best explanation is that the modern state of Israel seems to be a dramatic work of God in fulfillment of the Bible's predictions of a Jewish return to the land of Israel.

First, the Bible predicts that Israel would return to her land in unbelief. Biblical prophecy indicates that the Jewish people will turn to God only *after* returning to the land of Israel. Ezekiel 36:24 (NASB) says, "For I will take you from the nations, gather you from all the lands and bring you into your own land." The next two verses (25–26) continue, "*Then* I will sprinkle clean water on you, and you will be clean; I will cleanse you from all your filthiness and from all your idols. Moreover, I will give you a new heart and put a new spirit within you; and I will remove the heart of stone from your flesh and give you a heart of flesh" (italics added).

Note that the *national* restoration of the Jewish people will precede the *spiritual* regeneration of Israel. Israel has been reborn as a secular state by secular Jews. This is the precursor to the day when the entire nation turns in faith to Jesus Messiah Yeshua.

Second, the Bible predicts that Israel would return to her land in stages. Ezekiel 37 contains the vision of a valley of dry bones. The bones come to life in stages: first sinews on the bones, then flesh, then skin, and, finally, the breath of life (37:6–10). Then God told Ezekiel that "these bones are the whole house of Israel" (verse 11) and that their restoration is a picture of the way God will bring them "back to the land of Israel" (verse 12). So the regathering of Israel is not an event that will occur in one fell swoop. Rather, it is a process that culminates in the nation receiving the breath of life by turning to their Messiah.

This is precisely how the Jewish people have returned to the land. Through the different *aliyot,* beginning in 1881 to the recent wave of immigrants from the former Soviet Union, the Jewish people have returned in stages. The final step will be when the entire nation turns in faith to Jesus their Messiah and God breathes the breath of life on them.

Third, the Bible predicts that Israel would return to her land through persecution. God says of Israel through the prophet Jeremiah, "I will restore them to the land I gave their forefathers" (16:15). In the next verse, God says that He will use "fishermen" and "hunters" to pursue His people back to their land (verse 16). This metaphor for persecution has been literally fulfilled in the rebirth of Israel. Since the birth of modern Zionism, the primary motivation for return to the land of Israel has been anti-Jewish persecution. In the past one hundred years, God has used czarist pogroms, Polish economic discrimination, Nazi genocide, Arab hatred, and Soviet repression to drive Jewish people back to their homeland. Economic success and religious freedom in the Diaspora keep Jewish people complacent about returning, so God uses "fishermen" and "hunters" to drive them back to the Promised Land.

Fourth, the Bible predicts that Israel would return to her land to set the stage for end-time events. Daniel 9:27 speaks of a firm covenant between the future world dictator and the Jewish people, which will unleash the final events before Messiah Jesus' return. This prophecy assumes a reborn state of Israel. The Jewish state had to be restored so this prediction (and many others) could take place. A reborn state of Israel was necessary for this treaty/covenant to be signed, for the temple to be rebuilt, for Jerusalem to be surrounded by the nations during the campaign of Armageddon, even for Jesus to return to deliver the Jewish people from their enemies.

Since Israel has returned in unbelief, in stages, through persecution, it is likely that the modern state of Israel fulfills the predictions of the ancient Hebrew prophets . . . and sets the stage for events yet to come.

God established His plan for Israel in the ancient past by establishing His covenants with the Jewish people. On the basis of these covenants, God continues to work among the Jewish people in the present age. But God has much more in store for Israel in the future. In fact, He has given the Jewish people a featured role to play in the outworking of end-time events.

Israel's Future

Throughout history, God has caused the Jewish people to have an influence that far outweighs their size. Their influence will be even greater in the future. During the end times, Israel will be the focal point in God's future program in several ways.

A Role in the Future Tribulation

Israel will play a vital role in starting the future Tribulation. Although the Bible teaches that Jesus can return for His church at any moment (Matthew 25:1–13; 1 Thessalonians 5:1), it gives a specific requirement for the beginning of the future Tribulation period. The Tribulation will begin only when Israel signs a covenant (a treaty of some sort) with the future false messiah. According to Daniel 9:27, the seventieth "seven" of Daniel's vision begins when "he will confirm a covenant with many for one 'seven.'" The identity of the "he" in this verse, according to the rest of the verse, is a future world ruler who will set up an abomination in a yet to be built temple. This ruler is frequently called the "Antichrist" or the "Man of Sin," but I prefer to call him the "future false messiah."

This false messiah will make a covenant or treaty with *many*. From the context, it appears that *many* refers either to many in Israel or to Israel and her neighbors. This treaty, either between Israel and the false messiah or Israel and her neighbors but brokered by the false messiah, will most likely establish peace in the Middle East for the first half of the Tribulation (three and one-half years). But the false messiah will then break the covenant and unleash hell on earth, culminating in the campaign of Armageddon.

Significantly, the Messiah, Jesus, can return for the church at *any* time—even as you read this paragraph. However, the Tribulation will only begin when Israel and the future false messiah will make a treaty together

—showing Israel's vital role as a catalyst for the Tribulation period. Besides starting the Tribulation, Israel is crucial for other aspects of future events.

A Focal Point of the Tribulation

Israel will be the focus of the Tribulation. The prophet Jeremiah clarifies this when he calls the Tribulation period "a time of trouble for Jacob" (30:7). The name "Jacob" refers in this context not to the patriarch but the people who descended from him. Israel is God's primary concern during the Tribulation, since the church will have already been removed at the Rapture (when Jesus instantly calls His followers into heaven [1 Thessalonians 4:13–17]). Israel's central place in the Tribulation is evident in several ways.

First, Israel will face *persecution* during the Tribulation. In Revelation 12, God describes Satan's activity at both the Messiah's first and second comings. He uses the figure of "a woman clothed with the sun, with the moon under her feet and a crown of twelve stars on her head" (12:1). In light of Joseph's dream (Genesis 37:9), it is best to understand the woman as a reference to Israel. The woman (Israel) gave birth to a Son (Jesus, the Messianic King), who was persecuted by the dragon (Satan) at His birth (Revelation 12:1–6). This happened at Jesus' first coming through the attempt by Herod the Great to destroy the rightful King of the Jewish people (Matthew 2:13–18).

Prior to the second coming of the Messiah, the dragon will be cast to the earth and he will begin to persecute "the woman who had given birth to the male child" (Revelation 12:13), namely, Israel. Not only will the dragon be "enraged at the woman" (Israel) but he will make war "against the rest of her offspring" (Revelation 12:17). This refers to the future satanic attack on both the nation and the remnant of Israel who will come to faith during the Tribulation. During this time the Jewish people will endure unprecedented hatred and persecution.

Second, the people of Israel will experience *cleansing* during the Tribulation. God will permit the suffering of His chosen people in order to discipline them so that they will turn to Messiah Jesus in faith. The prophet Ezekiel speaks of the Tribulation as the time when Israel passes under God's rod of discipline (Ezekiel 20:37). This discipline will result in Israel being purged of rebels (those who have not yet trusted in Jesus as their Messiah) and the rest of the nation being brought into the bond of the covenant (Ezekiel 20:37–38).

The prophet Jeremiah records God's purpose for the Tribulation when

God says to Israel, "I will discipline you but only with justice" (Jeremiah 30:11). According to Zechariah, God will discipline the people of Israel in order to "refine them like silver and test them like gold." As a result, Israel will call on God's name and He will answer them. God will say, "'They are my people,' and they will say, 'The LORD is our God'" (Zechariah 13:9). God will use the suffering of the Jewish people to discipline them so that they will come to know the LORD through Jesus their Messiah.

Third, during the Tribulation many in Israel will devote themselves in *service* to God. Revelation 7:3–4 describes 144,000 Jewish people, from all the twelve tribes, who are called "the servants of our God." They are Jewish people who come to faith in Jesus after the removal of the church at the Rapture. No doubt there will be Bibles and other materials that will enable the 144,000 to understand and receive the Gospel. This remnant of Israel will be sealed by God and set apart for His service. What they will do in service to God is unclear. Perhaps they will be the evangelists of the Tribulation period, helping people all over the world to put their trust in Jesus the Messiah, even during the Tribulation.

Fourth, Israel will face *war* during the Tribulation. At the culmination of the Tribulation, world leaders will gather their armies in northern Israel, next to Mount Megiddo, to begin the campaign of Armageddon (Revelation 16:16). These nations will march on Jerusalem and besiege the Jewish people; there attacking armies of the world will fight against Jerusalem, capture and ransack the city, and commit horrible atrocities (Zechariah 12:2–3; 14:2). God will allow this so that Israel will turn to Him and then be saved. The Tribulation will be a time of war for the Jewish people.

God's wrath will fall on the earth during the Tribulation period. It will be a time of suffering for all peoples. But more than any other nation, God will focus His attention on the Jewish people, with the goal of bringing them to faith in Jesus and restoring them to Himself. Besides Israel's importance in starting and being the focus of the Tribulation, the nation will play an even more significant role in the second coming of Jesus the Messiah.

An Initiator in the Messiah's Return

Israel will initiate the second coming of the Messiah. Although no one knows the day or hour of Jesus' return for His church, we do know that He will return at the conclusion of the seven-year Tribulation period. What will bring about the end of that period and return the Messiah to the earth? The Scriptures teach that it will be Israel who will call for Jesus to return, and He will do so in His mercy.

Matthew 23:37–39 contains Jesus' response to Israel's national rejection of Him. He would have longed to gather Israel as a mother hen gathers her chicks, He said, but when the leadership of Israel rejected Jesus, they made that impossible. Therefore, Jesus said, Jerusalem and the temple would be destroyed. However, He did offer Israel hope in the midst of this judgment. "For I tell you, you will not see me again until you say, 'Blessed is he who comes in the name of the Lord'" (Matthew 23:39).

Jesus requires Israel to say the traditional Hebrew words of welcome and reception. In effect, Jesus is saying that He will not return to Israel until they welcome Him as the Messiah. What will cause Israel to do this?

The prophet Zechariah predicted that at the end of the Tribulation the nations will gather in Israel and attack Jerusalem (Zechariah 12:1–9). The suffering will have been so severe and the situation so grave that Israel's leaders will turn to God for deliverance. God will graciously open their eyes so that "they will look on me [in faith], the one they have pierced, and they will mourn for him as one mourns for an only child, and grieve bitterly for him as one grieves for a firstborn son" (12:10). Israel will mourn for all the years that they had rejected Jesus. The Messiah will return and "a fountain will be opened . . . to cleanse them from sin and impurity" (13:1). Then, as Paul had foretold, all the Jewish people alive in that day will put their faith in Jesus as their Messiah, "and so all Israel will be saved" (Romans 11:26).

Not only will the Lord deliver them from their sin, He will also deliver them from their attackers. According to Zechariah, "Then the LORD will go out and fight against those nations, as he fights in the day of battle. On that day his feet will stand on the Mount of Olives. . . . Then the LORD my God will come and all the holy ones with him" (14:3–5). It is only when Israel calls for Jesus to return and looks to Him in faith, that the Messiah will return. Israel is the key to the second coming of Jesus the Messiah. Even after Jesus returns, Israel will still have a crucial position in God's program.

A Special Place in the Messiah's Kingdom

Israel will be the head of the nations in the messianic kingdom. The messianic kingdom that Jesus will establish will have many marvelous components.

From the renovation of the earth to universal peace, it will be a glorious time. But for Israel, it will be remarkable. All Jewish people will have turned to Jesus whom they will now know as Lord. Those who are still scattered around the world will be returned to the land of Israel and will fully inhabit the land according to the provisions of the Abrahamic covenant.

The Messiah will begin His reign from the throne of David in Jerusalem and will rule over Israel and all the nations. Significantly, Israel will be the head of the nations then, even as the book of Deuteronomy had foretold: "The LORD will make you the head, not the tail" (28:13). Isaiah promised that God would again choose Israel and settle them in their land. Then "the house of Israel will possess the nations" (Isaiah 14:1–2).

Although many biblical passages speak of Israel's leadership of the Gentile nations in the messianic kingdom (Isaiah 49:22–23; 60:1–3; 61:4–9; Micah 7:14–17; Zephaniah 3:20), one is especially notable in that it speaks of the spiritual influence Israel will have over the nations. The Lord Almighty Himself describes the scene when "many peoples and powerful nations will come" to worship Him in Jerusalem. "In those days ten men from all languages and nations will take firm hold of one Jew by the hem of his robe and say, 'Let us go with you, because we have heard that God is with you'" (Zechariah 8:22–23).

When the Jewish people know the Lord, He will make them great, and they will lead the Gentile nations in worship of Him. This small nation of Israel will continue to have a large influence, even in the messianic kingdom. The ancient rabbis were right when they said, "Israel is like a vine: trodden underfoot; but some time later its wine is placed on the table of a king. So, Israel, at first oppressed, will eventually come to greatness."[5]

The "Immortal" Jew

This chapter began with a quote by Mark Twain. "All things are mortal but the Jew; all other forces pass, but he remains. What is the secret of his immortality?" Twain has asked the right question. What is the secret of this special people? At the outset of this chapter, we asked the same question. The answer, as we have seen, lies in the Abrahamic covenant.

Long ago, God, in His grace, chose Israel to be His special people. Therefore, even now, in the present age, Israel remains God's chosen people, the special object of His love and concern. Since this is true, God will be faithful to all the promises that He made to Abraham, Isaac, and Jacob.

9
Militant Islam
and the Arab-Israeli Conflict

The Palestinian question is not a national issue,
nor is it a political issue. It is first and foremost an
Islamic question.

> —The Supreme Islamic Research Council

To understand the Arab-Israeli conflict, it is essential to comprehend Islam.
More than 95 percent of the Arab world is Islamic and guided by Islam
in thinking about Israel. Islamic fundamentalism is on the rise around
the world and clearly making its presence felt. The 9/11 terrorist attacks
in 2001 against the United States heightened North America's awareness
of radical Islam. In a sense, Americans experienced what Israelis have been
dealing with for years.

Most Palestinians (98 percent) are Muslim, as are the Arab countries
that surround Israel. Although various Palestinian factions have differing
levels of commitment to Islam, from the more secular to the more funda-
mentalist, they are all committed to Islam and its teachings to some degree. Therefore, let us examine the relationship of Islam to the conflict.

In the aftermath of the 9/11 attacks, masterminded by fundamental-
ist followers of Osama bin Laden, Muslims were frequently heard in the
media condemning terrorism and claiming that Islam is a religion of peace.
Repeatedly, apologists for Islam asserted that "Islam means 'peace'" and
"taking one's own life is disapproved by Islam." Even President Bush made
similar assertions. It makes sense, since the United States was seeking to
build a coalition against terror that would include Islamic states. But are
those claims true? Is Islam truly a religion of peace?

Moderate Versus Militant Islam

The answer lies in the distinction between moderate and militant Islam. Most Americans are familiar with moderate Islam. The most essential element of Islam is adhering to the five pillars: confessing that Allah alone is God and that Muhammad is His prophet, praying five times daily, fasting during the month of Ramadan, almsgiving, and making a pilgrimage to Mecca once in a lifetime.

There are also six core beliefs of Islam, summarized as follows by Braswell:

- Monotheism. There is no other god but the one god Allah.
- Angels. Among the angels, Gabriel appeared to Muhammad from heaven with the words of the Qur'an.
- Prophets. There are many prophets, including Jesus, but Muhammad is the final prophet.
- Scriptures. The Qur'an is the infallible, inerrant scripture revealed to Muhammad. The Torah and the Gospel were revealed to Moses and Jesus as inerrant in their times but have since become corrupt.
- Judgment. Everyone will be judged by Allah.
- Paradise and hell. Distinctly different eternal destinies await the blessed and the damned.[1]

Militant Islam affirms another side of the religion, supporting violence "in the way of Allah." Originally, Islam was spread by the sword. Muhammad founded the religion in A.D. 622 in Medina, Saudi Arabia, with the support of various tribes. He spread the new religion, subduing other tribes, including Jewish ones, with dramatic loss of life. By the time he died in 632, Islam, through military conquest, ruled the Arabian Peninsula. His followers continued to spread the religion with the sword so that by 732, Islam controlled all the lands from the Indus River in the east to Spain in the west.[2] The violent spread of religion is a legacy of Islam.

Therefore, militant Islam is more than a religion; it is an ideology with a political agenda. Central to its beliefs is that all humanity is to live in submission to Allah. According to militant Islamists, Islam must extend its sovereignty over the whole world, even by force.

Why do some Muslims claim Islam as a religion of peace while others assert that it demands violence? First, moderate Islam and militant Islam emphasize different parts of the Qur'an. Twenty years after the death of Muhammad, his teachings were codified in the Qur'an. Some suras (chapters) reflect Muhammad's teachings in Mecca, coming from the early and middle years of his life, while other suras contain Muhammad's teachings from his later life in Medina. Since Muhammad's early life had less opposition and his later life had much antagonism, the early Meccan suras tend to advocate peaceful teachings, while the later Medina suras embrace violence and warfare. Moderate Islam emphasizes the early peaceful suras, but militant Islam accentuates the later, violent ones.

Second, moderate Islam limits the violent parts of the Qur'an to the historical periods in which they were written, while militant Islam generalizes them to all periods. Moderate Muslims would say that the calls for violence were not intended to be applied today but pertain to the events when they were written. Militant Muslims believe that the Qur'an's teachings about war must be applied at all times and in every circumstance.

Third, moderate Islam interprets the Qur'an's calls for battle in a spiritual sense, whereas militant Islam takes them literally. Moderates believe that Muslims must struggle within themselves in a spiritual sense but not aggressively with non-Muslims in a physical sense. Militant Muslims believe that they are obligated to obey the Qur'an's teachings about violence, killing, and war. They would view themselves as holy warriors, not terrorists or murderers.

Applying the Militant Perspective

Militant Islam began to reappear at the end of the nineteenth century and has grown rapidly since the fall of the Soviet Union. Today, it is taught in madrassahs (theological schools) in places like Pakistan and funded by Saudi Arabia and other oil-rich Arab countries. It is also embraced by many illiterate peasants who have difficulty making the fine distinctions necessary in moderate Islam.

Although media apologists tend to sharpen the distinctions between moderates and militants, in reality there is a significant blurring of the lines. For example, the Palestinian Authority and many Palestinians have embraced secular nationalism, but they also apply the Qur'an's teachings about Jewish people and violence to their views of Israel. Thus, the majority of Palestinians support Islamic terrorism and suicide bombers.[3]

The secular Fatah movement, under the leadership of Yasser Arafat, has developed a militant Islamic terrorist group called the Al-Aqsa Martyrs. Other Islamic terrorist groups, such as Hamas and Islamic Jihad, readily find support among secular and nationalist Palestinians. Palestinian support for militant Islam was evident in the jubilation in the West Bank and Gaza Strip, celebrating militant Islam's attack on the United States on September 11, 2001. Many Palestinians would identify themselves as moderates but would still endorse the teachings of militant Islam as it relates to Israel and the West.

The Call for Jihad

The word *jihad,* in its literal sense, means "struggle." Although most English speakers assume that *jihad* means "holy war," in reality Islam teaches four types of jihad. These refer to struggle waged with the heart, the tongue, the hand, and the sword. Obviously, only the last refers to "holy war," violent conflict in the name of Allah to advance Islam; the first three deal with inner struggle against moral temptations. These three also include struggle to obey the five pillars of Islam and proselytization of others to Islam.

Violent jihad can be further categorized as either offensive or defensive. Offensive warfare is designed to spread the sovereignty of Islam to non-Muslim areas. Muslims may take an active role in this category of jihad, or their participation may be passive, including both political and financial support. Defensive jihad refers to violent action to remove non-Muslim invaders who have taken lands previously held by Islam. According to Islam, territory once conquered by Islam belongs to Muslims forever. Therefore, Islam teaches that it is the obligation of every able-bodied Muslim to fight for any land that has been taken from Muslims. So, despite the distinctions between moderate and militant Islam, jihad, even violent jihad, is the obligation of every adherent of Islam.

One of the difficulties of the conflict between Israel and the Palestinians is Yasser Arafat's (and other Palestinian leaders') continual call for jihad, despite the signing of the Oslo peace agreement. For example, speaking at a rally in Dehaishe, near Bethlehem, on October 21, 1996, Arafat said, "We know only one word: jihad, jihad, and jihad. Whoever does not like it can drink from the Dead Sea or the Sea of Gaza."[4] In a speech at Al Azhar University in Gaza on June 19, 1995, Arafat said, "The commitment still stands and the oath is still valid: that we will continue this long jihad, this difficult jihad . . . via deaths, via battles."[5] Earlier in Gaza he declared, "All of us are willing to be martyrs along the way, until our flag flies over Jerusalem, the capital of Palestine. Let no one think they can scare us with weapons, for we have mightier weapons—the weapon of faith, the weapon of martyrdom, the weapon of jihad."[6]

When confronted by these quotes, Arafat frequently dissembles, saying he is only referring to internal jihad and not the violent type. But by saying he is willing to create martyrs and cause deaths and battles, it seems that the only logical way to understand these words is as referring to violent jihad. These frequent calls to jihad serve to diminish Israeli confidence that Yasser Arafat, or any who share in his calls for jihad, want to make a real peace deal.

Islam and Land

Islam divides the world into two zones: Dar as-Salaam (House of Peace) and Dar al-Harb (House of the Sword). Dar as-Salaam refers to lands that are under Islamic sovereignty, while Dar al-Harb refers to land that is no longer under Islamic sovereignty. Because Islamic thought is that once a land has been under Islamic sovereignty it forever belongs to Islam, if the previous owners retake a land, every able-bodied Muslim is expected to engage in jihad to reclaim the land for Islam.

Understanding this concept should clarify two questions that are repeatedly raised. First, is Islam a religion of peace? The answer is that although the term *Islam* is derived from the word *salaam,* the meaning is not exactly peace. It is more appropriately defined as submission or subjugation. Peace comes from submission to Allah and Islam. Lands only come under the House of Peace if they are subjugated by Islam, even if that is accomplished by the sword.

Second, why does it seem impossible for most Arab Muslim states to recognize Israel? The reason is that the Jewish people are not viewed as an indigenous people who held autonomy and sovereignty in the land years before the Islamic invasion. Rather, they are viewed as Western interlopers and colonialists that have taken a land that was previously under Dar as-Salaam. With Israel frequently compared to medieval Crusaders, it is alleged that there can be no peace until all the Holy Land is returned to Muslim sovereignty. This does not refer only to the West Bank and Gaza Strip, taken in the 1967 Six Day War, but Israel proper, as established in 1948.

Consequently, the militant Islamic terrorist group Hamas demands not just Israeli withdrawal from all of the West Bank and Gaza and the full right of return for four million Palestinian refugees to Israel proper but also the end of Israel as a state. According to the *New York Times,* Mahmoud al-Zahar, a leader of Hamas, has demanded that the Jewish state become "an Islamic state with Islamic law. From our ideological point of view, it is not allowed to recognize that Israel controls one square meter of historic Palestine."[7] Obviously, this Islamic view of land is a serious obstruction to a peaceful resolution to the conflict, even a two-state solution.

Islam and Martyrdom

Intifada II introduced a new form of terrorism: the suicide bomber. With a strap full of explosives, young men (for the most part) make their way onto Israeli buses, into open-air markets, night clubs, and restaurants, and kill themselves with the intention of murdering as many Israelis as possible. What could motivate a young person to do this? Some say frustration with the Israeli occupation or poverty or lack of hope.

But Islam plays a significant role in driving this form of terrorism. Muslim religious leaders characterize such actions as "martyrdom" for the sake of Islam and assure these "martyrs" (*shaheeds*) that they earn immediate entrance to paradise. By dying as supposed warriors (*mujahideen*) for Islam, the Qur'an promises such "martyrs" a special privileged place in paradise. Paradise for them will be especially sensual, with seventy-two perpetual virgins (called *houris*) fulfilling the erotic desires of the "martyrs." Moreover, the "martyrs" will be granted perpetual youth and increased sexual prowess (Sura 9:20; 55:54–55).

As a result, suicide bombers have now become Palestinian heroes. Yasser Arafat frequently calls for millions of martyrs, and Palestinian textbooks and children's television extol them. The Palestinian Authority has even set up camps for training children in military and terrorist operations. Palestinian children are taught to value dying as a "martyr" and promised immediate paradise. Islam has significantly contributed to the culture of violence and death in Palestinian society.

Islamic Attitudes Toward Peace Agreements

It appears that militant Islam's view of land, jihad, and martyrdom would prohibit the signing of any peace agreements with Israel. Nevertheless, Egypt and Jordan have both signed peace treaties and the Palestine Liberation Organization signed the Oslo framework for peace with the state of Israel. How could they do this?

"Temporary" Peace Agreements

Most Muslims would not consider these peace agreements to be permanent but rather temporary cease-fires. This is possible because Islam permits its adherents to lie for a variety of reasons. Although the Qur'an absolutely prohibits lies against Allah and against Muhammad, there are exemptions in several other areas. For example, a Muslim may lie to save one's life, to persuade a woman toward or maintain peace in marriage, to effect a peace or reconciliation with another Muslim, or for battle. Muslims also believe it is permissible to call a *hudna* (a temporary truce or cease-fire) until they are strong enough to take up arms again.

This appears to be Yasser Arafat's perspective. Two years after signing the Oslo Peace Accord and upon his return from receiving the Nobel Peace Prize, Arafat stopped in Stockholm to meet with Arab diplomats there. He stated, "We Palestinians will take over everything, including all of Jerusalem. . . . You understand that we plan to eliminate the State of Israel and establish a purely Palestinian State. We will make life unbearable for Jews by psychological warfare and population explosion; Jews won't want to live among us Arabs."[8]

Later Arafat would explain his signing of the peace agreement by saying, "We chose the 'Peace of the Brave' out of faith [in the conduct] of the Prophet [Muhammad] in the Hudaybiyeh agreement."[9] The Hudaybiyeh agreement refers to a ten-year peace agreement signed by Muhammad with a Quraish tribe. Eighteen months later, when his forces were stronger and the Quraish tribe was unsuspecting, Muhammad violated the agreement and captured Mecca. So Yasser Arafat has openly stated that he does not intend to keep the peace agreements that he signed with Israel.

The Trojan Horse

It is not only Arafat, but many Palestinian leaders unabashedly assert that all peace agreements with Israel are but a ruse. One of the clearest statements came from Faisal Husseini, the late PLO representative to Jerusalem and frequently hailed as a Palestinian moderate. Just prior to his death from a heart attack, Husseini gave an interview with the Egyptian daily newspaper *Al-Arabi*, in which he compared the Oslo accords to a Trojan horse. Additionally, he said,

Similarly, if we agree to declare our state over what is now only 22 percent of Palestine, meaning the West Bank and Gaza—our ultimate goal is [still] the liberation of all historical Palestine from the [Jordan] River to the [Mediterranean] sea, even if this means that the conflict will last for another thousand years or for many generations. . . .

We distinguish the strategic, long-term goals from the political phased goals, which we are compelled to temporarily accept due to international pressure. If you are asking me as a Pan-Arab nationalist what are the Palestinian borders according to the higher strategy, I will immediately reply: "from the river to the sea."

Palestine in its entirety is an Arab land, the land of the Arab nation, a land no one can sell or buy, and it is impossible to remain silent while someone is stealing it, even if this requires time and even [if it means paying] a high price.

If you are asking me, as a man who belongs to the Islamic faith, my answer is also "from the river to the sea," the entire land is an Islamic Waqf [religious endowment] which can not be bought or sold, and it is impossible to remain silent while someone is stealing it.[10]

Consistently, Palestinian leaders declare that peace agreements with Israel are all temporary. They are viewed as part of a phased plan for the elimination of Israel and the establishment of a Palestinian state, not just in the West Bank and Gaza, but including Israel proper as well. All this is justified by Muhammad's model of disingenuous peace agreements.

Islamic Attitudes Toward the Jewish People

Inferior Beings

Underlying all the other Islamic factors that contribute to the ongoing conflict is the pervasive and visceral anti-Semitism that permeates Islam. From its founding, Islam has classified Jews (and Christians) as *Dhimmis* (protected peoples) because of their status as peoples of the Book. Nevertheless, this was an inferior status that combined both tolerance and discrimination. Dhimmis were considered impure and were to be segregated from the Islamic community. They were never to forget that they were classified as inferior beings.

The Qur'an contains some extremely hostile passages about Jews. Historian Robert Wistrich summarizes them as follows:

Muhammad brands the Jews as enemies of Islam and depicts them as possessing a malevolent, rebellious spirit. There are also verses that speak of their justified abasement and poverty, of the Jews being "laden with God's anger" for their disobedience. They had to be humiliated "because they had disbelieved the signs of God and slain the prophets unrightfully" (Sura 2:61/58). According to another verse (Sura 5:78/82), "The unbelievers of the Children of Israel" were cursed by both David and Jesus. The penalty for disbelief in God's signs and in the miracles performed by the prophets was to be transformed into apes and swine or worshipers of idols (Sura 5:60/65).

The Koran particularly emphasizes that the Jews rejected Muhammad, even though (according to Muslim sources) they knew him to be a prophet—supposedly out of pure jealousy for the Arabs and resentment because he was not a Jew. . . . A variety of verses further charge the Jews with "falsehood" (Sura 3:71), distortion (4:46), cowardice, greed, and being "corrupters of Scripture.". . . The most basic anti-Jewish stereotype fostered by the Koran remains the charge that the Jews have stubbornly and willfully rejected Allah's truth. Not only that but according to the sacred text, they have always persecuted his prophets, including Muhammad. . . . The hadith (oral tradition) goes much further and claims that the Jews, in accordance with their perfidious nature, deliberately caused Muhammad's painful, protracted death from poisoning. Furthermore, malevolent, conspiratorial Jews are to blame for the sectarian strife in early Islam, for heresies and deviations that undermined or endangered the unity of the umma (the Muslim nation).[11]

Harsh Declarations and Falsehoods

As a result of this hostile perception of Jewish people, the Arab world has articulated all sorts of anti-Semitic polemic throughout this long conflict. In recent years, Muslim clerics, even those in the employ of the Palestinian Authority, have charged Jews with being descendants of apes, pigs, and other animals. Besides these harsh declarations, it is quite common for outright falsehoods to be declared as fact. For example, the current Syrian defense minister, Mustafa Tlass, wrote *The Matzo of Zion* in 1983, charging that the Jews used the blood of Muslims to make matzo.[12] In 2002, Dr. Umayma Jalahma wrote in the Saudi state-controlled daily newspaper *Al Riyadh*:

For [the Jewish] holiday [of Purim], the Jewish people must obtain human blood so that their clerics can prepare the holiday pastries. . . . That affords the Jewish vampires great delight as they carefully monitor every detail of the blood-shedding with pleasure. . . . After this barbaric display, the Jews take the spilled blood, in the bottle set in the bottom [of the needle-studded barrel], and the Jewish cleric makes his coreligionists completely happy on their holiday when he serves them the pastries in which human blood is mixed.[13]

Besides these blood libels, allegations abound that Israel is injecting Palestinian children with the AIDS virus and that Israel is poisoning Arab food to cause cancer and harm male virility.[14] Yasser Arafat has charged that Israel murders Arab children to use their organs "as spare parts,"[15] and his wife, Suha Arafat, accused Israel, in the presence of then–First Lady Hillary Clinton, of "daily and intensive use of poisonous gas," causing "cancer and other horrible diseases." She also claimed that Israel has contaminated 80 percent of Palestinian Arab water sources with "chemical materials."[16]

Furthermore, the Arab world has actively promoted the scandalous anti-Semitic forgery *The Protocols of Elders of Zion,* a book that alleges that Jewish leaders are plotting world domination. Egyptian state-run television even broadcast a forty-one-part series based on *The Protocols.* Moreover, Arab textbooks regularly depict Jews as "a wicked nation, characterized by bribery, slyness, deception, betrayal, aggressiveness, and haughtiness." *Islamic Education for the Eleventh Grade,* for example, says, "The Jews spare no effort to deceive us, hate us, deny our Prophet, incite against us, and distort the holy scriptures." A tenth-grade textbook asserts that "the logic of justice" demands that the Jewish people "be exterminated."[17]

Additionally, the Arab world, including governmental agencies and state-run media, regularly deny the Holocaust occurred.[18] Significantly, Mahmoud Abbas (also known by his nom de guerre, Abu Mazen), who became the first prime minister of the Palestinian Authority and is frequently identified as a moderate, has alleged that the total number of Jewish deaths at the hands of the Nazis was "fewer than one million."[19]

Likewise, Friday sermons broadcast across the Arab world repeatedly call for the destruction and murder of the Jews. One notable Palestinian preacher, Sheik Ibrahim Madhi, proclaimed at the Sheik 'Ijlin Mosque in Gaza, "Blessings for whoever has raised his sons on the education of Jihad and Martyrdom; blessings for whoever has saved a bullet in order to stick it in a Jew's head."[20] Islamic hatred of the Jewish people is aggressive and ubiquitous. It rivals—and at times, surpasses—Nazi anti-Semitic propaganda in its vileness and intensity.

Some consider Arab anti-Semitism to be an outgrowth of the Arab-Israeli conflict. For example, Bernard Lewis, a leading authority on Middle Eastern history, has described Arab anti-Semitism as an effect rather than a cause of the Arab-Israeli conflict. He explains it as "something that comes from above, from the leadership, rather than from below, from the society—a political and polemical weapon, to be discarded if and when it is no longer required."[21]

Since Lewis wrote that in 1986 other observers of the conflict have disagreed with him. The reason: If Arab anti-Semitism is a mere outgrowth of the political conflict and not the fuel that drives it, it would have begun to dissipate with the signing of the Oslo Peace Accord. However, once peace had arrived, Arab anti-Semitism not only continued, but it increased. Jonathan Rauch correctly observes that Arab anti-Semitism should not be dismissed "as an offshoot of the current Israeli-Palestinian dispute. . . . The reverse is more nearly true: Anti-Semitism perpetuates the conflict by preaching that Israel's very existence is an intolerable threat and insult to Islam."[22] In reality, Islam's hatred of the Jewish people is not an effect of the Arab-Israeli conflict, but a major cause of it.

"An Islamic Question"?

The Supreme Islamic Research Council's perspective, that the Arab-Israeli conflict "is first and foremost an Islamic question," has merit. Obviously, Islam has contributed greatly to the persistence of this conflict. Militant Islam's call for jihad, "martyrdom," and perpetual sovereignty over land are all factors, and its hateful perception of Jews fans the fires of conflict while obstructing peace initiatives and bringing greater suffering to both Jews and Arabs.

This conflict over the land raises the question, "Whose land is it?" In the next three chapters, we will begin to answer that question looking at the arguments from Scripture as well as those by Israeli and Arab proponents.

10
Whose Land?
A Biblical Perspective

Any attempt to impair the vital link between Israel
the people and Israel the land is an affront to
biblical faith.

—Rabbi Abraham Joshua Heschel

Conflicts about land are not unusual. India and Pakistan are in a conflict
over Kashmir; Russia is struggling with separatists who want to create an
autonomous state in Chechnya; and the Kurds want to be liberated from
Iraq so they can form an independent state. Meanwhile Northern Ireland
is part of a dispute between two peoples, one that wants to be governed
by the United Kingdom and the other that wants the land joined to Ireland.

It should be no surprise, then, that the biblical land of promise also
has a long history of disputes and continues to be part of a contention
between two peoples.

In each of the conflicts listed above, it seems nearly impossible to determine which side is right. When the arguments for one position are put
forth, they sound strong; when the other side presents their view, they
sound right as well. It reminds me of Tevye in the play *Fiddler on the Roof*.
He hears two men disagreeing and after listening to the first he says, "He's
right!" Then after listening to the second he says, "He's right!"

Finally a frustrated bystander challenges Tevye. "He's right and he's
right? How can they both be right?"

To which Tevye replies, "You know, you're also right!"[1]

Unfortunately, too often we become like Tevye when listening to land
disputes—everyone sounds right.

But when it comes to the Israeli/Palestinian conflict over the land, those who believe the Bible have a distinct advantage, for the Scriptures declare to whom the land belongs. While it is important to understand both historical and political arguments also, this chapter will examine only the scriptural answer to the question, "To whom does the biblical land of promise truly belong?" We will concisely state five propositions and consider the biblical evidence for each of them. Then, based on those propositions, some conclusions will be drawn from the evidence.

Five Primary Propositions

1. God promised the land of Israel to Abraham, Isaac, Jacob, and their descendants.

This proposition is derived from the covenant God made with Abraham, called the Abrahamic covenant. To begin, God made a promise to Abraham and then reiterated and expanded it several times. When the Scriptures are repetitious, the author's intent is to have readers mark the recurrence as important.

The first record of God's promise to Abraham is found in Genesis 12:1–7. There Abram (Abraham's original name; see Genesis 17:3–5) was told to leave his native country of Ur and go to the land the Lord would show him (12:1). When Abram finally arrived in the land of Canaan (as it was called then), the Lord told him, "To your descendants I will give this land" (12:7 NASB). This promise is repeated in the next chapter after the story of the dispute between the herdsmen of Abram and his nephew Lot (Genesis 13:7). To preserve the peace, Abram told Lot to select any part of the land that he wished, thus assuring Lot that Abram would go elsewhere (verses 8–10). In a sense, this put God's promise to Abram in jeopardy. If he gave up the land to his nephew, how could God fulfill His previous promise? So God assured Abram that despite this sacrificial attitude, all the land of Canaan would one day be his. The Lord said, "Now lift up your eyes and look from the place where you are, northward and southward and eastward and westward; for all the land which you see, I will give it to you and to your descendants forever" (verses 14–15 NASB).

A most significant recurrence of the land promise is found in Genesis 15:1–21. Following immediately upon Abram's rescue of Lot from Sodom (Genesis 14), the king of Sodom offered Abram all the spoils of battle. But Abram refused, lest it be said that the wicked king of Sodom made

Abram rich (14:21–23). Now, once again Abram demonstrated a sacrificial attitude and entrusted himself to the Lord's provision. In light of this, the Lord reiterated His covenant with Abram, assuring him that he would indeed have an heir. To confirm the covenant, the Lord caused Abram to fall into a deep sleep, and then He walked among the animal sacrifices (Genesis 15:12, 17).

As noted in chapter 8, this action was significant: By passing alone between the pieces of the sacrifices, God showed that this covenant did not depend on Abram but on the Lord alone. The covenant that was established was unconditional, subject only to the will and power of the God of Abram, not Abram at all. Then, having established the absolute nature of the covenant, God told Abram, "To your descendants I have given this land, from the river of Egypt as far as the great river, the river Euphrates" (15:18 NASB).

The Lord repeated the land promise in the context of establishing circumcision as an outward sign of the covenant, in Genesis 17. The Lord assured Abram, "I will establish my covenant as an everlasting covenant between me and you and your descendants after you for the generations to come, to be your God and the God of your descendants after you. The whole land of Canaan, where you are now an alien, I will give as an everlasting possession to you and your descendants after you; and I will be their God" (17:7–8).

Furthermore, God made it clear in this passage that the land would go to Abram's descendants through Isaac, not Ishmael. Although Abraham (renamed, verse 5) pled for Ishmael, the Lord refused and told Abraham, "My covenant I will establish with Isaac" (verse 21). Today many modern Arabs consider themselves to be descendants of Ishmael. Even if that were true, this passage makes it clear that the descendants of Abram to whom God gave the land are to be traced through Isaac and not Ishmael.

The Lord did indeed repeat the promise of land to Isaac, just as He assured Abraham that He would, and later God repeated it to Isaac's son Jacob (26:3; 35:12).

Clearly, the land grant of the Abrahamic covenant as found in Genesis, the first book of the Bible, was given to Abraham, Isaac, and Jacob, and then to the twelve tribes of Israel. Moreover, the land promise is reiterated in multiple passages throughout the Hebrew Scriptures. Additionally, the land promise is restated to all the people of Israel in 1 and 2 Chronicles, the last book of the Hebrew canon.[2] In 1 Chronicles 16:8–18, the psalmist David praises God for giving His covenant to Abraham, Isaac, and Jacob and so to "Israel as an everlasting covenant, [saying,] 'To you I will give the land of Canaan as the portion you will inherit'" (verses 17–18). Also, in 2 Chronicles 20:7 Jehoshaphat prayed, "O our God, did you not drive out the inhabitants of this land before your people Israel and give it forever to the descendants of Abraham your friend?"

So the Hebrew Bible, from the beginning to the end, recognizes that God gave the promise of the land to Abraham, Isaac, Jacob, and their descendants.

How did God have the right to give the land to the Jewish people when the Canaanites were obviously already there? The answer to this question is given by Rashi, the foundational medieval Jewish commentator (1040–1105) at the very inception of his commentary on the Torah.[3] From Rashi's point of view, the Sinai covenant and its laws form the substance of the Torah and are foundational to Judaism. Therefore, he asks why the Torah does not begin with the first commandment given at Sinai but rather begins with the creation of the heavens and the earth. His answer is most telling when he says Creation is tied to the land of promise:

> Why does [the Torah] begin with "In the beginning [referring to the book of Genesis and the story of creation]?" . . . Thus, should the nations of the world say to Israel, "You are robbers, for you have taken by force the lands of the Seven Nations [who inhabited the land of Canaan]"? They [Israel] will say to them: "All the earth belongs to God. He created it and gave it to whomever He saw fit. It was His will to give it to them and it was His will to take it from them and give it to us."[4]

This explanation makes perfect sense. Certainly, the author of the Torah did not include the creation of the world merely to satisfy his readers' curiosity. Instead, Moses wrote this account as a prologue to the Torah, establishing God's authority to give the land of His creation to His people Israel. Otherwise, the Canaanites or any other people that lived there might have a grievance. But the Creator and Owner of the land chose to give it to Abraham, Isaac, Jacob, and all their descendants forever as was His divine right.

2. God defined the boundaries of the land of Israel.

In Genesis 15:18, God established the boundaries of the land given to Abraham "from the river of Egypt to the great river, the Euphrates."

There is a dispute regarding the identification of the southwestern boundary, the river of Egypt. Some identify this as the Wadi El-Arish, a gully in the northern part of the Sinai Peninsula, that is dry in summer and filled with water during the rainy winter season. If this is correct it would exclude the Sinai Desert from the land grant. Others identify it as the Nile River. If this is correct, the Sinai Desert would be part of the land given to Israel.

It is unclear which view is correct. According to Exodus 23:31, the southern border is associated with the Red Sea, lending support to the Nile River view. But according to Numbers 34:4, the southern border is associated with Kadesh Barnea and the Wilderness of Zin, bolstering the Wadi El-Arish view. At this point, the evidence for either position is inconclusive but appears to favor the Wadi El-Arish as the southern border of the Promised Land.

In the north and east, the boundary is the Euphrates River, extending the land up to what is today's Lebanon, Syria, and Iraq. Obviously, Israel never obtained their entire land grant, either in the past or today. (Even at the zenith of David and Solomon's rule, the land they governed did not match the land grant God gave Abraham.) Nevertheless, God's promise is faithful (see proposition 5); thus at some future time these certainly will be the boundaries of Israel. This promise is foundational to the expectation of the literal future messianic kingdom when the land grant will be fulfilled in its entirety.

3. God gave the land of Israel to the Jewish people as an eternal inheritance.

Both Genesis 13:15 and 2 Chronicles 20:7 state that God gave the land to Israel as an inheritance "forever." Nevertheless, it is possible that the Hebrew word used in these passages (*olam*) and translated "forever" does not necessarily mean "for all eternity." For example, it is used in Exodus 21:6 of a slave who willingly accepts service to his master. When his ear is pierced, "he shall serve him forever [*olam*]." Clearly, Moses did not mean "for all eternity" but rather for the rest of his life or perhaps only until the year of jubilee. Therefore, since *olam* is the word used to describe the land grant, it could possibly mean that God gave the land to Israel for a long time, but not forever.

But let's extend our word study of *olam*. One Hebrew phrase used to describe that which is eternal is *min olam v'ad olam*. It is commonly translated "forever and ever" or "from everlasting to everlasting."[5] As a general rule, the phrase is used of matters pertaining to God alone. For example, it is used to describe the eternal blessedness of God (e.g., 1 Chronicles 16:36: "Praise be to the LORD, the God of Israel, from everlasting to everlasting").[6] The phrase declares the lovingkindness of God to be eternal (Psalm 103:17), and God's existence to be eternal (Psalm 90:2). Daniel uses the equivalent phrase in Aramaic to describe God's kingdom as existing "for all ages to come" (7:18 NASB). *"Min olam v'ad olam"* is the strongest expression in Hebrew to describe perpetuity and eternality. And, for the most part, it refers to God and His eternal nature.

There are only two exceptional usages in which the phrase does not refer to God. In both cases it refers to the nation of Israel's eternal possession of the land of Israel. In Jeremiah 7:7, God promises Israel, "I will let you dwell in this place, in the land that I gave to your fathers *for ever and ever.*" The prophet also uses the same phrase in Jeremiah 25:5, telling Israel that they will "dwell on the land which the Lord has given to you and your fathers *for ever and ever*" (emphasis added).

Biblical Hebrew usage simply has no stronger way to indicate eternality. Thus, Jeremiah's words could not be any clearer. God has given the land of Israel to the people of Israel as a perpetual and eternal inheritance.

4. God made total enjoyment and guaranteed habitation of the land of Israel contingent on Israel's faithfulness.

God's promise of the land as an eternal inheritance to Israel did not preclude the possibility that Israel might be temporarily removed from the Promised Land. In fact, God warned the nation that disobedience could, and would, lead to their exile and dispersion. In Leviticus 26:27–33, God alerted Israel. His warning included these words: If "you still do not listen to me but continue to be hostile toward me" (verse 27), God would indeed discipline them. After advising the nation that He would make the land of Israel desolate, He admonished them as follows: "I will scatter you among the nations and will draw out my sword and pursue you. Your land will be laid waste, and your cities will lie in ruins" (verse 33).

This severe warning passage does not end without hope. Despite Israel's disobedience to God's commands and the discipline of dispersion, God assured:

> *Yet in spite of this, when they are in the land of their enemies, I will not reject them or abhor them so as to destroy them completely, breaking my covenant*

with them. I am the LORD their God. But for their sake I will remember the covenant with their ancestors whom I brought out of Egypt in the sight of the nations to be their God. I am the LORD. (verses 44–45)

In Deuteronomy 4:40, Moses clarified the link between Israel's obedience to God and their enjoyment of the land. He commanded Israel to keep God's statutes and commandments "so that it may go well with you and with your children after you and that you may live long in the land the LORD your God gives you for all time." According to this verse, there is an ongoing paradox to the Jewish people's relationship to the land. On the one hand, God said that He is giving the land to the Jewish people for all time. On the other hand, the Jewish people's enjoyment and guaranteed tenancy of the land would be contingent on their obedience to God. Nevertheless, the Jewish people can be exiled from the land without forfeiting or nullifying the gift of the land as their eternal inheritance.

History confirms the accuracy of these warnings. After the failure of the Jewish revolts against Rome, the people of Israel gradually did go into exile. Although the land was never totally bereft of Jewish people, by the time of the birth of modern Zionism, Jewish people formed a tiny minority in a land that had indeed become desolate. Nevertheless, the promise of God as recorded in the Scriptures indicates Israel's ownership or title to the land remains eternal and unconditional. It belongs to them for all time because the land grant was not dependent on Israel's obedience but on God's faithfulness to His oath.

Because Israel is still in disobedience, some commentators have offered a different position. John Piper has argued,

A non-covenant-keeping people does not have a divine right to the present possession of the land of promise. Both the experience of divine blessing and the habitation of the land are conditional on Israel's keeping the covenant God made with her. . . . Israel has no warrant to a present experience of divine privilege when she is not keeping covenant with God. . . . Israel as a whole today rejects her Messiah, Jesus Christ, God's Son. This is the ultimate act of covenant-breaking with God.[7]

This position is plainly untenable. The land grant was both unconditional and eternal. Although the Jewish people might be disciplined with dispersion, their right to the land will never be removed. It belongs to them

for all time (or "for ever and ever"). Therefore, even in unbelief, the land
is theirs. Anytime the Lord returns the Jewish people to the land, it is theirs
by right of the Abrahamic covenant land grant. This is why God could
promise to return the Jewish people to the land of Israel in unbelief (see
Ezekiel 36:24–25; 37:1–14) as a precursor to their end of days return to
the Lord (Deuteronomy 4:29). At that time, *all* the Jewish people will trust
in their Messiah Jesus and the remaining Jewish people in dispersion will
all be returned to the land (see Matthew 23:37–39; Zechariah 12:10; Isaiah 11:11).

The point is that despite the disobedience and unbelief of the Jewish
people, whenever they are brought back to the land by God, whether in
faith or unbelief, the land belongs to them. This is by virtue of the Lord's
unconditional and eternal land grant found in the Abrahamic covenant.
The Jewish people may indeed temporarily lose the enjoyment and habitation of the land of Israel, but they never can lose the title to the land.

A further comment: Despite the frequent assertion that Israel's unbelief nullified the Jewish claim to the land, hardly anyone speaks of the
unbelief of the Palestinians. More than 95 percent of Palestinians are Muslim. Certainly, they, too, have rejected Jesus as both Lord and Messiah.
Moreover, the Palestinian Muslims never had any divine promises to claim.
Therefore, a Bible believer cannot justify transferring the right to the land
from unbelieving Jewish people who do have promises to claim, to unbelieving Arabs who do not have any promise to the land.

5. *God's promises to the Jewish people are irrevocable, regardless of their
unbelief.*

Some have argued that Israel's unbelief in Jesus as the Messiah has
caused God to transfer the nation's promises to the church, either permanently or temporarily. This is precisely Piper's position when he writes,

> When the builders rejected the beautiful Cornerstone, Jesus said,
> "The kingdom of God will be taken away from you and given to a peo-
> ple producing its fruits" (Matthew 21:43 [all NASB]).[8] He explained,
> "Many will come from east and west and recline at the table with
> Abraham . . . while the sons of the kingdom will be cast out into the
> outer darkness" (Matthew 8:11–12).[9]
> God has saving purposes for ethnic Israel (Romans 11:25–26). But
> for now most of the people are at enmity with God in rejecting the

gospel of Jesus their Messiah (Romans 11:28). God has expanded His saving work to embrace all peoples (including Palestinians) who will trust His Son and depend on His death and resurrection for salvation.[10]

It appears that Piper has confused the spiritual benefits of the Abrahamic covenant with the physical and material benefits of that covenant. Certainly, unbelieving Israel has been broken off from those spiritual promises, but the nation still has the physical and material benefits (Romans 11:17). That is why Paul can say that God has not cast off His people whom He foreknew (11:1) and that the gifts and calling of God are irrevocable (11:28–29).

Interestingly, Piper only partially quotes Romans 11:28 (NASB) about Israel's position of enmity with God.[11] The point Paul makes is actually the opposite of Piper's: "From the standpoint of the gospel they are enemies for your sake, but from the standpoint of God's choice they are beloved for the sake of the fathers; for the gifts and calling of God are irrevocable." Despite Israel's opposition to the Gospel, the Jewish people remain chosen because of the covenant made with Abraham, Isaac, and Jacob. Therefore, God's gifts, including the gift of land, belong irrevocably to the Jewish people.

Another passage that supports the irrevocable nature of Israel's promises is Romans 9:3–5. There Paul describes the privileges of his unbelieving "kinsmen according to the flesh, who are Israelites" (NASB). Using the present tense, Paul maintains that the privileges God granted to the Jewish people, such as the adoption as sons, the glory, the covenants, the Law, the worship of God, and the Messiah according to His physical birth, all remain intact. Paul specifically mentions the covenants and the promises as still belonging to his unbelieving brethren. Since the land grant is a promise connected to the Abrahamic covenant, it still remains in effect.

Colin Chapman, in his work *Whose Promised Land?*, argues for a permanent transfer of Israel's promises to the church and a figurative, rather than a literal, fulfillment of the land promises. He writes,

> Since the New Testament speaks of all followers of Jesus as "Abraham's seed and heirs according to the promise" (Galatians 3:29), it must mean that all four aspects of the covenant—the land, the nation, the covenant relationship between God and his people, and the blessing of all peoples of the world—find their fulfilment in Jesus and in those who put their faith in him. As a Christian, I feel bound to conclude that the promise of

the land to Abraham and his descendants "as an everlasting possession" finds its fulfilment in the kingdom of God, and therefore does *not* give the Jews a divine right to possess the land for all time.[12]

Chapman also confuses the spiritual promises of the Abrahamic covenant with the physical and material promises. Galatians 3:29 assures all those who have trusted in Jesus the Messiah alone that they will receive the spiritual promises given to Abraham, namely, that "through your offspring [the Messiah] all nations on earth will be blessed" (Genesis 22:18). Paul was not saying that God revoked or transferred all His promises from the physical descendants of Abraham, Isaac, and Jacob to the church. Otherwise Paul's assertion—that the promises continue to belong to unbelieving Israel, that God has not rejected Israel because of their unbelief, and that the Jewish people remain chosen and beloved by God with His irrevocable gifts and calling (Romans 9:3–5; 11:1–5, 28–29)—would all be untrue.

Jewish people (as all people) must trust in their Messiah Jesus to experience His forgiveness and spiritual renewal. Nevertheless, the physical and material promises given to the Jewish people remain fixed because they are not dependent on their obedience or faith but on the unconditional oath and faithfulness of God. Therefore, even in unbelief, the land of Israel belongs to the people of Israel.

Implications for Land Ownership

An Eternal Possession of the Jews

Three conclusions arise from the biblical foundations of these five statements. First, *the land of Israel is the inalienable and eternal possession of the Jewish people.*

Although other political and historical factors must be considered when evaluating to whom the land belongs, the most essential factor is the biblical. The Bible is plain—God gave the land of Israel to Abraham, Isaac, Jacob, and their descendants as an unconditional and eternal gift.

No Biblical Rights of Ownership for the Arabs

The second conclusion is that *the Palestinians do not have any* biblical *right to the land of Israel.* That is not to say that they cannot make historical or political claims. But as far as the Scriptures are concerned, the land does not belong to them. This conclusion regarding the Palestinian argument for the land must include several considerations.

To begin, it is inappropriate to call Israel "Palestine." The Bible never calls the land by this name, nor is there any sovereign state today by that name. The ancient biblical and contemporary political name is Israel. The name "Palestine" is derived from the Hebrew word for "Philistine" and referred to the coastal plain inhabited by the Philistines. The Roman emperor Hadrian officially called all of the land "Syria Palestina" in an attempt to sever it from its ancient association with the people of Israel in A.D. 135.

Additionally, some Palestinians make their claim to the land by identifying themselves as the descendants of the ancient Canaanites. Plainly, this is a false assertion—the Palestinian Arabs are a mixed people group that immigrated to the land a long time after the biblical period. Moreover, even if the claim to be Canaanites were true, God took the land from the Canaanites and gave it to the people of Israel.

Yet other Palestinians try to establish a biblical right to the land through their association with Jesus Christ. Palestinian spokeswoman Hanan Ashrawi declared, "I am a Palestinian Christian. I am a descendant of the first Christians in the world. Jesus Christ was born in my country and my land."[13] This sort of perspective led Yasser Arafat, a Muslim, to claim at a Bethlehem Christmas celebration, "Jesus was a Palestinian!"[14] The error of this is obvious: Jesus was not Palestinian but Jewish. Moreover, the vast majority of Palestinians—in fact, virtually all—are actually Muslims and not spiritually related to Jesus Christ at all. Jesus was not born in Palestine but Bethlehem of Judea, in Israel.

One other way Palestinian apologists deal with the biblical land grant to Israel is by attempting to label as illegitimate the biblical Jewish association to the land. For example, the mufti of Jerusalem, appointed by Yasser Arafat and the Palestinian Authority, said,

> There is not [even] the smallest indication of the existence of a Jewish temple on this place in the past. In the whole city [of Jerusalem] there is not even a single stone indicating Jewish history. This place belongs to us for 1,500 years. . . . The Jews do not even know exactly where their temple stood. Therefore, we do not accept that they have any rights, underneath the surface or above it.[15]

Yasser Arafat sought to use this position as a negotiating ploy at the Taba Negotiations in December 2000. In response to President Clinton's mention of the first temple on the Temple Mount, Arafat said, "There is nothing there [i.e., no trace of a temple on the Temple Mount]." Clinton responded, "Not only the Jews, but I, too, believe that under the surface there are the remains of Solomon's temple."[16] Denying the fact of the historical Jewish association with Jerusalem and the land of Israel will not negate its reality. God gave the land to the Jewish people. Archeology and history confirm the biblical record of the long Jewish presence in the land of Israel.

Negotiable Borders

A third and final conclusion is that until Messiah Jesus establishes his messianic kingdom, Israel may negotiate the boundaries of the land of Israel. This is based on the idea that the borders God established for the land have not yet been realized. While it is true that the land grant includes Judea and Samaria (or the West Bank of the Jordan), it is also true that the land grant extends to the land of the Hittites in the north and the Euphrates River in the east. Yet, at this time, the state of Israel has no desire or expectation of occupying or conquering Lebanon, Syria, and Iraq. Those holding a biblical perspective must be willing to wait for the messianic kingdom for Jewish sovereignty to extend that far. Similarly, political realities must also require waiting for the messianic kingdom before Israel will necessarily establish sovereignty over the Arab villages of the West Bank and the Gaza Strip.

Certainly, both Palestinians and Israelis will need to negotiate and compromise, making adjustments to the unacceptable cease-fire lines established in 1949. Nevertheless, the goal of a temporal peace will require Palestinians to accept Israel's existence as a Jewish state. Likewise, Israelis must recognize that the hope of a greater Israel, encompassing sovereignty over the West Bank and Gaza, must wait until the messianic kingdom.

Given by God

The biblical evidence clearly demonstrates that the land of Israel was given by the God of Israel to the people of Israel forever.

Jewish theologian and rabbi Abraham Joshua Heschel offered this distinctly biblical perspective when he wrote, "Any attempt to impair the vital link between Israel the people and Israel the land is an affront to biblical faith." He added that worshiping the golden calf was forgiven

but believing the calumnies of the ten spies was not. "The entire generation which left Egypt died in the wilderness. The Blessed Holy One could
forgo His own honor, but could not forgive the transgression in slander-
ing the Promised Land."[17]

The biblical mandate for the Jewish right to the land is clear. Of course,
in the world of international opinion as well as Arab assent, more than
the Holy Scriptures is needed to compel compromise. In the next two
chapters we will consider other arguments for Jewish possession of the
land—and Arab arguments for their own possession of the land.

11

Justice and Only Justice: The Case for Israel

No other nation in history faced with comparable challenges has ever adhered to a higher standard of human rights, been more sensitive to the safety of innocent civilians, tried harder to operate under the rule of law, or been willing to take more risks for peace.

—Alan Dershowitz
The Case for Israel

Naim Stifan Ateek, a pastor of an Arabic speaking congregation in Jerusalem, takes the title of his book *Justice and Only Justice* (Orbis) from Deuteronomy 16:20: "Justice, and only justice, you shall pursue, that you may live and possess the land which the Lord your God is giving you" (NASB). With passion and persuasiveness, Ateek contends that "the most basic and crucial issue of the Israel-Palestine conflict is that of justice."[1] According to him, the Palestinian claim to the land is only a matter of simple justice because the creation of Israel was a grave injustice perpetrated against the Palestinians.

Israel has its apologists as well. Recently, notable attorney Alan Dershowitz wrote *The Case for Israel* (Wiley). With equal passion and persuasiveness, Dershowitz maintains that a true understanding of history, politics, and law justifies Israel's right to exist within secure boundaries and to defend itself. For Dershowitz, Israel's existence is simply a matter of "justice and only justice."

Additional authors have lined up on both sides of this conflict, each claiming a just cause for his respective position. Whenever the situation in Israel heats up with another bombing or sometimes with a new peace proposal, other spokespersons on each side appear on television news programs making the case for justice.

How can a person sort through all the arguments and counterarguments? This chapter and the next will attempt to do just that. In this chapter I will present the Israeli positions for the Jewish right to the land followed by the typical Palestinian response to those arguments. Then, in the following chapter, I will invert the process, presenting the Palestinian position followed by the Israeli response. Only then will it be possible to assess the justice of both perspectives.

The Israeli Claims for Justice

The foundational assertion for many advocating the Israeli position is that God gave the land of Israel to the Jewish people forever as part of the Abrahamic covenant, a position detailed in the previous chapter. Those who support Israel also make their case based on other issues as well: history, politics, economics, and human rights.

The Historical Claims

The first of the historical claims is based on *the Jewish memory of the land*. Despite years of political exile, Jewish people never forgot their homeland. When Chaim Weizmann, then leader of the World Zionist Organization, was asked by the United Nations Special Committee on Palestine by what right the Jews claimed Palestine, Weizmann replied, "Memory is right." His point was that other nations have occupied lands and then abandoned them, but the Jewish people never abandoned nor forgot the land of Israel.

This memory of the land is evident in Jewish liturgy and law.[2] For example, Jewish people in the Diaspora have always prayed facing east, toward Jerusalem. In the daily liturgy Jewish people pray, "Gather us from the four corners of the earth" and "To Jerusalem Your city, return in mercy . . . rebuild it soon in our days." At the end of every Passover Seder and at the conclusion of the annual observance of Yom Kippur, Jewish people have always prayed, "Next year in Jerusalem," expressing the longing of a return to the land. Jewish people observe *Tisha B'av* (the Ninth of Av) as an annual fast day designed to remember the destruction of Jerusalem and the Exile. Traditionally Jewish homes built in the Diaspora always had some small corner left incomplete, to demonstrate that all homes in the Exile are temporary, awaiting the permanent return to the land of Israel. Even the joyous occasion of a traditional Jewish wedding includes the breaking of a glass, to recall that in every situation, even celebrations, Jews must remember the destruction of Jerusalem. The Jewish people have for nearly two thousand years taken seriously the words of the psalmist: "If I forget you O Jerusalem, may my right hand forget its skill" (Psalm 137:5).

Besides memory of the land, *Jewish movements back to the land* present a second historical claim. Throughout the history of exile, the persistent Jewish attachment to the land produced multiple and continuous attempts to return there and maintain a presence in the land of Israel. The first of these were the *Avelei Zion* ("Mourners of Zion"), Jews who arrived by the late first century and devoted themselves to mourning the destruction of the temple and to praying for the redemption of Zion. *Karaites,* a sect of Jews that only recognized the authority of the Hebrew Bible and rejected Rabbinic tradition, began to join the *Avelei Zion,* establishing communities in Israel as far back as the seventh century.

By the time of the Crusades, some 300,000 Jewish people were living in the land. The attacks by the Crusaders led to the death of many Jewish people and the flight of large numbers from the land of Israel. Nevertheless, a number of highly reputed Rabbinic scholars returned to the land in the medieval period. Poet Judah Halevy was famous for his devotion to the land of Israel. (See an excerpt from his *Odes to Zion* on page 61.) After writing his collection *Odes to Zion,* he attempted to move to the land of Israel. According to tradition he was murdered by a marauder upon arrival in the land but most likely he died while staying in Cairo, enroute to the Holy Land.

After the Ottoman Empire conquered Palestine (1517), Turkish leaders opened the doors to Jewish immigration. As a result, many Jewish people who had been expelled from Spain in 1492 made their way to Palestine. So many returned that the community of Safed in Galilee had a Jewish population of ten thousand by 1567. Shabbetai Zvi, a seventeenth-century false messiah, spurred thousands of Jewish people to sell their belongings in Europe and return to the land of Israel. In the eighteenth century, the sects of *Hasidim* ("pietists") made their way to the land. These immigrants laid the groundwork for the agricultural revival of the Galilee, paving the way for larger scale Jewish settlement there later. Jewish opponents of the *Hasidim,* known as *perushim* ("ascetics"), also made their way to the land at that time, establishing schools of Jewish learning and providing artisans and skilled laborers.

Since Rabbinic Judaism was committed to waiting for the Messiah to establish a government, all these movements to the land were uniformly religious. Nevertheless, they show the long commitment the Jewish people have had to their ancient homeland. Therefore, there had been a continuous Jewish presence in the land from the Roman to the Ottoman era. Although many of the Jewish people in the land throughout these periods had returned from various parts of the Diaspora, some Jewish people had never left Israel. Even today, there are Israelis who maintain a direct line of ancestry in the land back to the period of the second temple. The Jewish people have maintained their historical ties to their ancient homeland through memory of the land, religious movements to the land, and a continuous presence there.

The Political Claims

The principle of self-determination is the first political argument to be made for Israel's right to the land. Israel supporters regularly adduce that the Jewish people were the last indigenous people to exercise self-rule in the land. After the Hasmoneans, the Jewish dynasty that governed the land from 142 to 63 B.C., no indigenous people had political autonomy in Israel. From the end of their rule until the birth of the state of Israel, the land was consistently governed by foreign imperial rulers. The six ruling forces were: Roman/Byzantine, 63 B.C.–A.D. 636; Arabia, 636–1099; Crusaders, 1099–1291; Mamluk, 1291–1516; Ottoman, 1516–1917; and Britain, 1917–1948.

Even during the Arabian period, the government was imperial and not related to an indigenous Arab population. The Arabian Empire always governed the land as outsiders from imperial capitals in Damascus, Baghdad, or Cairo. While many ethnic peoples came and went as did a variety of rulers, the land remained uniquely tied to the Jewish people.

World sanction is yet another political argument in favor of Israel. The Balfour Declaration, issued by the British government during World War I in support of Zionist aspirations, "viewed with favour the establishment in Palestine of a national home for the Jewish people, and will use their best endeavours to facilitate the achievement of this object." Twenty years later, the British Peel Commission (1937), after interviewing the principle individuals involved in issuing the Balfour Declaration, reported that "the field in which the Jewish National Home was to be established was understood, at the time of the Balfour Declaration, to be the whole of historic Palestine, including Transjordan."[3]

The Council of San Remo (1921) recommended that the British receive the mandate for Palestine, using the Balfour Declaration as the basis for their decision. The League of Nations also recognized the significance of the Balfour Declaration and included the text of it in their official mandatory award to Britain in 1922. The League's Permanent Mandates Commission required the British not to just permit but to "secure" the Jewish national home and to "use their best endeavors to facilitate" Jewish immigration and Jewish settlement in Palestine.[4] Otherwise, the mandate would be revoked.

Ultimately, the United Nations General Assembly voted (in 1947) to partition western Palestine into two states, one Jewish and one Arab. With this vote, the world body recognized the legality of Jewish aspirations for a reconstituted state. From the Balfour Declaration to the League of Nations Mandates Commission all the way to the United Nations General Assembly, the world has recognized the Jewish right of self-determination in the land of Israel. Therefore, Israel claims its political right to the land by emphasizing both the principle of self-determination and international recognition.

The Economic Claims

Israel cites two factors in making an economic claim for the land. The first is *the deterioration of the land* under the Arab population. Israel claims that by 1882, the land was underpopulated with just 250,000 people. Moreover, when Zionist Jewish settlers returned they found the land to be denuded of trees with its corollary loss of topsoil. The northern part of the land was swamp-laden due to clogging of rivers. The cities and towns were in ruins and disease was rampant. The biblical land of milk and honey, noted for its great fertility, was now a wasteland.

The second argument put forward by Israel is *the Jewish renewal of the land*. Jewish settlers purchased (at exorbitant prices) land for their settlements. By planting trees, irrigating barren areas, and draining swamps, returning Jewish settlers began industry and farm exports. The Jewish people reclaimed their forsaken land with their own blood and sweat, making it productive once again. Working a land that was no longer economically viable, Israel claims that Jewish commitment to the land caused an economic rebirth. As a result, Arabs from surrounding areas moved to Palestine to share in the wealth created by the Jewish economic revival. Israel claims its right to the land by restoring its economic viability.

The Human Rights Claim

Additionally, Israel claims a legitimate human right to the land. The first of these human rights claims is the nation's consistent *peaceful desires.* From the outset, Zionist settlers have extended their hands in peace to their Arab neighbors. At the creation of the state, the Declaration of Independence proclaimed,

> In the midst of wanton aggression, we yet call upon the Arab inhabitants of the State of Israel to return to the ways of peace and play their part in the development of the State, with full and equal citizenship and due representation in its bodies and institutions—provisional or permanent. . . . We offer peace and unity to all the neighboring states and their peoples, and invite them to cooperate with the independent Jewish nation for the common good of all.

Israel claims to have been consistent in offering peace since the creation of the modern state. Additionally, they claim *a willingness to compromise* in order to make peace. Historian Paul Johnson suggests that a reason for the ongoing conflict has been a difference in cultural perspectives on compromise. The Jewish people have a history of compromise that developed as a survival technique throughout all the years of oppression in Christian Europe. Arab Muslims, influenced by the uncompromising nature of the Qur'an, have been unwilling to make concessions to establish peace. As a result, Johnson concludes, "A truce, an armistice might be necessary and was acceptable because it preserved the option of force for use later. A treaty, on the other hand, appeared to them a kind of surrender."[5]

Thus, the Arab nations have refused to recognize or even negotiate with Israel. Even today, after several years of terrorist bombings and shootings, the majority of Israelis are committed to achieving peace through compromise. This is evident in the most recent survey of Israelis which show that three-fourths still believe in a two-state solution to the conflict.[6]

Yet another of Israel's human rights arguments is derived from *the Holocaust and the need for a safe haven from anti-Semitism.* Hitler's genocide of European Jewry—six million Jewish people murdered, solely for being Jewish—entitles the people to a sovereign state. The world community had abandoned the Jewish people to Hitler's "Final Solution." While it was still possible to have Jewish people escape Nazi

Germany, no nation was willing to take them. During the war, the Allies did next to nothing to intervene on behalf of Jewish people going to their slaughter. Israel claims that with a Jewish state, the Jewish people would not have been betrayed so callously. And with a land of its own, world Jewry would have a safe haven from anti-Semitism and any further threats of genocide.

Another human rights claim to national status is that Israel has been subjected to *terrorism* from its inception as a state. Amazingly, prior to the most current uprising, the period with the most Israeli deaths due to Palestinian terror was after signing the Oslo Peace Accord with Yasser Arafat and the PLO. Furthermore, those Palestinian terrorists, in killing innocent civilians, deny people the most basic of human rights, the right to life. These terrorists, whose actions are supported by the majority of Palestinians, are not "freedom fighters" but cruel murderers. Thus, the right of the Jewish people to the land of Israel is also supported by human rights principles that oppose the cruelty of Palestinian terrorists.

The Jewish claim to the land is more than just a biblical contention. The Israelis claim the moral high ground. Their cause is supported by history, politics, economics, and human rights. Their position is that Israel exists because of justice and only justice.

The Palestinian Response

Palestinians and their supporters see very little credibility in these arguments for Israel's right to the land. As to the historical arguments, most Palestinians deny the long Jewish association with the land. Instead, they argue that the Jewish people of Israel are not descendants of biblical Israel but rather the Khazars, a medieval Ukrainian kingdom whose nobility adopted Judaism. The Egyptian daily newspaper *Al-Akhbar* asserts,

> Jews have no right or title in Palestine because they are not the offspring of Abraham Isaac and Jacob. . . . Jacob is not Israel, and the latter is a different person who had nothing to do with the Patriarchs or the Prophets; he was the forefather of the Jews. . . . It is a pure act of arrogance on the part of the Jews, the killers of Prophets, to advance the claim that they are the Prophets' descendants.[7]

Moreover, Palestinians claim the Jewish tie to the land was eliminated with the dispersion of the Jewish people and that the Arab Palestinians have the right to the land. They would further argue that the Palestinians are the modern descendants of the Canaanites, that they have lived in the land since biblical days and thus are the occupants of the land from time immemorial.

As to the political claims, Palestinians argue that as the occupants of the land, they have had their right to self-determination violated by the creation of a Jewish state. Moreover, they claim that the Balfour Declaration, the League of Nations Mandates Commission, and the United Nations General Assembly, by sanctioning a Jewish homeland and state in Palestine, all denied the legal rights of the Palestinian Arabs to self-determination.[8]

With respect to the economic claims to the land, Palestinian supporters argue that Zionist descriptions of the land are erroneous. With respect to population figures, they contend that the population of Palestine in 1881 was 500,000, of which only 20,000 were Jews. Additionally, Palestinians assert that the land was fruitful and lush, filled with farms, orange groves, and thriving olive trees.[9]

Palestinians also dismiss the Israeli human rights claim. They deny that Israel has always had peaceful desires and a willingness to compromise. Thus, Palestinian apologists Rosemary and Herman Ruether have argued that the perceptions of Jewish peacefulness and reasonableness are merely a result of superior Jewish communication with the Western world. Therefore, they write,

> Vehement Arab anti-Zionist (sometimes anti-Jewish) rhetoric has been exploited by world Zionism to convince Jews and Christians that Arabs are irrationally violent, in contrast to Israel "reasonableness."
>
> While Arab leaders tend to be militant in rhetoric but conservative and often indecisive in practice, Israeli leaders are usually carefully moderate in public rhetoric but decisively opportunistic in diplomatic and military action. They have typically concealed the continually expansionist nature of their project from their Western sponsors and pursued a "step by step" process toward these goals. While pointing to militant Arab rhetoric to frighten Jews and convince them that the Arab world is genocidal toward Jews and that no peace is possible with them, Israeli leaders have been quite aware of the actual inability of the Arab world to deliver on this militant rhetoric. But they have preferred to cultivate the militant, rather than the moderate, side of the Arab world, in order to avoid responses from Jews and Western sponsor

governments that might force them to limit their expansionist ambitions.[10]

Additionally, Palestinians argue that the Holocaust should have no bearing on the dispute. To begin, much of the Arab world denies that the Holocaust occurred and thus the Jewish people's need for a homeland. For example, Mahmoud Abbas (Abu Mazen), who was Palestinian prime minister for a short time, wrote a doctoral dissertation intended to delegitimize Zionism by arguing that the Holocaust did not happen. He wrote,

It seems that the Zionist movement's stake in inflating the number of murdered in the war aimed at [ensuring] great gains. This led it to confirm the number [6 million], to establish it in world opinion, and by doing so to arouse more pangs of conscience and sympathy for Zionism in general. Many scholars have debated the question of the 6 million figure, and reached perplexing conclusions, according to which the Jewish victims total hundreds of thousands. The well-known Canadian author Roger Delarom said on this matter: "To date, no proof whatsoever exists that the number of Jewish victims in the Nazi concentration camps reached four million or six million. Zionism first spoke of twelve million exterminated in these camps, but then the number decreased greatly, to half, that is, only six million. Then the number decreased further, and became four million, as the Germans could not have killed or exterminated more Jews than there were in the world at that time. In effect, the true number is much smaller than these fictitious millions." The [American] historian and author Raul Hilberg thinks that this number is no greater than 896,000.[11] [In truth, Hilberg's studies set the figure of Jewish dead at six million.][12]

Holocaust denial is rampant in the Arab media, including the Palestinian areas, Egypt, Syria, Saudi Arabia, and the rest of the Arab world.

Other Palestinian proponents accept the historicity of the Holocaust but contend that the Palestinians should not have been made to pay for the crimes of the Europeans. They argue that the true *Nakba* (the Arabic word for "catastrophe" and a play on the Hebrew word *Shoah*, which means "catastrophe") occurred with the creation of the Jewish state. Their conviction is that European persecution of the Jewish people should not have led to the mistreatment of the Palestinian Arabs. Furthermore, the Israelis in their alleged oppression of the Palestinians have become "the racist

Nazis" of the Middle East, denying the human rights of the Palestinian people. (This charge by Palestinian proponents moves beyond political advocacy to anti-Semitic rhetoric. The Israeli repudiation of it will be presented in the next chapter.) Thus Ateek asks, "Why should the price of Jewish empowerment after the Holocaust in the creation of the State of Israel be the oppression and misery of the Palestinians?"[12]

Plainly, Palestinians and their apologists reject the Israeli historical, political, economic, and human rights arguments. But even more than rejecting the contentions of Israelis, these proponents of the Palestinian position make a claim to the land in their own right. Their assertions that the land rightfully belongs to the Palestinians are just as forcefully denied by Israel and its proponents. In the next chapter, the Palestinian claim for justice will be presented and the Jewish response examined. Only then can a fair assessment be made.

12
Justice and Only Justice: The Case for Palestine

There is no symmetry in this conflict. One would
have to say that. I deeply believe that. There is a
guilty side and there are victims. The Palestinians
are the victims.

—Edward Said
Professor of comparative literature,
Columbia University

The suffering of Palestinians is undeniable. They have been abandoned and
abused by their fellow Arabs. The United Nations has fostered a Palestinian culture of poverty and dependency. The Israeli government has
restricted Palestinian freedoms in its attempts to restrain terrorism.

As a result, the Palestinians are an aggrieved people, demanding recognition of their plight, restitution for the wrongs done to them, and an independent state in Palestine. They contend that the land they call Palestine
wholly belongs to them. Let's examine their cry for justice by identifying
their claims and stating the Israeli responses.

The Palestinian Claim for Justice

The Palestinians base the justice of their claim for Palestine on history,
politics, economics, and human rights. But foundational to their argument
is the religious claim to the land. Like the Israelis, who find sanction in the
Scriptures, the Palestinians cite both the Bible and Qur'an as supporting
their right to the land.

The Religious Claims

Islamic nationalists frequently cite Qur'anic sources as the foundation of their title to Jerusalem. For example, although the Qur'an does not mention Jerusalem by name, Palestinian supporters argue that the Qur'an does allude to it as "the far distant place of worship." They allege that Muhammad visited Jerusalem on his night journey and state that the Qur'an calls Jerusalem "the third of the sanctities," referring to its status as the third most holy site in Islam. Additionally, because of Muhammad's early practice of praying towards Jerusalem, the Qur'an calls Jerusalem "the first of two directions."[1]

Besides Jerusalem, Islamic nationalists claim that the biblical land promises belong to the Arabs and not the Jewish people. For example, Islam identifies Abraham as a Muslim: "Abraham was neither Jew nor Christian; but he was sound in the faith, a Muslim; and not of those who add gods to God" (Sura III, The Family of Imran, verse 60).[2] According to Bernard Lewis, "From the Muslim point of view, the Jewish revelation was a divine revelation that was corrupted." As such, both Old and New Testaments were "superceded and replaced by the Koran in Islamic belief. They no longer have validity."[3]

Furthermore, Islam claims that the Arabs descended from Ishmael and that he, rather than Isaac, was the true son of promise. Their argument is based on Ishmael being the older son and as such, according to Middle Eastern culture, he would have been the favored son and the one to receive the promises.

Thus, most Palestinians maintain that as Muslims, they have a divine right to the land of promise. Beyond religion, however, Palestinians also assert their right to the land on other secular grounds, beginning with their long presence in Palestine.

The Historical Claim

Naim Stifan Ateek expresses the first historical argument succinctly, *the long presence of the Palestinians in the land,* when he writes, "The Palestinians base their claim on the observed facts of history: they have lived in the land for many centuries. It is quite probable that the ancestors of some have lived in the land from time immemorial."[4] The basic assertion, that Palestinians have lived in the land from the dawn of history, is offered in *The Arab Case for Palestine,* submitted to the Anglo-American Committee in March of 1946:

"The Arabs of Palestine are descendants of the indigenous inhabitants of the country, who have been in occupation of it since the beginning of history."[5]

When to mark the beginning of "time immemorial" is a subject of dispute, even for Palestinian claimants. Some Palestinians claim their descent from the ancient Canaanites while others from the ancient Philistines. For example, Palestinian archeologist Adel Yahya argues that "Palestinians are the descendants of the ancient Canaanites themselves, who were present in the land before the Israelites arrived."[6] According to the Dutch Palestinian Information Internet site, "The Palestinian Arabs of today, Muslims and Christians, are not, as popularly believed, the descendants of the Arabian desert conquerors of 1300 years ago. In fact, they are mainly the descendants of the original native population—Canaanites, Edomites, and Philistines."[7] The intention of these assertions is to prove that Palestinians predated the Jewish people in the land.

Some make the more accepted historical claim that the Palestinians are descended from the Arab invasion in the seventh century. Thus, the argument of historical priority is that Palestinians have lived as the indigenous people of Palestine for at least thirteen hundred years—and even more than three millennia. Proponents argue that the Arabs most likely predated the biblical Israelites in the land and they were most certainly present prior to the modern Zionist return to the land. Hence, Zionist aspirations and colonization were nothing more than an illegitimate land grab from its indigenous people.

Yet a second historical argument refers to *the displacement of the Palestinian population by Zionist Jews*. Proponents contend that Zionists were nothing more than colonial settlers who displaced the indigenous Palestinian population, initially by their aggressive land purchases. Ultimately, however, the Zionist enterprise deliberately evicted up to one million Palestinians in an aggressive war launched in 1948. As a result, this displaced Palestinian population became a people without citizenship in any country, and most were forced to live within refugee camps established and still administered by the United Nations.

The refugees now number approximately five million Palestinians who lost their villages, homes, orchards, and farmland to the invading Zionists.

The Political Claim

Building on their historical claims, Palestinians further assert political rights to the land, the first being *the right of self-determination*. A starting point of this argument is the McMahon-Hussein Correspondence of 1915–16. In the First World War, Britain and France affirmed that one of their goals was to establish national governments deriving their authority from indigenous populations. At that time, Sir Henry McMahon, the British High Commissioner in Cairo, sought to divide Arabs from their allegiance to the Ottoman Empire by negotiating with Hussein Ibn Ali, the Sherif of Mecca. In a series of letters from 1915–16, McMahon pledged the British government's support for the reestablishment of the caliphate in an independent Arab state, if Hussein would support the British war effort against the Turks. Following World War I, the Arabs claimed that the British had promised to include all of Palestine in the independent Arab state. Although Palestine is not mentioned in the correspondence, McMahon did promise Hussein that "Great Britain is prepared to recognize and support the independence of the Arabs in all the regions within the limits demanded by the Sherif of Mecca."[8]

Therefore, it is argued that while the British initially recognized the legitimate Palestinian right of self-determination, they betrayed their promises by issuing the Balfour Declaration in 1917. Edward Said puts it this way: The Balfour Declaration "was made (a) by a European power, (b) about a non-European territory, (c) in a flat disregard of both the presence and the wishes of the native majority resident in that territory, and (d) it took the form of a promise about this same territory to another foreign group, so that this foreign group might, quite literally, *make* this territory a national home for the Jewish people."[9]

Palestinian proponents further argued that the 1947 partition of Palestine by the United Nations violated this right of Arab self-determination. They maintain that after the establishment of the British Mandate by the League of Nations, the British sought to establish a Jewish majority in Palestine by pursuing an aggressive Jewish immigration policy. When this policy failed, the United Nations partitioned Palestine with total disregard for the indigenous population. Despite this, even at the time of partition, Palestinian Arabs were still in the majority.

Brazilian journalist Cecilia Toledo wrote, "In 1947 there were 600,000 Jews and a million three hundred thousand Palestinian Arabs. So, when the United Nations divide [sic] Palestine, the Jews were a minority (31% of the population). This division, promoted by the main imperialist powers—with the support from Stalin—gave 54% of the fertile land to the Zionist movement."[10] Thus, by virtue of the right of self-determination, the very presence of Jewish people in the land and the establishment of the state of Israel is considered a violation of Arab rights. But this is not the only political argument to be made.

The second political argument is what the Palestinians call *the right of return* to all of Palestine. Foundational to this position is the contention that Israel forcibly expelled up to one million Palestinians during the 1948–49 war, thereby creating the continuing Palestinian refugee problem. The Israeli state leadership did this deliberately to ensure a significant Jewish majority in the new Jewish state they were creating. Thus, Palestinians claim that the refugee problem can only be resolved politically by allowing all Palestinian refugees and their descendants to return to their former homes and villages. Additionally, they claim that United Nations Resolution 194, issued on December 11, 1948, guarantees all Palestinians and their descendants the right to return to their former homes, even in Israel proper (i.e., those borders Israel established during the 1967 Six Day War).

Edward Said maintains that Israel did indeed forcibly exile the Palestinians in 1948; nevertheless, he argues that Resolution 194 makes the cause of the refugee problem immaterial. He writes: "*What matters is that they are entitled to return,* as international law stipulates, as numerous United Nations resolutions (voted for by the United States) have averred, and as they themselves have willed. (The first UN General Assembly resolution— Number 194 . . . has been repassed *no less than twenty-eight times* since that first date.)"[11]

Palestinian advocates assert that only Israeli intransigence has kept the Palestinian refugees from returning. Israelis object that flooding the state of Israel with millions of Palestinian refugees and their descendants will undermine the Jewish character of Israel. It will cease to be a Jewish state and undermine a two-state solution. To this the Palestinians reply that they are not concerned with maintaining the Jewishness of Israel but only in obtaining justice, namely, the right of return.

The third Palestinian political claim is that the UN Security Council Resolution 242, issued after the Six Day War, demands *the end of the Israeli occupation of the West Bank and Gaza.* The recent Intifada II, begun on September 30, 2000, is nothing more than resistance to a cruel occupation of Palestinian land with its indigenous people. Palestinians argue that Resolution 242 demands that Israel return to the June 4, 1967, borders. Moreover, it is only Israel's unwillingness to do so that has produced the current violence. It is the political right of the Palestinians to oppose, even with violence, this oppressive Israeli occupation.

Palestinians object most vociferously to Jewish settlements on the West Bank and in Gaza. They argue that Israeli settlements are a violation of the Fourth Geneva Convention, which prohibits the forcible transfer of populations from occupied territory and the transfer of its own civilian population into the occupied territory.[12] Hence, the occupation is perceived as the cause of Israeli settlements which in turn illegally jeopardize the political rights of the Palestinian people in the West Bank and Gaza.

The Economic Claim

Palestinians make an economic case for the land by rejecting fully the Zionist descriptions of nineteenth-century Palestine as barren, swamp-laden, and underpopulated. Palestinian apologists state that at the time of the Zionist invasion a large Arab community inhabited a lush land. The land was fertile and fruitful, filled with both orange groves and olive trees. Yasser Arafat said of that time: "Palestine was then a verdant land, inhabited mainly by an Arab people in the course of building its life and dynamically enriching its indigenous culture."[13]

The Palestinians also contend that population records are inaccurate because many Arab peasants were undocumented in 1882 as a result of their refusal to participate in the land censuses taken at that time, and that 500,000 Palestinians were in the land. Palestinian proponents also cite the 1921 census, carried out at the official beginning of the British Mandate, which identified an Arab population of 590,000 Muslims and 89,000 Christians.[14]

Thus, to Palestinians, the creation of the state of Israel was nothing less than theft by European colonialists of their economically thriving and well-populated land.

The Human Rights Claim

Arafat and other Palestinian advocates argue that Israel has become "the prime example of human rights violators in the world."[15] The allegations of human rights abuses vary. Israel's desire to maintain a Jewish majority in the state of Israel is called racist; so is the law of return, which allows Jews to become citizens of Israel. Critics term the Israeli occupation of the West Bank and Gaza "a crime against humanity," charging Israel with being an apartheid state, like the former South African state. They charge Israel with multiple human rights violations, including the use of checkpoints to humiliate Palestinians and curfews in Palestinian areas to obstruct the ability of Palestinians to go about their lives, earn their livelihoods, or go to school. Palestinians allege that Israel demolishes homes as a form of collective punishment, uses deadly force against children who merely throw stones, and assassinates Palestinians without trial (frequently called "extrajudicial killings").

It is further alleged that Israel commits these human rights violations despite the Palestinian Authority's desire for peace. In his *New York Times* article in which he condemned terrorism (see page 47), Yasser Arafat also reaffirmed his commitment to a two-state solution to the conflict.[16] In response, Palestinians say, Israel has isolated Arafat, the elected leader of the Palestinians, putting him under virtual house arrest in Ramallah and threatened him with exile. According to the Palestinians, these violations of human rights demand violent resistance, and those who perform terrorist acts are truly freedom fighters waging a war of national liberation.

The Palestinians contend that they are the victims of injustice and that their cause is supported by religion, history, politics, economics, and human rights. Their position is that Palestine should be theirs because of justice and only justice.

The Israeli Response

Israelis contend there is yet another side to the claims made by Palestinians and that a more careful examination would yield alternate conclusions. To begin, Israelis challenge the *religious claims* Palestinian Muslims make. With respect to Jerusalem, the Qur'anic title "Far Distant Worship Place" did not originally refer to Jerusalem. Nearly a century after the writing of the Qur'an, the Ummayad dynasty based in Damascus built the Al-Aqsa Mosque in Jerusalem, which later came to be known as the "Far Distant Worship Place."[17] Additionally, according to the Qur'an, Muhammad never physically set foot in Jerusalem but merely did so in a vision. In fact, early Muslims prayed toward Jerusalem for only a short period in an attempt to obtain Jewish converts. When this failed, Muhammad directed his followers to pray toward Mecca.

Actually, a serious strain of anti-Jerusalem perspectives runs through Islam. According to Bernard Lewis, "There was strong resistance among many theologians and jurists" to viewing Jerusalem as a sacred city because this was considered a Judaizing error.[18] Ibn Taymiya (1263–1328), a highly regarded medieval Muslim scholar, dismissed Jerusalem as a holy city, viewing the claim as an idea borrowed from Jews and Christians and springing from the earlier rivalry between the Ummayad Dynasty and Mecca.[19] Thus, Daniel Pipes concludes, "Politics, not religious sensibility, has fueled the Muslim attachment to Jerusalem for nearly fourteen centuries."[20]

Besides Jerusalem, there is Qur'anic evidence for considering the land of Israel the homeland of the Jewish people. Iconoclastic Islamic cleric Shaykh Professor Abdul Hadi Palazzi, imam of the Italian Islamic Community Center, believes the Qur'an states that God made the Jewish people heirs of the Holy Land, citing Sura 5:20–21.[21]

He also argues that the Qur'an "explicitly refers to the return of the Jews to the Land of Israel before the Last Judgment," citing 17:104.[22] Other Muslims recognize this as well, including Rustam Issaev, ambassador to Israel from Uzbekistan, an Islamic nation.[23] Therefore, even according to Muslim sources, Jerusalem and the land of Israel must be considered the land God gave the Jewish people.

With regard to the promises given to Ishmael, Israelis would point out that the Scriptures make these promises to Isaac, not Ishmael. That the Torah was written two thousand years before the Qur'an would indicate that the biblical presentation is more authentic than the Qur'anic version. Additionally, although the Bible does make promises to Ishmael and his descendants (Genesis 17:20), they are not the land promises given to Abraham, Isaac, Jacob, and their descendants. Moreover, even the biblical promises given to Ishmael do not necessarily apply to the Arabs. As S. D. Goitein writes, "To be sure, there is no record in the Bible showing that Ishmael was the forefather of the Arabs."[24] This idea is a much later Jewish tradition that was given life in the Qur'an rather than in the Scriptures. Israelis plainly repudiate the Palestinian religious claims to the land.

Israelis also dispute Palestinian *historical claims*, the first being the long residency of Palestinian Arabs in the land. In response, Israelis argue that identifying the Palestinian Arabs with the Canaanites or Philistines lacks any scholarly credibility. As to their identification with the seventh-century Islamic conquest, there may indeed be a slight relationship to those Arabian military colonists. But for the most part, the Palestinian Arabs are descendants of immigrants who entered the land from surrounding areas in the second half of the nineteenth and the first half of the twentieth century.[25] Palestinians only truly began to identify as a separate people group after the birth of modern Israel. Before that they were simply Arabs who considered themselves part of Syria, with no distinct Palestinian national identity.[26]

"Palestine was part of the province of Syria," noted the Arab Higher Committee representative to the United Nations, adding, "politically, the Arabs of Palestine were not independent in the sense of forming a separate political entity." Even the first chairman of the PLO, Ahmed Shuqeiri, told the Security Council, "It is common knowledge that Palestine is nothing but southern Syria."[27] Palestinian nationalism only began after the First World War and developed after Israel's birth.

In contrast, Jewish nationalism persisted despite long years of exile with the hope and expectation of a Jewish return to their ancient land, not unlike the Spanish Reconquista.[28]

Therefore, Israelis contend that the Jewish return to Zion was not a colonial land grab, as is claimed, but the restoration of the original inhabitants to their ancient homeland.

But what of the displacement of the Arab population? Israeli apologists assert that the commonly claimed 750,000 to 1,000,000 original refugees is impossible. The number is no more than 650,000 Arab refugees and, according to the United Nations mediator at the time, it was as low as 472,000.[29]

Second, Israelis claim that they did not expel the Palestinian Arabs but actually begged them to stay. Israel claims that the vast majority of Arab refugees fled out of (unfounded) fear of atrocities[30] and at the urging of Arab leaders. (A few Arab villages were indeed destroyed and their people expelled for military purposes, since they were being used to besiege Jerusalem.) They cite the exhortations of then–Iraqi Prime Minister Nuri Said to tell the Arabs to "conduct your wives and children to safe areas until the fighting has died down." Habib Issa, secretary general of the Arab League, reported in 1951 that his predecessor, Azzam Pasha, had assured the Arab peoples that the occupation of Palestine and of Tel Aviv would be "easy booty . . . it will be a simple matter to throw Jews into the Mediterranean."[31] Thus, Israelis contend that their alleged "original sin" of expelling the Palestinians is a product of propaganda rather than history.

Besides disputing Palestinian religious and historical assertions, Israelis also challenge their *political claims*. With respect to Palestinian self-determination, Israelis assert that the Balfour Declaration in no way contradicted British promises to the Arabs as found in the McMahon-Hussein correspondence. In fact, McMahon identified the areas in which Great Britain would support Arab independence and then specifically excluded

Palestine from those areas. He then qualified Britain's promise to the Arabs by stating, "With *the above modification* Great Britain is prepared to recognize and support the independence of the Arabs in all the regions within the limits demanded by the Sherif of Mecca" (italics added)[32] Years later, McMahon confirmed that Palestine was never "on the table," writing, "I feel it my duty to state, and I do so definitely and emphatically, that it was not intended by me in giving this pledge to King Hussein to include Palestine in the area in which Arab independence was promised."[33]

Israelis also contend that the Balfour Declaration was a legitimate recognition of the reality of a Jewish community already present in Palestine. This was confirmed by the League of Nations and included in its granting the British a mandate for Palestine. Moreover, the British carved an Arab state out of eastern Palestine, making Jordan the original country for the Palestinians.

Israelis also reject the alleged Palestinian right of return. One reason is that the number of Palestinian refugees has been inflated. By defining as a refugee any Arab that had lived in Israel for as little as two years before departure, the United Nations used a different standard for Palestinians than UN agencies use for any other refugees. They even included as refugees Palestinians who may have merely moved from one part of Palestine to another only to find themselves separated from their original village by the 1949 armistice line. By using the different standards, the United Nations number Palestinian refugees to be more than four million. If the United Nations would apply the standards it uses for all other refugees in the world, there would be fewer than one million.[34] For example, in all other cases, except for the Palestinians, refugee status is not hereditary.

Israelis also reject the Palestinian interpretation of UN Resolution 194 upon which the right of return is based. To begin, it was the General Assembly that agreed upon Resolution 194, making it nonbinding. Besides, the Arab states unanimously rejected it when it was issued. Also, the resolution calls for repatriation only of "refugees wishing to return to their homes and *live at peace with their neighbours,*" something Palestinian refugees have not been willing to do. Furthermore, it does not limit resolution of the refugee problem to repatriation but also calls for "*resettlement* and economic and social rehabilitation of the refugees" (all italics added). Moreover, the overall purpose of the resolution never was to solve the refugee problem but to establish a conciliation commission. Thus historian Efraim Karsh wrote, "Only in the 1960s, and with the connivance of their Soviet and third-world supporters, did the Arabs begin to transform Resolution 194 into the cornerstone of an utterly spurious legal claim to a 'right of return,' buttressing it with thinly argued and easily refutable appeals to other international covenants on the treatment of refugees and displaced persons."[35]

As an alternative to return, Israelis propose a permanent exchange of refugees as the more reasonable solution to the problem, noting that process happened successfully in 1950, when Turkey and Bulgaria exchanged 150,000 refugees, and on a much larger scale in 1947, when India and Pakistan exchanged eight million and six million refugees, respectively.[36] Israelis perceive the Palestinian insistence on a "right of return" for the refugees and their descendants not as a means of making peace but an attempt to destroy the Jewish state via demographics instead of war.

Regarding their occupation of the West Bank and Gaza, the Israelis believe their presence is legal and certainly not the source of the current conflict. (They had in effect ended the occupation with the Oslo agreements that gave the Palestinian Authority governmental responsibility over 98 percent of the Palestinian population in these areas, and the conflict still resumed. Moreover, Ehud Barak attempted to negotiate the creation of a Palestinian state in 97 percent of the Palestinian territories but was unceremoniously rejected by Arafat.)

Israelis insist, with respect to the occupation, that Security Council Resolution 242 did not demand withdrawal from all the territories. Rather the resolution called for Israel, in exchange for termination of belligerency and recognition of the Israeli right "to live in peace within secure recognized boundaries," to withdraw "from territories occupied in the recent conflict." The U.K. and U.S. ambassadors who framed the resolution denied it was intended to force a return to the exact prewar boundaries.[37] Israel regards the boundaries that existed prior to the Six Day War as indefensible and insecure, "Auschwitz borders."[38]

Furthermore, Israelis allege that the settlements are in no way illegal because they are built in lands where Jewish people had historically lived, which had never had final internationally recognized borders, and which had been seized in a defensive war.[39] Thus, whether referring to self-determination, the right of return, or the occupation, Israelis contend that the political arguments favor their position and not the Palestinians.

The Israelis reject Palestinian *economic claims* as well. They assert that the whole land, which supports some nine million people today, had an

Arab population of only 260,000 in 1882. They contend that immigration from surrounding Arab countries because of the Jewish economic development of the land produced the growth of the Arab population. Photographs and journals written by travelers confirm that the land itself was swamp-laden in the north and barren in the south.

As to the alleged vast orange groves of the Palestinians, in 1937 the Peel Commission concluded that "much of the land now carrying orange groves was sand dunes or swamp and uncultivated when it was purchased [by Jews]. . . . There was at that time of the earlier sales little evidence that the owners possessed either the resources or training needed to develop the land." According to this British commission, the Jewish presence in Palestine had produced higher wages, a better living standard, and increased employment.[40] Israelis insist that they did not steal a lush and prosperous land from its Arab population but rather they purchased and developed an infertile and largely abandoned barren land.

Finally, Israel and its defenders contend that Israel's record on *human rights* is strong. Accusations of abuse are the outgrowth of an unjust double standard that measures Israel's rights record in ways different from all other nations. According to Harvard law professor Alan Dershowitz,

> [Israel's] record on human rights compares favorably to that of any
> country in the world that has faced comparable dangers. Its Supreme
> Court is among the best in the world, and it has repeatedly overruled
> the army and the government and made them operate under the rule of
> law. . . . It also has freedom of speech, press, dissent, association and
> religion.[41]

With respect to the Israeli law of return, calling it racist is a reflection of an unfair double standard. Many nations have similar laws, including Russia, Germany, and Jordan. Additionally, non-Jews may apply and have been granted citizenship via naturalization. Also, Israel has approximately one million Arab citizens who have the right to vote and serve in the Knesset. On the other hand, Arab nations, such as Jordan and Saudi Arabia, specifically prohibit Jews from becoming citizens.

The racist charge by Arabs extends to Israel's treatment of Palestinians in refugee camps by equating them with Nazi treatment of Jewish people. This accusation is particularly offensive to Israelis, who believe such a charge minimizes the true horror of the Holocaust. Palestinian spokesmen accuse Israel of being like the Nazis, which moves the debate from anti-Israel rhetoric to overt anti-Semitism. To say Israel's actions compare with Nazi Germany's systematic racial killings, concentration camps, and genocide is patently untrue.

Israel contends that Palestinian life has significantly improved under the administrative occupation. Arab life expectancy has increased, and infant mortality has decreased dramatically. Economic conditions surged to the extent that Palestinian per capita income was double that of Syria's and quadruple that of Yemen's. Only after Israel began to administer these territories did most Palestinians begin to receive running water and obtain electricity, ranges for cooking, as well as televisions, refrigerators, and cars. As a result of the "occupation," Palestinian literacy surged, universities began, and freedom of the press became normative. These advances all ground to a halt and regressed only after the Palestinian Authority took over administrative control.[42]

Israel asserts that it does not desire to have humiliating checkpoints. Rather these are necessary to thwart terror against Israeli citizens. If the terror would stop, so would the checkpoints. Israelis also deny demolishing homes indiscriminately but do so to protect its citizens. Israel only destroys homes which are used as cover for terrorists or those that are built over tunnels used for smuggling illegal weapons.

Finally, Israelis assert that they are in the midst of a war. As such, targeting enemy military leaders during such a time is perfectly legitimate under the rules of warfare. This is not only Israel's practice, but also that of the United States and other democracies. Israel's restraint is evident in the relatively low number of Palestinian casualties, compared with 65,000 killed during conflicts between Indians and Pakistanis.

With respect to Arafat's offer of peace, Israel has come to repudiate him as a peace partner. After years of seeking to negotiate with Arafat as a peace partner, Israel concluded that Arafat had no intention of making peace. Israel now understands Arafat's offers of peace as merely part of the "phased strategy" spoken of by Arafat, with the ultimate goal of building a Palestinian state in Israel proper.[43]

Four Realities in the Arab-Israeli Conflict

In light of the claims and counterclaims, what should we think? In evaluating the arguments on both sides, there appear four realities that the world community must not ignore.

First, Israel does have a right to exist. That this has become an issue is profoundly shocking. The world is a better place because there is a Jewish state. It can be said that Israel does indeed want to come to a compromise and an accommodation with the Palestinians, even if it requires great sacrifice on the part of the nation. While by no means perfect, Israel has accomplished much. It established a legitimate democracy in the Middle East; achieved scientific, agricultural, and medical advances that have served the world; provided sanctuary for the Jewish people, one of the most persecuted people in history; guarded the religious liberty of all its citizens including Jews, Christians, and Muslims; and protected and maintained free access to the holy places of all three major religions.

Second, there has been a dangerous revival of anti-Semitism around the world. It is seen in the Conference against Racism in Durban, South Africa, (September 2001), the harsh rhetoric of the Muslim world, and the attacks against Jews and Jewish sites in France, the rest of Europe, Africa, and Turkey. This is a frightening resurrection of a hatred that was thought to finally have died. Unfortunately, those who politically oppose Israel feel justified by allegations of Israeli misdeeds in attacking Jews around the world. Moreover, others excuse their own anti-Semitism by cloaking it as merely political opposition to Israel. *New York Times* columnist Thomas Friedman correctly observed, "Criticizing Israel is not anti-Semitic, and saying so is vile. But singling out Israel for opprobrium and international sanction—out of all proportion to any other party in the Middle East—is anti-Semitic, and not saying so is dishonest."[44]

Third, it must be acknowledged that the Palestinians have suffered greatly and deserve compassion. Some have lived in refugee camps and without real homes for entire lifetimes. Unfortunately, Palestinians blame Israel for all their anguish when others are responsible as well. For example, the United Nations Relief Works Agency has fostered a dependency on the part of the Palestinians; the Arab states have kept Palestinians in refugee camps as a propaganda tool rather than integrating them into normal life; and the Palestinian Authority has not prepared their people for peace but continue to assure them of a maximalist resolution to their suffering. Palestinians should also consider how their persistent use of terrorism has brought hardship and heartache to their own lives.

The time has come to make the compromises necessary for ending the conflict. Palestinians should be granted their own state, but only if they will authentically accept the two-state solution and genuinely abandon terrorism.

Fourth, the Israelis and Palestinians need to look forward rather than to the past in order to find a solution. Alan Dershowitz has rightly observed:

[There must be] some kind of statute of limitations for ancient grievances. Just as the case for Israel can no longer rely exclusively on the expulsion of the Jews from the land of Israel in the first century, so too the Arab case must move beyond a reliance on events that allegedly occurred more than a century ago. One reason for statutes of limitations is the recognition that as time passes it becomes increasingly difficult to reconstruct the past with any degree of precision, and political memories harden and replace the facts.[45]

All the grievances and countergrievances on both sides seem intractable. The conflict, with all its arguments and counterarguments, has become like a bowl of spaghetti that can no longer be separated into individual strands. That is why throughout the last century partition has consistently been proposed as the resolution of the problem. The British initially did this with their creation of Transjordan; the Peel Commission also proposed partition to bring peace; the United Nations also offered partition as the answer; finally, President Clinton tried to obtain a two-state solution, a form of partition, at Camp David in July of 2000.

Unless both aggrieved parties are willing to look to the future rather than to the past, peace will not be conceivable.

13
Islam in Prophecy:
The Future Islamic Invasion of Israel

The last hour would not come till the Muslims fight
against the Jews and the Muslims kill them, until
the Jews hide themselves, and the stones and trees
would speak up saying, "There is a Jew hiding
behind me, come and kill him."

—Saying of the Prophet Muhammad
Hadith Sahih Muslim, Book 40:6985

According to Islam, at the end of days, Islam will be victorious over all
nations and religions, particularly the Jewish people and Israel. This perspective was plainly evident in a *Jerusalem Post* interview with some Palestinian Muslims shortly after the 2001 terrorist attacks on the United States.
A Muslim named Karam argued that the United States and Israel were
trying to resist an inevitable historical process. "Everyone knows that in
the end the whole world is going to become Muslims."

When the interviewer asked what will become of the state of Israel,
another young Muslim who was listening interrupted by saying, "Israel?
Israel will be the world capital of Islam."[1]

This view of the future governs modern militant Islam. Muslims who
adopt an aggressive posture against Israel believe Islam is ascendant and
Israel will be defeated. Nevertheless, the Bible has a competing end-time
scenario. The Bible anticipates a conflict in which Islamic nations one
day will unite, surround Israel, and then invade the Jewish state with the
intention of destroying it. However, the Bible outlines a wholly different
outcome. The prophet Ezekiel previewed this final conflict and its ultimate
outcome.

The Identity of the Invaders

Ezekiel 38 indicates that there will be a future invasion of Israel, although interpreters disagree as to the identity of the invaders. Ezekiel describes the invaders this way:

Son of man, set your face against Gog, of the land of Magog, the chief [or rosh] prince of Meshech and Tubal; prophesy against him and say: "This is what the Sovereign LORD says: I am against you, O Gog, chief prince of Meshech and Tubal . . . also Gomer with all its troops, and Beth Togarmah from the far north with all its troops—the many nations with you." (verses 2–3, 6)

Of what nations does Ezekiel speak? Some interpreters, particularly during the period of the Cold War, inaccurately identified Israel's attackers as Russia.[2] This was based primarily on the similarity of sound in the words used: *Rosh* to Russia, *Meshech* to Moscow, and *Tubal* to Tobolsk (Ezekiel 38:2). This approach seems to take its interpretation more from Cold War headlines than the biblical text.

The countries that are named in Ezekiel 38 existed during the biblical period. The book of Genesis lists the nations that descended from Noah's son Japheth (Genesis 10:2–5) and there is considerable overlap with Ezekiel's invading armies. They include Magog, Meshech, Tubal, Gomer, and Togarmah, but not Rosh. That is because *rosh* is an adjective best translated *head* or *chief* and refers to the "*chief* prince of Meshech" (as in the New International and English Standard Versions), not to a country named Russia.

The Role of the Commonwealth of Independent States

In order to identify the armies that will assault Israel we must identify those nations mentioned in Ezekiel 38 that existed in biblical times and then ascertain what modern countries are present there now.[3] Magog was a nation that occupied the area between the Black and Caspian Seas, from which the Scythians descended. Gomer probably refers to the Cimmerians, who lived in eastern Asia Minor, near modern Armenia, and were called Gimirrai in Assyrian writings and Kimmerioi in Greek writings.[4] All these nations inhabited what is now modern Armenia, Azerbaijan, and Georgia. While formerly part of the Soviet Union, they are now independent nations with separate foreign policies.

The Bible always places Meshech and Tubal together, and Assyrian documents describe a land of Tabal(u) by the land of Musku. Old Testament scholar Allen Ross locates these nations as having moved from eastern Asia Minor north to the Black Sea.[5] This would place these nations in what is now eastern Turkey.

Togarmah, described in Genesis 10 as a descendant of Gomer, is mentioned in ancient texts as the district and city of Tagarma, located north of the ancient road from Haran to Carchemish.[6] On a modern map, Togarmah would be located in eastern Turkey.

Based on the evidence, most of the group of nations described in Ezekiel 38:2–3, 6, with the exception of Togarmah, appear to be the states of the former Soviet Union, now members of the Commonwealth of Independent States, or CIS. They maintain separate foreign policies and are independent of Russia. What is more, they all share the same Islamic religious heritage. Map 6, "Countries in the Coming Islamic Invasion," shows the probable locations of these and other Ezekiel 38 nations.

The Role of Turkey

Of the above nations, Turkey alone is not part of the CIS, but it is indeed Islamic. Some would object that although Turkey is predominantly Muslim by religion, it is an unlikely invader of Israel. The government is secular as are most of the people. Furthermore, Israel and Turkey have a strong alliance, even sharing in joint military exercises. Yet biblical prophecy foretells that Turkey will participate in an Islamic invasion.

The credibility of this biblical prediction is bolstered by the rapid change in political realities. For example, before the fall of the Shah of Iran, the Iranian government was secular and shared close relations with Israel. However, with the rise of the Islamic republic of the Ayatollah Khomeini, Iran became hostile to Israel; today it is one of Israel's most implacable enemies. In the same way, Turkey could very well adopt an Islamic government and change its disposition towards Israel.

In November of 2002, Turkey's citizens gave the Justice and Development party a majority in the parliament. Led by the new prime minister, Recep Tayyip Erdogan, this party has its roots in banned Islamic parties. In fact, the prime minister had been imprisoned on the charge of incitement. Although Turkey has yet to change its posture on Israel, its unwillingness to allow U.S. troops to attack Iraq from Turkish lands shows that its Islamic allegiance is increasing rapidly. In the future, Turkey may take a stronger Islamist position, leading it into an Islamic alliance against Israel.

Map 6
COUNTRIES IN THE COMING ISLAMIC INVASION

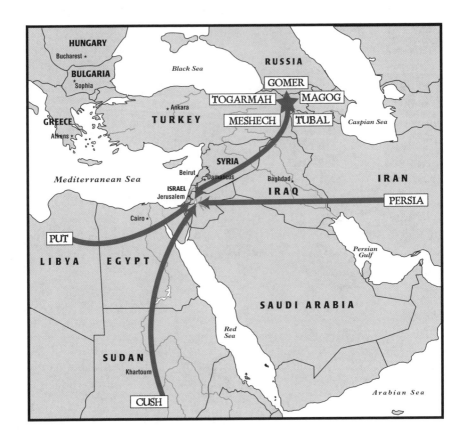

The Roles of Iran, Sudan, and Libya

Additionally, Ezekiel describes three other nations that will join the attack on Israel from the north: "Persia, Cush and Put will be with them, all with shields and helmets" (38:5). Today Persia is called Iran. As noted above, it is dominated by a strict Islamic government and is a source of anti-Israel terrorism. Tehran's heated rhetoric against Israel along with its missile development and nuclear aspirations has led Israel to view Iran as its most dangerous enemy in the Middle East.

Moreover, the Hezbollah terrorists that frequently attack Israel from Lebanon are funded, supplied, and trained by Iran. Recall that Iran sent the *Karine A* weapons ship to the Palestinian Authority, which Israel seized before it could drop its terrorist cargo. It will be no surprise if Iran joins an attack on Israel.

The second ally named by Ezekiel is Cush, now called Sudan, a country known for its Islamic militancy. It harbored Islamic terrorist Osama bin Laden prior to his establishment of a base in Afghanistan.

The last ally mentioned by Ezekiel is Put, which is modern-day Libya. Led by Mohammar Khadaffi, Libya has long been known for its extremism and radical anti-Israel posture. Based on Ezekiel's prophecy, militant Islam will coalesce and form an alliance that will one day attack Israel. The alliance will include the Islamic republics that were formerly part of the USSR, Turkey, Iran, Sudan, and Libya—all joining to surround and invade Israel. According to the Bible, the hatred of Israel among militant Muslims will increase to the point of all-out war with the Jewish state.

The Time of the Invasion

When will the Islamic invasion of Israel take place? In his description of the invasion, Ezekiel gives some clues that this will take place sometime in the future period of tribulation on the earth.

Clue One: A Restored Israel

First, this will take place after Israel has been restored as a nation. Ezekiel makes this clear when he writes, "In future years you will invade a land that has recovered from war, whose people were gathered from many nations to the mountains of Israel, which had long been desolate. They had been brought out from the nations, and now all of them live in safety" (38:8).

In Ezekiel 37 the prophet had described the regathering of Israel in his vision of the dry bones. There he showed how Israel would be brought back from the nations of the earth to her ancient homeland. This would occur in stages. It appears that this prophecy was fulfilled, at least partially, in the rebirth of the nation of Israel. The state of Israel will also be in existence during that future tribulation.

Clue Two: Israel at Peace

A second clue is that Israel will be living in peace and security when the invasion comes. Ezekiel wrote,

> You will say, "I will invade a land of unwalled villages; I will attack a peaceful and unsuspecting people—all of them living without walls and without gates and bars." . . . In that day, when my people Israel are living in safety, will you not take notice of it? You will come from your place in the far north, you and many nations with you. . . . You will advance against my people Israel like a cloud that covers the land. (38:11, 14–16)

How will Israel find peace and security? The tribulation period will only begin when Israel signs a covenant with the future false Messiah[7] (Daniel 9:27). Most likely, Israel will be willing to sign this treaty with the coming world ruler because he will guarantee their peace and security. That is why Paul says that the Tribulation will begin "while people are saying, 'Peace and safety'" (1 Thessalonians 5:3). Therefore, sometime in the Tribulation, after Israel has experienced this false, temporary peace, the Islamic invasion will begin.

Clue Three: Israel Will Not "Know . . . the Lord Their God"

A third clue for determining the time of the invasion is that it will take place before Israel as a nation comes to know the Lord. Ezekiel promised that as a result of God's protection "the house of Israel will know that I am the LORD their God" (39:22) and God "will pour out [His] Spirit on the house of Israel" (39:29).

Sometime after this invasion, the nation of Israel will understand God's protection and turn in faith to their Messiah Jesus. That will only occur immediately before the second coming of Jesus at the end of the Tribulation. Therefore, the Islamic invasion must take place during the Tribulation but sometime prior to its end.

The Final Clue: A Further Regathering in Israel

A last element for identifying when this will take place is in Ezekiel 39:25–28. There Ezekiel assured Israel that after the defeat of the invading armies, God "will now bring Jacob back from captivity" (verse 25). Although Ezekiel had said that the invasion would take place only after Israel has been restored as a nation, here he promised a further regathering of all the Jewish people who had not yet returned to their ancient homeland.

Although Israel has already been restored as a nation, millions of Jewish people remain in dispersion. Only when Messiah Jesus returns will those Jewish people be regathered by Him from the rest of the world. So once again, the Islamic invasion will take place after Israel has been restored as a nation and the false peace of the Tribulation has begun. But it must take place before Jesus returns, when all Jewish people will put their trust in Him and be regathered to the land of their fathers.

Most likely, the Islamic invasion will take place in the middle of the future seven-year tribulation. Recall that according to Daniel 9:27, Israel will sign a covenant with the false messiah. The covenant will be for seven years, yet right in the middle of that period, the future false messiah will break that covenant. It is possible that the Islamic invasion will take place just prior to the breaking of the covenant. Perhaps, with God's removal of the bloc of Islamic nations, the Antichrist will no longer feel the need to maintain his political alliance with Israel. With the Islamic threat removed, he will turn on Israel and unleash a horrific period of anti-Semitism.

Although we cannot be dogmatic about the timing of the Islamic invasion, it appears that it will take place during the Tribulation and most likely just before the midpoint. But more important than the timing of the Islamic invasion is the way God will resolve it.

The Defeat of the Invaders

Ezekiel assured his people that God would not abandon them to defeat at the hands of the invaders. Instead, God declares, "When Gog attacks the land of Israel, my hot anger will be aroused" (38:18). God will intervene when the nations attack Israel by causing "a great earthquake in the land of Israel" (verse 19). Since Israel is situated on the Jordan Rift, an earthquake fault line running north-south through the heart of the land, any earthquake can have a devastating effect. In the confusion of broken roads and bridges, the invading armies will turn on each other. "Every man's sword will be against his brother" (verse 21). Perhaps the earthquake will disrupt command and control of the invading armies or maybe the different languages spoken by the armies (Farsi, Turkish, Arabic) will bring confusion, or possibly a combination of these two factors. The result will be the invaders will be killing each other with friendly fire; then, as the bodies pile up, God will send plague and further bloodshed (verse 22).

In the midst of this confusion, God will bring "torrents of rain" (verse 22) on those who attack Israel. In Israel, which is dry nine months a year, a heavy rain can cause flash floods and swell rivers and wadis to such an extent that armies can be entirely halted or swept away. While they are stopped in their tracks, God will rain "hailstones and burning sulfur" (verse 22) on the invading armies, devastating the armies of militant Islam.

Both Israel and its invaders will understand that Israel did not rescue herself with her own military strength but that God delivered His nation with supernatural intervention. God says, "I will show my greatness and my holiness, and I will make myself known in the sight of many nations" (38:23). God alone will send a massive earthquake, plague and bloodshed, torrential rains, hailstones, and fiery sulfur to defeat the Islamic invasion of Israel.

How Soon?

How soon these events will take place is unknown to anyone. The Bible promises that the next event on the prophetic calendar is the removal of the followers of Messiah—the church—prior to the Tribulation (1 Thessalonians 1:10; 5:9). Yet the rise of Islamic militancy in our day and its associated hatred of Israel could be hints that these events are certainly getting closer. Militant Muslims, citing the prophet Muhammad's words in Hadith 40:6985 (see the opening quotation), fully expect Islam to dominate the world in general and Israel in particular. On the other hand, the Scriptures paint a drastically different outcome. When these Islamic militants attack, the God of Israel will rush to the aid of His people and use His protection as a means of ultimately bringing them to trust in the Messiah Jesus.

But what of the Arab nations that surround Israel? They are not mentioned in Ezekiel 38–39. What does the Bible say about them? It is to this we next turn our attention.

14
The Arab States in Prophecy

The biblical legacy of Arabs and Jews has the potential to reconcile both antagonistic parties under the Abrahamic umbrella and to offer the hope of the gospel of peace in an area tyrannized by war.

—Tony Maalouf
Arabs in the Shadow of Israel

Peace between Israel and her Arab neighbors remains the priority of the United States and other nations, who have expended much time and effort in trying to find the way to lasting peace. The process has had its ups and downs. Who would have thought that the joy and excitement of the signing of the Oslo accords would give way to the anger and bitterness spawned by the violence of the Intifada just seven years later?

Will there ever be peace between the Arabs and the Israelis?

The Bible foretells that peace between the Arab nations and Israel will indeed come! This peace will arrive, however, not through the successful peace brokering of the United States and other countries. Instead, peace will appear when the Peacemaker, Messiah Jesus, returns to set up His throne and reign over the kingdoms of the earth.

At that time, peace will be established for the Arab world and the Jewish nation in three ways: (1) through the desolation of some Arab nations, (2) through the annexation of some Arab lands by Israel, and (3) through the spiritual transformation of some Arab countries.[1]

To see what the future holds for the Arab states, it is important to recognize that the Bible speaks of the future of specific biblical nations. In the previous chapter we uncovered several biblical nations and their modern counterparts in a future Islamic invasion. Now lets identify further modern Arab countries existing in the same geographic places as those biblical nations in order to discern what the future holds for key Arab states.

Peace Through Desolation

Although desolation is truly tragic, for some nations it appears to be God's only recourse for achieving peace. The perpetual animosity of these peoples towards Israel has led God to declare the ultimate destruction of these nations.

Southern Jordan

The southern area of the modern Hashemite kingdom of Jordan was inhabited by the biblical nation of Edom. Several Bible prophets foretold the complete desolation of the Edomites, revealing the future of this part of Jordan.

God declared that the Edomites would be completely destroyed (see Ezekiel 35:1–15) because they "had everlasting enmity and have delivered the sons of Israel to the power of the sword" (verse 5 NASB). The Lord assured the complete desolation of Edom (verse 9) since they "rejoiced over . . . Israel because it was desolate" (verse 15 NASB). The same promise is found in Obadiah, where God compared the house of Jacob to a fire and Edom to stubble. Edom would be set on fire so that "there will be no survivors from the house of Esau" (Obadiah 18). In Jeremiah, God proclaimed that Edom would become "an object of horror, of reproach and of cursing; and all its towns will be in ruins forever" (Jeremiah 49:13). The future is bleak for the southern area of Jordan. In the messianic kingdom, it will be completely desolate.

Iraq and the Future of Babylon

The first Gulf War (1991) thrust Iraq—ancient Babylonia—into the thinking of most Americans for the first time in modern history. At that time, there was a tremendous surge in interest in Bible prophecy, with people wondering if Armageddon was upon us. Obviously, those who painted end-time scenarios around that war were mistaken. Additionally, most Americans became interested in Iraq once again with the prelude, fighting, and aftermath of "Gulf War II," the move (in 2003) to free Iraq of the brutal regime of Saddam Hussein. Yet this was perceived by most Americans as a political and security issue, and not some sort of fulfillment of end-time prophecy. While I am in agreement with this assessment, the events in Iraq could lay the groundwork for the events foretold in the Bible about that nation.

The ancient Hebrew prophets foretold that Babylon, a large town in central Iraq today and the great capital of the ancient Babylonian Empire, would ultimately be desolate for all time (Isaiah 13 and Jeremiah 50–51). Isaiah said that Babylon "will never be inhabited or lived in through all generations; no Arab will pitch his tent there" (13:20). Jeremiah confirmed Isaiah's words, comparing Babylon's destruction to that of Sodom and Gomorrah (50:39–40).

While the city of Babylon was indeed destroyed, the extent of its demise as described in the Bible has not yet occurred. As Charles Dyer points out, "The city did not fall suddenly, and the houses were not burned. No great slaughter of inhabitants took place. If we take the descriptions of Isaiah and Jeremiah at face value, then Cyrus's capture of the city did not fulfill their predictions."[2] Additionally, both Isaiah and Jeremiah associated the fall of Babylon with the final spiritual restoration of Israel (Isaiah 14:1; Jeremiah 50:4–5), an event that will take place at the return of Messiah Jesus. For these reasons, it is best to expect the Bible's prediction about Babylon's demise to be fulfilled yet in the future.

To discover what the Bible says about the ultimate destiny of Babylon, let's examine Revelation 17–18. The apostle John's vision of the future links the various strands of biblical data to give a final picture of what will become of Babylon.

Some Bible scholars believe that the Babylon described in Revelation 17 is not a literal city but symbolic of a future corrupt world religious system. Additionally, they view Revelation 18 as describing this "Babylon's" central economic role and its being the political capital of the future world ruler (frequently called the Antichrist).[3]

It is much better, since the two chapters describe Babylon in much the same way, to interpret the Bible passage as describing the very same Babylon. Moreover, since both chapters identify Babylon the Great as a "great city," a growing number of scholars view Revelation 17–18 as a compilation of the biblical data regarding the ultimate destiny of the *city* of Babylon.[4]

These two chapters describe the ultimate destiny of Babylon because of her spiritual harlotry and resistance to God. Babylon has been the seat of rebellion against God since the building of the city and tower of

Babel.[5] In the tribulation period, while the future false Messiah will exercise political and military control over the earth, the corrupt city of Babylon will exercise economic control over the kingdoms of the earth (17:2; 18:3, 9). She will even dominate the Antichrist economically. That is why the city of Babylon is described as a harlot riding the back of the beast, referring to Babylon's economic control of the Antichrist.

The Bible does not state how Babylon, a city that is not even fully rebuilt yet and residing in a nation that is economically weak after years of UN sanctions, will become the world economic power. While this is only conjecture, it is possible to see the rapid economic turnaround of Iraq. Today, Iraq sits on the second largest oil reserves in the world (next to Saudi Arabia). Amazingly, the country's oil reserves have not yet been fully explored. Once that is done, it could very well have the greatest oil reserves on the earth. If the United States is successful in rebuilding Iraq and restoring its oil business, Iraq could very well become an economic powerhouse. In the future tribulation, the false messiah will need to move his armies and mechanized weaponry to maintain his military dominance. That could possibly be the reason Revelation 17 describes Iraq as economically dominant over the Antichrist.

Nevertheless, the future world ruler will not accept his position of subservience permanently. Revelation 17:16 says that he and the nations he dominates will hate Babylon and "bring her to ruin . . . ; they will eat her flesh and burn her with fire." This will cause the angels of heaven and the people of God to rejoice over Babylon's judgment (18:20). Someone might object that if it is the Antichrist and his armies that defeat Babylon, how could this be viewed as the judgment of God? The answer is that even the Antichrist and his allies are under the sovereignty of God who has "put it into their hearts to accomplish his purpose" (17:17). As a result of this attack, Babylon and much of Iraq will become a place of continual burning (19:3) and the abode of demons (18:2) during the kingdom period.[6] Although the desolation of this city in Iraq is foretold in Scripture, as we shall see, it is not the sole destiny of the Iraqi nation.

Peace Through Annexation

Ezekiel 47:13–20 describes the boundaries of Israel during the messianic kingdom. These look quite similar to Israel's borders during the reigns of David and Solomon. The northern border will also include the Hethlon Road and the city of Lebo (verse 15; probably modern Lebwah), both of which are in Lebanon. Additionally, it will include the city of Damascus (verse 16), which is in Syria. So, although the Bible does not explicitly state the future of these two nations, clearly Lebanon and parts of Syria will experience peace with Israel by being annexed into the Jewish state during the messianic kingdom.

Peace Through Transformation

The most encouraging news to be found in the biblical prophecies regarding the Arab nations is that several of these will experience spiritual transformations. There will be some Arab states that will come to a genuine faith in Messiah Jesus and share in the worldwide blessings of the messianic kingdom. This will be the way that they finally achieve peace with Israel.

Central and Northern Jordan

The biblical nations of Moab and Ammon were situated in what is now the central and northern parts of the Hashemite kingdom of Jordan. The destiny of Jordan includes not only desolation in the south (as was discussed above), but also hope of a remnant who will come to faith in the Messiah Jesus. In Jeremiah 48, the Lord predicted the future destruction of Moab, which did indeed occur. However, at the end of the oracle, God provides hope by promising, "I will restore the fortunes of Moab in the days to come [literally "the end of days"]" (48:47).

The end-time hope of Ammon is found in the next oracle of Jeremiah. First, the Lord declared the future destruction of Ammon (49:1–5) but then included hope of restoration. The Lord said, "Afterward, I will restore the fortunes of the Ammonites" (49:6). These passages in Jeremiah look forward to the end of days, when a remnant of these two biblical nations will put their faith in the Messiah and experience spiritual transformation. Thus, it seems that the northern and central parts of the modern kingdom of Jordan will find peace with Messiah and peace with Israel.

Egypt

From the time of birth of the state of Israel in 1948 until Egyptian President Anwar el-Sadat addressed the Knesset (the Israeli parliament) thirty years later, Egypt had been an implacable enemy of Israel. Today, there is a peace treaty that has been sustained for twenty-five years, even though many consider it to be a "cold peace." However, the prophet Isaiah foresees Israel and Egypt experiencing a friendly peace, when they both will know the Lord.

Isaiah foretells that Egypt will "cry to the LORD because of oppressors, and He will send them a Savior and a Champion, and He will deliver them" (19:20 NASB). At that time, Egypt will have an altar to the Lord and will worship Him (verses 19, 21). According to Zechariah, the Egyptians will also celebrate Sukkot (the Feast of Booths) together with Israel in the messianic kingdom (Zechariah 14:16–19). Egypt will be at peace with both her ancient enemies, Assyria and Israel, with this threesome providing blessing to the whole earth (Isaiah 19:24–25).

Syria and Iraq

What was once the land of Assyria today includes parts of modern Iraq and Syria. In the great prophecy of Egypt's future redemption, the prophet Isaiah also indicates that Assyria will know the Lord, and through this spiritual transformation the Assyrians will be peace partners with both Israel and Egypt. The ancient Via Maris, which has been closed since the birth of modern Israel, will be restored, providing an open highway from Egypt, through Israel, and up to Assyria (or parts of modern Syria and northern Iraq). Assyria will worship with Egypt and Israel, indicating that people in Syria and Iraq will come to know Messiah Jesus and enter the messianic kingdom (Isaiah 19:23).

In that great day, "Israel will be the third [party] along with Egypt and Assyria, a blessing on the earth. The LORD Almighty will bless them, saying, 'Blessed be Egypt my people, Assyria my handiwork, and Israel my inheritance'" (Isaiah 19:24–25).

Peace Today?

On a warm June evening in 1997, a unique group gathered in a meeting room at Chicago's Moody Bible Institute. The leaders of the various Arab fellowships and ministries dialogued with the messianic congregations and Jewish ministries of Chicago. Certainly different political opinions were represented in that room, yet a peace and unity prevailed —derived from the faith that all the participants had in the Messiah, Jesus.

It was a fantastic evening of a shared meal, shared stories, and shared joy; in fact, it was a little bit of the "not yet" future kingdom experienced "right now" in our midst. Beyond that, it gave a lesson for all who long for peace between the Arabs and Israel.

Regardless of efforts toward political peace (which should be pursued), the ultimate hope for true peace exists only through spiritual transformation. When these Jewish and Arab peoples united around their faith in Jesus, they were able to experience peace. That is true today and it will be true in the messianic kingdom. Only when Israel and the Arab nations experience a spiritual transformation, will peace arrive. And ultimately, that will only fully happen when the Peacemaker comes.

15
Is Peace Possible?

Enough of blood and tears. Enough.

—Yitzhak Rabin

When Yitzhak Rabin and Yasser Arafat signed the 1993 Declaration of Principles on the White House lawn, the impossible dream seemed to have turned into reality. After more than seventy years of conflict, three Arab uprisings, five wars, innumerable attacks and reprisals, bombings, and shootings, Jews and Arabs appeared to have achieved peace at last. Reluctant as he was to do so, Yitzhak Rabin shook hands with Yasser Arafat, explaining, "You make peace with enemies, not with friends."

Hopes were very high that day because, as Yasser Arafat later said in his Nobel Prize acceptance speech, the national cause of the Palestinians was "the guardian of the gate of Arab-Israeli peace." He recognized that Israeli-Palestinian peace would result in the whole Arab world making peace with Israel as well.

Signing the Declaration of Principles, however, was only the beginning and not the final peace agreement. As Rabin said, "We are in the midst of building the peace. . . . Mistakes could topple the whole structure and bring disaster down upon us."[1]

Indeed, the building did collapse: Intifada II, ongoing for more than three years and continuing as of this writing, has brought greater pessimism about the prospects for Arab-Israeli peace than ever before. Is peace even possible? This chapter will investigate that question by summarizing attempts at peace in the past, and looking at possibilities in the present and prospects for the future.

Attempts at Peace in the Past

Although subject to occasional outbreaks of violence, for the most part Jewish people had far more advantages in the Islamic world than their fellow Jews experienced under the leadership of Christian empires. That is why initially there were hopes for a peaceful and fruitful relationship between Arabs and Jews when the modern return to the land was just underway.

Before the War of Independence

After the British issued the Balfour Declaration and World War I had ended, the Zionist leadership recognized the need to have amenable relationships with the Arabs. Therefore, Chaim Weizmann began to seek a negotiating partner to establish a working agreement with the Arabs. He met with Emir Feisal, leader of the Arab movement, to obtain independence from colonial powers in the Middle East. In an atmosphere of warmth and welcome, Feisal reminded those present that "no true Arab can be suspicious or afraid of Jewish nationalism." He even stated that it would be unworthy of the Arabs not to say "welcome back home" to the Jewish people.[2]

As a result of the warm relations, Feisal and Weizmann were able to come to an agreement at the 1919 Paris Peace Conference. There they concluded an agreement that established boundaries between Palestine (a Jewish state) and the Arab state, large-scale Jewish immigration to Palestine, and protection of the Arab population of Palestine and all holy places.[3] Under his signature, Feisal added this codicil: "Provided the Arabs obtain their independence as demanded in my Memorandum dated the 4th of January, 1919, to the Foreign Office of the Government of Great Britain, I shall concur in the above articles."[4]

That proviso undid the agreement, for the Zionist leadership later refused to join Feisal in opposing French claims in the Middle East, and the British failed to withdraw its colonial control of all Arab areas. Emir Feisal terminated his relationship with the Zionists. No major peace attempts would be made until the outbreak of hostilities after the birth of Israel.

Just prior to the outbreak of the War of Independence (1948), David Ben-Gurion, leader of the Jewish Agency in Palestine, sent Golda Meir (who would later become foreign minister and ultimately prime minister of Israel) to negotiate secretly with King Abdullah of Transjordan. Crossing into Transjordan secretly, dressed as an Arab woman, Mrs. Meir sought to prevent the king from joining the impending attack against Israel. While receptive towards the Zionists, Abdullah wanted to grant the Jewish community of Palestine limited autonomy under an enlarged kingdom of Jordan, consisting of both sides of the Jordan River, of which he would be king. This was unacceptable to the Jewish leadership, and King Abdullah joined the war.

A New Nation and the Rhodes Armistice Talks

After the birth of Israel and the 1948–49 War of Independence, the United Nations mediated armistice talks between Israel and the Arab nations that had invaded Israel. They were designed to set temporary armistice lines between the belligerent states. The United Nations appointed American Ralph Bunche to guide the process, and he succeeded in bringing Arab and Jewish participants together for face-to-face talks.

During the Rhodes Armistice Talks, when the Israeli and Jordanian military officers came to agreement about the boundary between Israel and Jordan, they drew the line on a map using a green pen. That is why, even today, the boundary between Israel proper and the West Bank is still called the Green Line.

These talks, begun in the context of hostility, ultimately were conducted with professionalism and a good deal of friendliness. The negotiations were successful in setting temporary boundaries and granting Jewish people promises of access to pray at the Western Wall in Jerusalem. (That promise would remain unfulfilled as long as Jordan controlled the Old City of Jerusalem.) These talks were considered the precursor to a final peace agreement between Israel and the Arab states.

The anticipated peace failed because of the Arab states' insistence that Israel return to the borders set in the 1947 United Nations Partition Agreement rather than the Rhodes Armistice Lines. Israel claimed that returning to the partition lines would amount to allowing the Arab states to engage in a "limited liability war." In other words, nations could aggressively invade a sovereign state, lose territory and the war, and then demand that there be no consequences. As a result of this disagreement, there would be no final peace treaty, only an armistice between Israel and her Arab neighbors.

The Six Day War and the Khartoum Declaration

Israel believed that the Six Day War (1967) afforded the greatest promise of peace since its birth as an independent nation. Although attacked by the surrounding Arab nations, Israel won a decisive victory in only six days. Having taken the West Bank from Jordan, the Sinai Peninsula from Egypt, and the Golan Heights from Syria, Israeli leaders were certain that these nations would be willing to negotiate a final peace agreement in exchange for these lands. They could not have been more mistaken. The war simply hardened Arab attitudes against Israel. Their hardening was expressed in August 1968, when the Arab nations gathered for its first Pan-Arab summit since 1965. After meeting for several days, the summit issued a communiqué committing the Arab states to "no recognition of Israel, no peace and no negotiations with her" and to taking "all steps necessary to consolidate military preparedness."[5]

This outcome only served to make Israel more reliant on military superiority for survival. The 1973 Yom Kippur War would open Israel once again to peace negotiations.

Shuttle Diplomacy of 1973–74

In the first days of the Yom Kippur War, Egypt and Syria's surprise 1973 invasion of Israel brought the Jewish state to the brink of destruction. It need not have come to that. In 1971, Egyptian President Anwar Sadat wanted to negotiate the return of the Sinai to Egypt. Addressing the Egyptian parliament on February 4, 1971, Sadat said,

> If Israel withdrew her forces in Sinai to the Passes, I would be willing to reopen the Suez Canal; to have my forces cross to the East Bank; . . . to make a solemn official declaration of a cease fire; to restore diplomatic relations with the United States; and to sign a peace agreement with Israel through the efforts of Dr. Jarring, the representative of the Secretary-General of the United Nations.[6]

No one seemed to take Sadat seriously. Although Sadat had confirmed his offer in a letter to the United States on February 14, 1971, the United

States failed to act in any decisive way to initiate discussions. Gunnar Jarring, a Swedish diplomat and linguist, continued to have contacts with Israel and her Arab neighbors but did not realize the import of Sadat's stunning initiative. Worst of all, Sadat's initiative was not seized by Israeli Prime Minister Golda Meir and her cabinet. Overconfident of the military superiority made evident by the Six Day War and becoming accustomed to enlarged borders, Mrs. Meir responded by insisting in advance of negotiations that Israel would not return the entire Sinai. This lost the opportunity to make peace and led to the disastrous Yom Kippur War.[7]

Sadat's desire to have the Sinai returned motivated his surprise attack with Syria against Israel. After Israel turned the tide of the war and stopped just short of destroying the Egyptian Third Army (under threat of Soviet involvement), U.S. Secretary of State Henry Kissinger sprang into action. Using his so-called "shuttle diplomacy," Kissinger traveled from capital to capital, mediating between the parties. By 1974, he was able to engineer a disengagement of forces between Israel and Egypt and Israel and Syria. This led, in turn, to the next opportunity for peacemaking.

The 1979 Israel-Egypt Peace Treaty

Having fought Israel to a standstill (the near-destruction of the Egyptian Third Army notwithstanding), Anwar Sadat still had not succeeded in returning the Sinai to Egypt. Coupled with that, the Egyptian economy was failing and in desperate need of American support. Sadat decided to make a bold move to shore up his political situation, telling the Egyptian parliament once again he was ready to go "to the ends of the earth for peace. Israel will be astonished to hear me say now, before you, that I am prepared to go to their own house, to the Knesset itself, to talk to them."[8]

Within days, Sadat was denounced in Arab capitals as a traitor. Even U.S. President Jimmy Carter missed the significance of Sadat's offer, desiring instead a comprehensive international settlement at a Geneva conference with the Soviet Union participating. The only leader to seize the opportunity was the hawkish Israeli prime minister, Menachem Begin. He promptly invited Sadat to Jerusalem where, welcomed with pomp and unbelievably wild greetings, Sadat did indeed speak to the Israeli parliament just eleven days after making the offer in his own parliament.

This began a period of negotiations between Israel and Egypt brokered by the United States, which now understood the opportunity Sadat had provided. President Carter ultimately convened talks at Camp David, where the three leaders and their negotiating teams worked out the framework of a settlement. Egypt would agree to peace with Israel in return for Israel surrendering the entire Sinai Peninsula, dismantling the Jewish settlements built there, and offering the Palestinians autonomy in the West Bank and Gaza (which they rejected). (The United States would also sell Egypt military hardware and also grant billions of dollars in foreign aid to the Egyptians to rebuild their economy.)

On March 26, 1979, Sadat, Begin, and Carter signed the first formal peace treaty between Israel and an Arab country. Although there was great hope for warm relations between Israel and Egypt, the assassination of Anwar Sadat by Islamic terrorists resulted in a new Egyptian administration that would maintain the formal peace but keep relations with Israel cold.

The Oslo Accords

After the U.S.-led coalition's victory in the 1991 Gulf War, President Bush and Secretary of State James Baker decided to capitalize on the unprecedented unity of the Arab world and the influence of the United States. With Soviet President Mikhail Gorbachev, President Bush convened the Madrid Conference, bringing together Israel, Syria, Lebanon, and a joint Jordanian-Palestinian delegation. This inaugurated the first official direct talks between Israel and these countries and laid the foundation for the future peace process.

Israel had insisted on the exclusion of the terrorist Palestine Liberation Organization (PLO), so the Palestinians participated under the aegis of Jordan. Nevertheless, all Palestinian participants were in constant communication with PLO leadership in Tunis. In this sense, the exclusion of the PLO was mere fiction. The conference ended without any agreements, but all the participants indicated they would meet again.

Several factors slowed official peace negotiations. First, President Bush began to focus on his reelection campaign; Israel elected a new prime minister, Yitzhak Rabin; and Arab states began to resist further direct meetings with Israel. Meanwhile, Israeli academic Ya'ir Hirschfield and Israeli journalist Ron Pundak began secret negotiations with Abu Alaa, the PLO second in command in Oslo, Norway. Supported by the Norwegians, the secret negotiations grew more serious, producing the framework for an agreement between Israel and the PLO. This was brought to the Rabin government that agreed to a draft Declaration of Principles. First, among the principles was the agreement to exchange letters of mutual recognition, which took place on September 9, 1993.

Several factors led to this surprising agreement. We have already mentioned the loss of a sponsor in the USSR after Soviet communism collapsed, as well as Arafat's loss of support within the Arab world when Iraq lost the first Persian Gulf War. That war also changed Israel's perspective about the need for an enlarged territory as a means of security. After Saddam Hussein had rained Scud missiles from Iraq against the Israeli populace, the Israeli government realized that the West Bank granted them scant protection in a missile attack. They believed a peace agreement would yield far more security. Other factors already noted were the election of Yitzhak Rabin and the Labor Party, which brought a government more willing to make compromises for the sake of peace.

In addition, the first Intifada had wearied Israel and convinced the majority of Israelis that they could not go on governing the Palestinians interminably. Finally, the rise in popularity among Palestinians of the radical Islamic terrorist group Hamas had convinced Israel that the PLO was a more reasonable potential peace partner.

All these factors came together by 1993, producing the surprising Oslo accords.

The United States came to play a mediating role in the ensuing negotiations. On September 13, 1993, Yitzhak Rabin and Yasser Arafat signed an official Declaration of Principles, also known as Oslo I, providing gradual self-rule to the Palestinians in the West Bank and Gaza. The newly formed Palestinian Authority agreed to combat terror and to resolve all future differences through negotiations and not violence. Both parties committed to a five-year process, including final status talks which would deal with the most contentious issues: Jerusalem, the final borders, Jewish settlements in the West Bank and Gaza Strip, and the Palestinian refugees. Forty-three nations together pledged some $2.5 billion dollars to help the new Palestinian government, with the United States contributing $500 million.

The next step in the Oslo process was the Gaza-Jericho Agreement (May 4, 1994), signaling the beginning of Palestinian self-government in the territories. Israel withdrew from Gaza City and Jericho, leaving these areas under the authority of the Palestinian Authority.

The Israel-Jordan Peace Treaty

Meanwhile, Israel's Rabin and Jordan's King Hussein signed The Washington Declaration, a non-belligerency agreement ending the forty-six-year state of war between Israel and Jordan. This in turn led to negotiations toward reaching a formal peace treaty, which was accomplished and signed on October 26, 1994. This second formal peace agreement between Israel and an Arab country called for joint economic projects, cooperation in the war against terrorism, and sharing of water rights.

Oslo II

On September 28, 1995, Rabin and Arafat signed another interim agreement, known as Oslo II. This committed Israel to withdrawing from six major Palestinian cities on the West Bank. The PA assumed responsibility for civil affairs and security in the cities—mainly preventing terrorist attacks—and civilian control of Palestinian villages. The Israel Defense Forces retained responsibility for the safety of Israelis but withdrew from 27 percent of the West Bank. Now 90 percent of all Palestinians would live under Palestinian government.

At this point the process slowed significantly, for several reasons. First and foremost was the Palestinian Authority's failure to deal with terrorism. In fact, after signing the Oslo accords, more Israelis were killed via Palestinian terrorism than the entire period since the end of the Six Day War. Second, the assassination of Prime Minister Rabin in November 1995 took the negotiations out of the hands of the leader most trusted by Israelis to negotiate with Arafat. Third, the rise in terrorism resulted in the election of Benjamin Netanyahu of the less compromising Likud party.

A Protocol, a Memorandum, and an Agreement

Nevertheless, on January 15, 1997, Netanyahu and Arafat signed the Hebron Protocol: Israel withdrew from Hebron, and the PA recommitted to combating terrorism and preventing incitement of the Palestinian population.

The following year, with President Bill Clinton putting heavy pressure on Israeli Prime Minister Netanyahu, Israel and the PA agreed to the Wye River Memorandum. Israel would withdraw fully from another 13 percent of the West Bank, while the PA would take more verifiable steps to fight terrorism. At this point, the PA had full control of 40 percent of the West Bank, had governmental authority over all major Palestinian cities and most villages, and governed 98 percent of the Palestinian population. The occupation was virtually over.

With Israel's election of Ehud Barak and the labor party, Barak and Arafat signed the Sharm el-Sheikh Agreement on September 5, 1999, reaffirming the commitment of Israel and the Palestinians to the full implementation of all previous agreements. Both sides agreed to tackle the toughest permanent status issues and come to a final status agreement within one year.

President Clinton invited Barak and Arafat to Camp David in July 2000 to hammer out the final agreement. There Barak made various proposals for an end of conflict. He offered a Palestinian state on all of Gaza and 95 percent of the West Bank, provision of land from Israel proper to compensate for the 5 percent Israel would retain from the West Bank, and shared sovereignty of Jerusalem. President Clinton made various bridging proposals—all of which were rejected by Arafat without even offering a counterproposal.

According to PA government representatives, this is when Arafat determined to break his Oslo agreements by turning to violence to achieve his goals. Thus, the hopeful Oslo accords were destroyed by Intifada II. The more conservative elements within Israel had warned against the Oslo agreements, pointing to Arafat's history of duplicity. Particularly worrisome was his "phased strategy," which called for taking what could be had but ultimately obtaining all of historic Palestine, including Israel. Now, after more than three years of violence for most Israelis and Palestinians, the hope for peace lies in ruins.

Despite the failure of the Oslo accords, the peace treaties with Jordan and Egypt have held firm. Although both Arab countries recalled their ambassadors to Israel with the outbreak of the violence of Intifada II, they continue to engage Israel and seek to mediate between Israel and the Palestinians.

Proposals for Peace in the Present

The breakdown of the Oslo agreements has caused many to despair of hope for peace. Nevertheless, several proposals exist at this writing to end the fighting and establish a permanent peace.

The Road Map to Peace

The first of the peace plans now on the table is the so-called Road Map, drafted by the European Union, Russia, the United Nations, and the United

States. After the second Gulf War (2003), President Bush threw his weight behind this proposal and obtained agreement to it by both Israel and the Palestinian Authority.

The Road Map offers the establishment of a Palestinian state in short order, but it requires a new Palestinian leadership to "declare an unequivocal end to violence and terrorism and . . . to arrest, disrupt, and restrain" terrorist groups. It further demands that they begin the "dismantlement of terrorist groups" and the "confiscation of illegal weapons." The Road Map also calls upon Israel to dismantle some settlements that had not been legally approved by the Israeli government.

Both Mahmoud Abbas and Ahmed Qureia, the first and second Palestinian prime ministers, respectively, have accepted the Road Map but refuse to risk civil war with Palestinian terrorists by meeting the security requirements of dismantling the terrorist groups. At this point the Road Map is virtually dead, but the United States continues to cling to it as the only acceptable plan for peace.

Private Peace Proposals

Some Israelis and Palestinians, frustrated by their leadership's inability to come to a settlement, have put forward private peace proposals. The first, The People's Voice initiative, presented by former *Shin Bet* (General Security Service) director Ami Ayalon, and Al-Quds University president Sari Nusseibeh, calls on both sides to make major concessions. Significantly, it proposes a two-state solution and a return to the 1967 borders, with some modifications, and a reinterpretation of the rights of return so that Palestinians can return only to their new state and not to Israel.[9] By January 2004, 150,000 Israelis and 100,000 Palestinians had signed a petition supporting this agreement.

Another private initiative is the Geneva Accord, developed by Yossi Beilin, a former Israeli justice minister, and Yasser Abed Rabbo, a former Palestinian information minister. It has the support of several Nobel Peace Prize winners, including former U.S. President Jimmy Carter; however, the agreement has no official backing from Israel or the PA. First presented on December 1, 2003, it has little chance of being adopted, since it does not end the Palestinian claim to a right of return to Israel proper. Most Israelis feel this agreement sides heavily with the Palestinian position.

Unilateral Disengagement: The Fence

Besides these private initiatives, another proposal, unilateral separation, first articulated by a private citizen, now appears to be finding support as a government proposal. Israeli Dan Shueftan, a senior fellow at Haifa University's Center for National Security Studies, has long argued that a negotiated settlement is virtually impossible.[10] Therefore, he calls on Israel to disengage from the Palestinians unilaterally, a view that is gaining acceptance among the Israeli populace and government. Foundational to a unilateral separation is the building of a boundary between Israel and the West Bank.

Now, after three years of ongoing terrorist attacks, Israel is building a security fence in an attempt to block infiltration by terrorists from the West Bank. The fence that already exists surrounding Gaza provided a model of effective deterrence—not one terrorist attack has been launched from Gaza. Plans calls for the fence to run close to the 1949 Green Line but not strictly so. Some of it will enter some lands conquered in 1967 to provide protection for Israeli settlements.

The Palestinian Authority has objected vociferously to the fence, calling it an "Apartheid Wall." While complaining that the wall separates Palestinian farmers from their farmland and orchards, the biggest grievance is that it appears that Israel is establishing a nonnegotiated final border. Israel claims that this is not the case; the fence is merely being built for security purposes to keep terrorists out.

Nevertheless, in December 2003, first Ehud Olmert, deputy prime minister of Israel, and then Ariel Sharon, prime minister, warned that if the Palestinians will not follow the Road Map to peace, within a few months Israel will take unilateral steps to disengage. Prior to these announcements, the most notable politician to push for unilateral separation was former Labor Prime Minister Ehud Barak. Now it appears that the Likud leadership is adopting the same strategy.

Embracing Shueftan's unilateral disengagement plan requires establishing a border of Israel's choosing while dismantling some Israeli settlements in the West Bank. Although the fence is not said to represent the unilateral border, it could very well become that. Proponents of unilateral separation say that if the Palestinians want to change the border at a later date, they will have to negotiate with Israel. In other words, the Palestinian Authority must become a responsible peace partner. Should Israel disengage unilaterally it would not by any means provide peace, but perhaps it would deter terrorism.

Hope for Peace in the Future

The question remains, is there any hope for peace in the Middle East?

The only certain hope for peace in the Middle East and the world is found in the Bible. In addressing end-time events, the Scriptures foretell two kinds of future peace, the false messiah's peace, and the True Messiah's peace.

The False Messiah's Peace

The tribulation period, discussed in chapter 8, will be a time of war, although a false messiah (also known as the Antichrist) will succeed in making a temporary peace for the world.

How this will occur is not made plain in Scripture. What is known is that the prophet Daniel foretold that this seven-year period would begin when "the prince who is to come" (the false messiah, or Antichrist) makes a covenant with "the many" (Daniel 9:26–27 NASB), most likely referring to many in Israel or to Israel and her neighbors. This treaty, either between Israel and the false messiah or Israel and her neighbors (but brokered by the false messiah), will most likely establish peace in the Middle East for the first half of the Tribulation (three and one-half years).

This peace will hold because no nation in the Tribulation will be powerful enough to wage war with the false messiah (Revelation 13:4). But then the false messiah will break the covenant, commit the abomination of desolation, demand worship as God, and unleash hell on earth (Daniel 9:27; 11:36; 2 Thessalonians 2:4). The point is this: There will indeed be peace in the future, but a temporary peace guaranteed by the future false messiah. (That is not to say any political ruler that might mediate peace between Israel and her Arab neighbors today is the Antichrist; rather, someday in the future, the false messiah will make peace but then bring the worst of wars upon Israel and the world.)

The True Messiah's Peace

True peace will ultimately come not through negotiations but after a final, cataclysmic war, called Armageddon. The true peace will arrive when

Jesus the Messiah comes at the end of the Tribulation to deliver His people Israel, who have come to believe in Him and called for His return (Zechariah 12:10). Then the Messiah Jesus will indeed return, stand on the Mount of Olives, and split it, thereby providing a way of escape for besieged Israel (Zechariah 14:3–4). The New Testament describes the appearance of the Messiah Jesus at that time in magnificent terms:

> *And I saw heaven opened; and behold, a white horse, and He who sat on it is called Faithful and True, and in righteousness He judges and wages war. . . . And He will rule them with a rod of iron; and He treads the wine press of the fierce wrath of God, the Almighty. And on His robe and on His thigh He has a name written, "KING OF KINGS, AND LORD OF LORDS."* (Revelation 19:11, 15–16 NASB)

After Messiah Jesus slays His enemies with the sword of His mouth and casts the future false messiah and his false prophet into the lake of fire, He will take his seat on the throne of David. Then, according to the prophet Isaiah, "of the increase of his government and peace there will be no end" (9:7), and "the wolf will live with the lamb" because "the earth will be full of the knowledge of the LORD" (11:6, 9). No matter how dismal or dire the situation in the Middle East becomes, those who love the Lord Jesus and believe in His Word can look to the future with ultimate joy and expectation, because the true Messiah Jesus will bring permanent peace to Israel, the Arab nations, and the world.

How Christians Can Help

During the first day of a high school course called "War and Peace in the 20th Century," the teacher began by asking the students, including me, whether we believed there would ever be peace in the world. Most of the class said they thought peace would arrive because the world will finally realize the horrors of war. Since I had just become a follower of Jesus, I said that I believed what the Scriptures said—that there would be an end to war, but only when Messiah Jesus returned to establish peace.

It has now been thirty years since I shocked my class with my outrageous (to them) statement. Nevertheless, nothing in the world has convinced me that we can or will ever bring lasting peace. Resolution of the Arab-Israeli conflict, and ultimately world peace, does depend on Messiah Jesus.

Until then, I believe that those of us who follow Jesus have three responsibilities:

- We must pray for peace. This is in obedience to Psalm 122:6: "Pray for the peace of Jerusalem: 'May those who love you be secure.'" Praying for peace is not limited to praying for Israel but for all the people, Jews and Arabs, Israelis and Palestinians, who are suffering because of the violence. If Messiah delays His return, perhaps He will grant a season of peace to His troubled land.
- We must work for peace. Jesus taught, "Blessed are the peacemakers, for they will be called sons of God" (Matthew 5:9). When we work for peace, we reflect our family relationship to God. Just as God is the ultimate peacemaker, reconciling the world to Himself through the death and resurrection of the Messiah Jesus, so as we work for peace we will look like God's children.
- We must proclaim God's peace through Messiah Jesus. Even if we are unsuccessful in reconciling warring peoples, we can announce the reconciliation provided by Messiah's death and resurrection to individual Jews and Arabs, so that they can find peace with God and with each other.

These are our responsibilities until Messiah returns; then He will finally bring peace to Israel, the Arabs, and the world. At that time,

He will judge between the nations,
And will render decisions for many peoples;
And they will hammer their swords into plowshares, and their spears into
    pruning hooks.
Nation will not lift up sword against nation,
And never again will they learn war. (Isaiah 2:4 NASB)

Appendix I
Key Dates

C. 2000 B.C. Abraham receives the Abrahamic covenant; beginning of the patriarchal period.

1446 B.C. The Exodus from Egypt.

1406 The Israelites, under Joshua's leadership, begin the conquest of Canaan.

1010 David becomes second king of Israel.

931 The northern tribes secede from the Davidic dynasty's leadership and the kingdom is divided into Israel (ten northern tribes) and Judah (two southern tribes).

721 The northern kingdom of Israel is conquered and exiled by the Assyrian Empire.

586 The southern kingdom of Judah is conquered and exiled by the Babylonian Empire; Solomon's temple is destroyed.

537   Edict of Cyrus the Great of Persia allowing exiled Jewish people to return.

516   Jewish people who have returned to the land complete the second temple.

331   Alexander the Great conquers the land of Israel; Greek domination begins.

142–63   Jewish autonomy in the land of Israel under the Hasmonean dynasty.

63   Pompey takes control of Judea, bringing Roman domination.

C. 4 B.C.   The birth of Jesus of Nazareth.

A.D. 33   Death and resurrection of Jesus the Messiah.

66–73   The First Jewish Revolt against Rome.

70   The Roman destruction of Jerusalem and the temple.

132–35   The Second Jewish Revolt led by Bar Kokhba against Rome.

C. 135   The Romans rename Judea "Syria Palestina" in an attempt to obliterate the land's Jewish identity.

C. 135–636   Rabbinic Period; Jewish life moves to Galilee.

313–636   Byzantine rule over the land of Israel, then known as Palestine.

630–32   Muhammad conquers Mecca; mass conversions to Islam.

636   Muslims from Arabia conquer the land of Israel.

636–1099   Muslim military rule over the land, based first in Damascus, then Baghdad and Egypt.

646–52   The Qur'an is written.

685   The Dome of the Rock, the oldest surviving mosque, is built on the Temple Mount (called the *Haram El-Sharif* by Muslims), where the two Jewish temples had stood.

1099–1291   The Crusader Period; Europeans make war and maintain limited control of Palestine through a network of fortified castles.

1291–1516   Mamluk rule; Egyptian Muslim military class comes to power in Egypt and dominates Palestine from Egypt.

1517–1917   Ottoman rule; the Turkish Empire attached the land to the province of Damascus and governed it from Istanbul.

1881   Pogroms in Russia motivate many Jewish people to immigrate to America, but some rekindle their hope for restoration to the land of Israel.

1882–1903   First *aliyah* (immigration wave); Jews arrive mainly from Russia.

1894–95   Captain Alfred Dreyfus is convicted of betraying French military secrets, and anti-Semitism erupts in liberal France, leading Theodore Herzl to develop the Zionist idea.

1896   Theodore Herzl publishes *The Jewish State*.

1897   The First International Zionist Congress convened in Basel, Switzerland.

1904–14   Second *aliyah*; Jews arrive mainly from Russia.

1915–16   British and French sign the secret Sykes-Picot Agreement demarcating spheres of influence.

1916   Arab revolt against Ottoman rule begins.

1917   The British issue the Balfour Declaration favoring the establishment of a Jewish national home in Palestine; T. E. Lawrence takes Aqaba; General Allenby takes Jerusalem.

1919–23   Third *aliyah*; Jews arrive mainly from Russia.

1920   Arabs riot against Jews during the Nebi Musa observances. San Remo Conference gives Great Britain the Mandate for Palestine with the intention of facilitating the creation of the Jewish national home.

1921   The British appoint Haj Amin al-Husseini the Grand Mufti of Jerusalem; the Arabs riot against the Jews.

1922   The League of Nations ratifies the British Mandate for Palestine with the intention of facilitating the creation of the Jewish national home. The Churchill White Paper establishes the kingdom of Transjordan on 75 percent of Palestine, leaving only 25 percent for the Jewish national home.

1924–32   Fourth *aliyah*; Jews arrive mainly from Poland.

1929   Orthodox Jews set up a screen to separate women and men at the Western Wall on Yom Kippur. The mufti declares this to be a threat to the Al-Aqsa mosque complex on the Temple Mount and instigates riots in Jerusalem, Hebron, and Safed. Arabs demand an end to Jewish immigration.

1930   The Passfield White Paper severely limits Jewish immigration, following Arabs' demand to end Jewish immigration.

1931   The MacDonald Letter of Clarification reinstates Jewish immigration.

1933   Adolph Hitler becomes Chancellor of Germany.

1933–39   Fifth *aliyah*; Jews arrive mainly from Germany.

1936–39	The mufti instigates riots (called the Arab Revolt) that kill more than five hundred Jews and many more Arabs that refused to carry out his orders for a general strike.
1937	The Peel Commission first proposes partitioning Palestine.
1939	A British white paper severely limits Jewish immigration and repudiates the Balfour Declaration.
1939–45	World War II; six million Jews murdered by Nazi Germany.
1946	The Irgun, a Zionist paramilitary group led by Menachem Begin, bombs the British military and civil headquarters at the King David Hotel.
1947	The United Nations votes to partition Palestine into two states, one Jewish and the other Arab; the Jews accept partition while the Arabs reject it.
1948	The British end their mandate in Palestine.
	The state of Israel declares independence; David Ben-Gurion becomes the first Israeli prime minister.
	Five Arab armies invade Israel.
1948–49	650,000 Arabs flee from Israel and are placed in refugee camps in Arab areas; Israel is victorious in its War of Independence.
1948–52	820,000 Jews flee Arab lands, with 586,000 settling in the new state of Israel.
1949	Jerusalem is divided with the New City under Jewish rule and the Old City under Jordanian rule.
1952–56	Terrorists raid Israel from adjoining Arab states, particularly from Egypt; Israel adopts a retaliation policy.

1956   Israel, allied with Great Britain and France, captures the Sinai in order to clear out terrorist bases and open the Straits of Tiran international waterway to Israeli shipping.

1964   The Palestine Liberation Organization (PLO) is established in Cairo, uniting various Arab terrorist groups under one umbrella with the sworn goal of destroying Israel.

1967   In the Six Day War, Israel defeats Egypt, Syria, and Jordan, gaining control of all Jerusalem, the Golan Heights, the west bank of the Jordan River, and the Gaza Strip.

1970   King Hussein has troops expel the PLO from Jordan.

1972   PLO terrorists murder eleven Israeli athletes at the Munich Olympics.

1973   Egypt and Syria launch a surprise attack against Israel on Yom Kippur but Israel repels them; the Arab oil embargo causes the price of oil to skyrocket.

1975   The United Nations passes a resolution calling Zionism racist.

1976   Israel raids Entebbe Airport in Uganda in a dramatic rescue of 102 hostages taken by terrorists.

1977   Menachem Begin becomes Prime Minister of Israel after years in opposition; Egyptian President Anwar Sadat visits Israel at Begin's invitation.

1979   Israel and Egypt sign the Camp David Peace Agreement resulting in Israel's return of the Sinai Peninsula to Egypt in exchange for peace.

1981   Muslim extremists assassinate Anwar Sadat; the Israeli air force destroys the Iraqi nuclear reactor before it becomes operative.

1982   Israel invades Lebanon in Operation Peace for Galilee and removes the PLO from Lebanon.

1987–93   Widespread rioting, called the Intifada (uprising), erupts in the West Bank and Gaza Strip.

1989   Jewish immigrants begin to arrive from the former Soviet Union, with nearly one million arriving within ten years.

1991   The Gulf War; a U.S.-led coalition drives Iraqi forces out of Kuwait while Israel is attacked by Iraqi Scud missiles; the United Nations repeals its "Zionism is Racism" declaration.

1993   The secret Oslo accords between Israel and the PLO are announced, followed by the signing of the "Declaration of Principles on Interim Self-Government Arrangements for the Palestinians." Prime Minister Yitzhak Rabin and PLO Chairman Yasser Arafat shake hands on the White House lawn.

1994   The Oslo accords begin to be implemented in Gaza and Jericho; Israel and Jordan sign a peace treaty.

1995   A Jewish extremist assassinates Yitzhak Rabin.

1997   Prime Minister Benjamin Netanyahu and Arafat conclude the Hebron Agreement, granting autonomy to the Palestinians in Hebron.

1998   Netanyahu and Arafat conclude the Wye River Plantation Agreement, resulting in another 13 percent of disputed land being placed under the Palestinian Authority.

2000   Israel withdraws from the security zone in Lebanon.

      The Camp David II summit ends in failure as Arafat summarily rejects the significant offer by Prime Minister Ehud Barak.

Ariel Sharon visits the Temple Mount. The second Intifada erupts in September, and Israel responds with military closures of Palestinian cities.

2001   Palestinian suicide bombers kill and maim Jewish civilians; Ariel Sharon is elected Prime Minister of Israel.

On September 11, Islamic terrorists hijack airplanes and use them as flying missiles, destroying the World Trade Center and parts of the Pentagon; the United States launches Operation Enduring Freedom in Afghanistan.

2002   On June 24, United States President George W. Bush presents his vision of peace in the Middle East, calling for a Palestinian state and the reform of the Palestinian Authority including a new leadership not tainted by terrorism.

2003   The United States releases the "Road Map" plan for peace.

Mahmoud Abbas becomes first Palestinian prime minister on April 29; resigns on September 6. Ahmed Qureia becomes second Palestinian prime minister.

Appendix II
United States Policy Toward Israel

The United States, even while trying to bring a peaceful resolution to the Arab-Israeli conflict, has maintained strong support for the state of Israel. As a result, periodically questions arise regarding whether U.S. support is appropriate. Let's address some of these questions.

Is not the U.S. support of Israel against its own interests?

As a matter of fact, U.S. support of Israel has not jeopardized relations with the Arab world. The United States has a deep and longstanding relationship with the Arab states. Those states need U.S. military and political support, as seen in the leading role played by the U.S. in the 1991 Gulf War. Moreover, several Arab states, such as Egypt, Kuwait, and Saudi Arabia, are threatened by Islamic extremists, so they rely on U.S. support. Some of these Arab nations need the United States as a market for their oil, and therefore they are committed to strong relations with the United States. The U.S. support of Israel has not hindered these strong relationships.

The United States has always supported nations like Israel that are democratic, have a free press, and maintain an independent judiciary. It's in America's interest to support a country that battles worldwide terror. In fact, Israel is the United States' most strategic ally in the volatile Middle East.

Did not the United States' support of Israel cause the September 11 terrorist attacks?

In the aftermath of the horrific attacks against the United States by Islamic terrorists, the Al-Qaeda leader, Osama bin Laden, issued statements tying that terrorist group's actions to the U.S. support of Israel. As a result, people on both ends of the U.S. political spectrum began to call for the United States to cease supporting Israel. They asserted that this response to the terror attacks would bring an end to Islamic terror, since the terrorists would no longer have a reason to attack.

This contention misunderstands the cause of the terror attacks. Osama bin Laden and radical Islam do not hate and oppose the United States because of its support for Israel. Rather, their opposition stems from their belief that the United States and its allies in the Middle East, which not only include Israel but also Saudi Arabia and Egypt, stand in the way of the establishment of radical Islam in their region.

Bin Laden and other Islamic extremists are radically opposed to American values such as democracy, modernism, freedom, globalism, and diversity. In fact, prior to 9/11, bin Laden's great complaint against the United States was the stationing of U.S. troops in Saudi Arabia after the first Gulf War. Only after the United States launched the war on terror in response to the 9/11 attacks did he champion the Palestinian cause in a blatant attempt to win support from the "Arab street."

Former Prime Minister Benjamin Netanyahu, in his address to the United States House of Representatives Government Reform Committee in the days after the 9/11 attacks, said it well: "The soldiers of militant Islam do not hate the West because of Israel; they hate Israel because of the West—because they see it as an island of Western democratic values in a Moslem-Arab sea of despotism. That is why they call Israel the Little Satan, to distinguish it clearly from the country that has always been and will always be the Great Satan—the United States of America."[1]

Does not the United States maintain a double standard in its relationship with Israel, as compared to Iraq and other nations?

The United States invaded Iraq in 2003 and removed the regime of Saddam Hussein because the U.S. believed that Hussein had the beginning of a nuclear weapons program and had been in defiance of seventeen United Nations resolutions since the end of the Gulf War. Yet Israel does indeed already unofficially have nuclear weapons and is in defiance of many UN resolutions. Why does the United States maintain such a bold-faced double standard?

This question, frequently posed by opponents of Israel, betrays a lack of understanding of the United Nations and international treaties. With respect to United Nations Security Council resolutions, the UN distinguishes between "chapter six resolutions," which are nonbinding, and "chapter seven resolutions," which are binding and include the potential of military force to compel compliance. While Iraq defied seventeen chapter seven resolutions, none of the resolutions rejected by Israel during the Arab-Israeli conflict comes under chapter seven. They are all non-binding chapter six resolutions, and no penalty has ever been assessed by the United Nations. By imposing sanctions against Iraq but not Israel, the UN was simply following its own rules. The same is true for the U.S. use of force to compel Iraqi compliance.

With regard to Israel possessing nuclear weapons, Israel never signed the Nuclear Non-Proliferation Treaty. As with any treaty, governments are free not to sign. However, any nation that does sign will receive international civilian help in developing nuclear power for nonmilitary purposes. According to international law, signatories may not then secretly use that aid to develop nuclear weapons. Iraq and other nations did, in fact, attempt to do this—Israel did not. Being a nuclear power, as Israel is, does not in and of itself constitute a breach of international law.[2]

United States support of Israel is consistent with the values of this country despite the accusations leveled. The United States supports Israel because it is indeed an island of democracy in a sea of despotism. For many Americans, there is an even more compelling reason. That is, based on the Abrahamic covenant, God will bless those who bless Israel and curse those who do not (Genesis 12:3). For the United States to maintain God's blessing, it is essential to maintain the strong alliance with Israel.

Notes

Chapter 1—The Vanishing Peace

1. *Intifada* is Arabic for "uprising." From 1987–93, Palestinians engaged in widespread violence against Israel. Initially led by teens throwing stones, the uprising gradually grew more violent, but it did not reach the levels of the second uprising that began in 2000. Now known as Intifada II, Israelis have called it the *Terror Intifada* and Palestinians have called it the *Al-Aqsa Intifada*.

2. Ben Barber, "Clinton Ignored Arafat's Offenses," *Washington Times,* April 10, 2002.

3. Efraim Karsh, *Arafat's War* (New York: Grove Press, 2003), 149–50.

4. Itamar Rabinovich, *Waging Peace* (New York: Farrar, Strauss, and Giroux, 1999), 104.

5. Khalil Osman, "Palestinians Want New Intifada as Camp David II Ends Without Deal After 15 Days," *Crescent International,* August 1–15, 2000.

6. Israelis and Arabs have interpreted UN resolution 242,which changed Israel's borders, in different ways. Israelis believe it only requires them to give up some of the lands taken in the 1967 Six Day War and allows for new defensible borders to be drawn. The Arab states believe that the resolution calls for a return to the 1949 armistice lines. This will be discussed in Chapter 12.

7. "President William J. Clinton Statement of the Middle East Peace Talks at Camp David;" July 25, 2000, transcript, the White House, Washington, D.C. http://www.yale.edu/lawweb/avalon/mideast/mid027.htm

Chapter 2—Intifada II: Armed Conflict in the Middle East

1. Afterward, the Israel Defense Forces investigation concluded that the child was struck by Palestinian gunmen, not Israeli troops. The German ARD television network

concluded in its investigative documentary "Three Bullets and a Child" that Mohammed al-Dura was not killed by IDF gunfire. Rather, the Palestinians arranged a well-staged production of his death. See Amnon Lord, "Who Killed Muhammad al-Dura? Blood Libel—Model 2000," *Jerusalem Letters/Viewpoints,* July 15, 2002, Jerusalem Center for Public Affairs, http://www.jcpa.org/jl/vp482.htm. Also see Joshua Muravchik, *Covering the Intifada* (Washington, D.C.: Washington Institute for Near East Policy, 2002), 15–17, in which Muravchik concludes, "Because the Palestinian hospital where [Muhammad] and his father were taken claimed to have recovered not a single one of the roughly two dozen bullets that hit the two, it will never be known which side's fire killed [Muhammad]."

2. "PA TV Broadcasts Call for Killing Americans," Middle East Media Research Institute, Special Dispatch Series, no. 138, October 14, 2000.

3. Some media identify these terrorists with the inappropriate phrase "suicide bombers." The phrase is incorrect because the bombers' primary goal is not to kill themselves (which is suicide), but to murder as many Israelis as possible (which is homicide). That is why President George Bush and his spokesmen, as well as Secretary of State Colin Powell and Fox News Channel, all use the phrase "homicide bombers."

4. "Palestinian Ambulance Driver Caught Transporting Bomb," *Jerusalem Post,* March 27, 2002; "Suicide Bomber Found in Ambulance," *Jerusalem Post,* March 27, 2002.

5. "Arafat to Barak: Go to Hell!" *Jerusalem Post,* October 23, 2000.

Chapter 3—Understanding Intifada II

1. Nina Gilbert and Lamia Lahoud, "Ben-Ami: Rajoub Said Sharon Temple Mount Visit Would Pose No Problem," *Jerusalem Post,* October 4, 2000.

2. Avishai Margalit, "The Middle East: Snakes and Ladders," *The New York Review of Books,* May 17, 2001.

3. Quoted in Marshall Roth, "Did Sharon Spark the Riots?" May 7, 2001, http://www.aish.com/jewishissues/middleeast/Did_Sharon_Spark_the_Riots$.asp.

4. Lamia Lahoud, "PA Minister: Intifada Planned Since July," *Jerusalem Post,* March 4, 2001.

5. "Which Came First—Terrorism or 'Occupation'?" Israel Ministry of Foreign Affairs web site; http://www.mfa.gov.il/mfa/go.asp?MFAH0ldc0.

6. Letter from George Mitchell and Warren Rudman to ADL Director Abraham Foxman, May 11, 2001, cited in Mitchell Bard, *Myths and Facts: A Guide to the Arab-Israeli Conflict* (Chevy Chase, MD: AICE, 2001), 262.

7. Stephen Schwebel, *American Journal of International Law* 84 (1990): 72.

8. Eugene Rostow, "Resolved; Are the Settlements Legal?" *New Republic,* October 21, 1991, 14.

9. Arafat's terrorist activities and philosophy are chronicled in Barry Rubin and Judith Colp Rubin, *Yasir Arafat: A Political Biography* (New York: Oxford Univ. Press, 2003). See also Barry Rubin, "Yasir Arafat: Mystery Inside an Enigma," *Chronicle of Higher Education,* September 5, 2003.

10. Yasir Arafat, "The Palestinian Vision of Peace," *New York Times,* February 3, 2002.

11. As cited in *CyberAlert,* web magazine of the Media Research Center, March 15, 2002, http://www.mediaresearch.org/cyberalerts/2002/cyb20020315.asp.

12. "Jenin Camp Is a Scene of Devastation but Yields No Evidence of Massacre," *Washington Post*, April 16, 2002.

13. Janine Zacharia, "Powell: No Evidence of Massacre," *Jerusalem Post*, April 25, 2002.

14. Matthew Guttman, "Human Rights Watch: No Evidence of Massacre in Jenin," *Jerusalem Post*, April 28, 2002.

15. Agence France-Presse on April 28 reported the conclusion of Maj. David Holley, a British military adviser to Amnesty International, who told the news agency that he did not see "any evidence of a massacre. The Israeli army was fighting against some desperate [Palestinian] fighters here." The next day the *Boston Globe* reported, "Palestinian Authority allegations appear to be crumbling under the weight of eyewitness accounts from Palestinian fighters who participated in the battle and camp residents who remained in their homes until the final hours of the fighting. . . . All said they were allowed to surrender or evacuate." Charles A. Radin and Dan Ephron, "Claims of Massacre Go Unsupported by Palestinian Fighters," *Boston Globe*, April 29, 2002.

16. Joshua Muravchik, *Covering the Intifada* (Washington, D.C.: Washington Institute for Near East Policy, 2003), 115.

Chapter 4—The Land of Israel: From Roman to British Rule

1. For an expanded treatment of Jewish life in this period, see Gedaliah Alon, *The Jews in Their Land in the Talmudic Age*, trans. Gershon Levi (Cambridge, MA: Harvard Univ. Press, 1984).

2. Carl Hermann Voss, *The Palestinian Problem Today* (Boston: Beacon, 1953), 13, as quoted in Joan Peters, *From Time Immemorial* (New York: Harper & Row, 1984), 157.

3. Peters, *From Time Immemorial*, 157–59.

4. Ibid., 159.

5. Ibid.

6. Mark Twain, *The Innocents Abroad* (New York: Penguin Putnam, 1980), 360.

7. Ibid., 454–55.

8. Howard M. Sachar, *A History of Israel from the Rise of Zionism to Our Time*, 2nd ed. (New York: Knopf, 1996), 24, 167.

9. Peters, *From Time Immemorial*, 155–56. See also Arieh L. Avneri, *The Claim of Dispossession* (New Brunswick, NJ: Transaction Books, 1984), 16.

10. Ibid., 156.

11. Ibid., 157.

12. Ibid., 198–99.

13. Ibid., 197.

Chapter 5—The Return to Zion

1. *Encyclopaedia Britannica* (Chicago: Encyclopaedia Britannica, 2002), s.v. "Zionism."

2. Walter Laqueur and Barry Rubin, eds., *The Israel-Arab Reader*, 5th rev. ed. (New York: Penguin, 1995), 19.

3. Daniel Patrick Moynihan, the United States representative to the UN at the time, said, "The United States . . . does not acknowledge, it will not abide by, it will never acquiesce in this infamous act."

4. Alan Dershowitz, *Chutzpah* (Boston: Little Brown, 1991), 241.

5. A false charge, leveled since the Middle Ages, that Jewish people murdered Christian children and used their blood to make Passover matzo.

6. An acronym from the Hebrew words of Isaiah 2:5: "Come, O house of Jacob."

7. Chaim Weizmann, *Trial and Error* (New York: Harper, 1949), 43.

8. Laqueur and Rubin, *The Israel-Arab Reader,* 16.

9. An example of the way Weizmann persuaded Balfour occurred once when Balfour suggested to Weizmann that another land might be suitable for the Jewish people. Weizmann responded, "Mr. Balfour, supposing I were to offer you Paris instead of London, would you take it?" Balfour replied, "But Dr. Weizmann, we have London." "That is true," Weizmann said. "But we had Jerusalem when London was a marsh." Barbara W. Tuchman, *Bible and Sword* (New York: Ballantine, 1984), 314–15.

10. Lord Shaftsbury had influenced a number of political leaders with his biblical understanding of the Jewish people. See Tuchman, *Bible and Sword,* 175–207; 311–12.

11. Tuchman, *Bible and Sword,* 311.

12. Laqueur and Rubin, *The Israel-Arab Reader,* 15.

13. Tuchman, *Bible and Sword,* 328.

14. Letter to the editor, *London Times,* July 23, 1937.

15. Laqueur and Rubin, *The Israel-Arab Reader,* 41.

16. Yehoshua Porath, *The Emergence of the Palestinian-Arab National Movement, 1918–29* (London: Frank Cass, 1974), 112–14.

17. Howard M. Sachar, *A History of Israel from the Rise of Zionism to Our Time,* 2nd ed. (New York: Knopf, 1996), 190.

18. See David Wyman, *The Abandonment of the Jews* (New York: Random, 1990). Most Jews who attempted to flee Nazism faced closed doors, including those aboard the refugee ships *The St. Louis* and *The Strumer.*

19. For documentation of the world's passivity, see Arthur Morse, *While Six Million Died* (New York: Overlook, 1998 reprint) and Wyman, *The Abandonment of the Jews.*

Chapter 6—The Birth of Israel

1. Photograph of Israel's Declaration of Independence, trans. Jewish National Council, *Encyclopedia Judaica* (Jerusalem: Keter, 1971), 5:1453–54.

2. Literally "Immigration B," but the phrase could be defined as "Plan B."

3. The seven nations approving the report were Canada, Czechoslovakia, Guatemala, the Netherlands, Peru, Sweden, and Uruguay. The dissenting minority report came from India, Iran, and Yugoslavia. (Australia abstained in the vote.)

4. For the most thorough and readable history of the conflict, beginning with the partition vote and ending after the 1948 Israeli War of Independence, see Larry Collins and Dominic Lapierre, *O Jerusalem!* (New York: Simon & Schuster, 1972).

5. Walter Laqueur and Barry Rubin, eds., *The Israel-Arab Reader,* 5th rev. ed. (New York: Penguin, 1995), 107–9.

6. Current revisionist historians erroneously claim that Israel held the strategic advantage. For example, see Baylis Thomas, *How Israel Was Won* (Lanham, MD: Lexington, 1999), 81. These arguments and many other spurious claims are effectively rebutted by Efraim Karsh, *Fabricating Israel's History* (London: Frank Cass, 2000).

7. Howard M. Sachar, *A History of Israel* (New York: Knopf, 1996), 333.

8. Benny Morris, *Righteous Victims* (New York: Vintage, 2001), 214, 204.

9. Sachar, *A History of Israel,* 335.

10. Efraim Karsh, "Were the Palestinians Expelled?" *Commentary* 110 (July/August 2000): 29–34.

11. Sachar, *A History of Israel,* 353.

Chapter 7—Growing Pains

1. "Arab Asks British [to] Curb Terrorist," *New York Times,* February 19, 1947, 12.

2. "Interview with David Ben Gurion," *New York Herald Tribune,* April 28, 1963.

3. Michael Oren, *Six Days of War* (New York: Oxford Univ. Press, 2002), 92.

4. Howard M. Sachar, *A History of Israel* (New York: Knopf, 1996), 633.

5. Mark Tessler, *A History of the Israeli-Palestinian Conflict* (Bloomington, IN.: Indiana Univ., 1994), 393.

6. Ibid; Sean Anderson and Stephen Sloan, *Historical Dictionary of Terrorism* (Metuchen, NJ: Scarecrow Press, 1995), 268.

7. Chaim Herzog, *The Arab-Israeli Wars* (New York: Vintage, 1984), 149.

8. Arthur Goldberg, speech to American Israel Public Affairs Committee Policy Conference, May 8, 1973, as quoted in Mitchell Bard, *Myths and Facts: A Guide to the Arab-Israeli Conflict* (Chevy Chase, MD: AICE, 2001), 98.

9. "An Oppressive Foreign Ruler," *Beirut Daily Star,* June 12, 1974, as quoted in Bard, *Myths and Facts,* 98.

10. For an excellent review of Israel's improvement of Palestinian lives under the occupation, see Efraim Karsh, "What Occupation?" *Commentary* 114:1 (July-August 2002), 46–51.

11. The operation was directed by Yonatan Netanyahu, whose brother Benjamin would later become prime minister.

12. Oren, *Six Days of War,* 86.

13. Avner Cohen, "The Last Nuclear Moment," *New York Times,* October 6, 2003.

14. This and other peace initiatives will be explained in greater detail in chapter 15, "Is Peace Possible?"

Chapter 8—Israel in the Center of History and Prophecy

1. Gail Lichtman, "Beating the Odds: Why Jews Win So Many Nobel Prizes," *Jerusalem Post,* May 11,1997.

2. The *personal* promises God gave to Abraham included a great name, vast wealth, and abundant spiritual blessing for himself. The life of Abraham as recorded in Scripture confirms that these promises were fulfilled. Significantly, the *national* promise of a future land called it an "everlasting possession." The *universal* promise would be that through Abraham the whole world would be blessed through Messiah (Genesis 12:3).

3. Many Bible scholars call this "The Palestinian Covenant." However, since the use of the term "Palestine" is part of the political dispute today and never used in the Bible to describe the land of Israel, it is best to rename this promise from God the "Land Covenant."

4. The foretold descendant from "the stump of Jesse" and "the house of David" is announced in Isaiah 11:1,10; 16:5; Jeremiah 23:5; 30:9; 33:15–17; Ezekiel 34:23–24; 37:24–28; Hosea 3:4–5; and Amos 9:11–15.

5. The Talmud, Nedarim 49b.

Chapter 9—Militant Islam and the Arab–Israeli Conflict

1. George W. Braswell Jr., *What You Need to Know About Islam and Muslims* (Nashville: Broadman Holman, 2000), 19.

2. Islam was defeated in 732 by Charles Martel at the Battle of Tours, thereby keeping Islam from spreading through western Europe.

3. According to a June 2002 poll taken by the Palestinian research organization The Jerusalem Media and Communications Center, 71 percent of Palestinians support terrorist attacks against Israeli civilians and 68 percent support suicide bombings. Significantly, more than half (51 percent) also believe the end result of the conflict should be the liberation of all "historic Palestine," which would demand the end of the state of Israel (report in *Jerusalem Post,* June 21, 2002).

4. "Arafat Urges Jihad Against Israel," *Yediot Ahronot,* October 23, 1996.

5. Evelyn Gordon, "Zissman: Arafat Violating Accord Through Speeches," *Jerusalem Post,* August 3, 1995.

6. "The Weapons of Jihad," *Parade,* June 25, 1995.

7. "Bombers Gloating in Gaza as They See Goal Within Reach: No More Israel," *New York Times,* April 4, 2002.

8. Arutz Sheva News Service, February 27, 1996.

9. Arafat's speech to a "Fatah" conference, November 15, 1998; as cited in Memri Special Dispatch Series, no. 13, November 17, 1998.

10. *Al-Arabi,* June 24, 2001, trans. Middle East Media Research Institute.

11. Robert S. Wistrich, "Muslim Anti-Semitism: A Clear and Present Danger" (New York: The American Jewish Committee, 2003), 6–7.

12. As cited in Wistrich, "Muslim Anti-Semitism," 8. This is a restatement of the outrageous medieval ritual murder charge that Jews use the blood of Gentiles to make Passover matzo.

13. Umayma Jalahma, "The Jewish Vampires," *Al Riyadh,* March 12, 2002.

14. "The Israeli authorities infected by injection 300 Palestinian children with the HIV virus during the years of the Intifada," Nabil Ramlawi, PLO Representative to the

UN in Geneva; as quoted in *Jerusalem Post*, March 17, 1997. The poisoning charge was published in *Yediot Ahronot*, June 25, 1997.

15. *Hayat Al-Jadidah,* December 24, 2001; Al Jazeera television, January 13, 2002.

16. Reuters News Service, November 11, 1999.

17. Jonathan Rauch, *National Journal,* June 30, 2003.

18. Wistrich, "Muslim Anti-Semitism," 16–19.

19. Ibid., 16. Abbas also alleged the Zionists were in league with the Nazis in his 1983 book entitled *The Other Side: The Secret Relationship between Nazism and the Zionist Movement.*

20. Palestinian Authority Television, August 3, 2001; trans. Middle East Media Research Institute, August 7, 2001.

21. Bernard Lewis, *Semites and Anti-Semites* (New York: Norton, 1986), 259.

22. Rauch, *National Journal,* June 27, 2003.

Chapter 10—Whose Land? A Biblical Perspective

1. Sholom Alechem, *Fiddler on the Roof,* adapted as a play by Joseph Stein, Jerry Block, and Sheldon Harnick (New York: Crown, 1972), 30.

2. The order of the books in the English Bible is different from the order in the Hebrew Bible. First and 2 Chronicles close the canon of the Hebrew Bible and are considered one book.

3. *Torah* is the Hebrew word for Law, and refers to the Pentateuch, i.e., Genesis through Deuteronomy.

4. Rashi, "Bereishis," *The Metsudah Chumash/Rashi,* vol. 1, trans. Avrohom Davis (Hoboken, NJ: Ktav, 1993), 1.

5. I am indebted to Stuart Dauermann, rabbi of Ahavat Zion Messianic Synagogue in Beverly Hills, California, for this word study and the insights into the meaning of the phrase *min olam v'ad olam.*

6. See also 1 Chronicles 29:10; Psalm 41:13; 106:48; Daniel 2:20; Nehemiah 9:5.

7. John Piper, "Land Divine?" *World,* May 11, 2002.

8. This passage is not talking about a transfer of God's promises from Israel to the church but rather the transfer of leadership of the Jewish people to the believing remnant. Note that two verses later (verse 45) Jesus identifies the Jewish leaders as the subject of this parable, not the nation of Israel as a whole. Cf. David L. Turner, "Matthew 21:43 and the Future of Israel," *Bibliotheca Sacra* 159 (January–March 2002): 46–61.

9. Jesus' point is that faith, not Jewish descent, is the only guarantee to a place in the kingdom. He is not in any way declaring the removal of the national promises from the Jewish people to someone else.

10. Piper, "Land Divine?" *World.*

11. Note that Romans 11:28 does not really speak of enmity with God but with believers in Messiah.

12. Colin Chapman, *Whose Promised Land?* 3rd ed. (Oxford: Lion, 1992), 243.

13. As quoted in Calvin E. Shenk, "The Middle Eastern Jesus: Messianic Jewish and Palestinian Christian Understandings," *Missiology* 29, no. 4 (October 2001): 408.

14. Ibid., 403.

15. In an interview in *Die Welt* (a German newspaper), as quoted in *Moment,* April 2001, 31.

16. Benny Morris, "Camp David and After: An Exchange," in *The New York Review of Books,* June 13, 2002.

17. Abraham Joshua Heschel, *Israel: An Echo of Eternity* (New York: Farrar, Straus, and Giroux, 1969), 66.

Chapter 11—Justice and Only Justice: The Case for Israel

1. Naim Stifan Ateek, *Justice and Only Justice* (Maryknoll, NY: Orbis, 1989), 115.

2. Abraham Joshua Heschel, *Israel: An Echo of Eternity* (New York: Farrar, Straus, and Giroux, 1969), 60–67.

3. Ben Halpern, *The Idea of the Jewish State* (Cambridge, MA: Harvard Univ. Press, 1969), 201. Winston Churchill's white paper (see page 73) called for and led to Transjordan, an Arab state in eastern Palestine.

4. Howard M. Sachar, *A History of Israel* (New York: Knopf, 1996), 129.

5. Paul Johnson, *A History of the Jews* (New York: Perennial, 1988), 530. For the entire discussion of the differing approaches to negotiations and compromise among Israelis and Palestinians, see pp. 529–33.

6. According to a June 2003 survey conducted by the Tami Steinmetz Center for Peace Research, 78 percent of surveyed Israeli Jews support the "Road Map" plan for peace which leads to a two-state solution; see http://www.ipforum.org/serial.cfm?rid=877.

7. David Shipler, *Arab and Jew: Wounded Spirits in a Promised Land* (New York: Penguin, 2002), 236.

8. For example, the illegality of the partition is claimed by asserting that although Jewish settlement only consisted of 7 percent of Palestine at the time of partition, the Jewish state was granted 60 percent of the land in Palestine (cf. Colin Chapman, *Whose Promised Land?* 3rd ed. [Oxford: Lion, 1992], 50.) On the other hand, statistics are tricky. Israel supporters point out that (1) most of the land was government owned (then the British Mandatory government) and Arab land ownership was only 3 percent, (2) almost two-thirds of the land given for the Jewish state was the infertile Negev Desert, and (3) the largest part of historic Palestine had already been given to the Arabs in 1922 to create Transjordan. If this land is factored into the equation, then the Jewish section in the partition was about 20 percent of historic Palestine and the Arab sections were 80 percent.

9. Yasser Arafat, "Address to the UN General Assembly," Walter Laqueur and Barry Rubin, eds., *The Israel-Arab Reader,* 5th rev. ed. (New York: Penguin, 1995), 331.

10. Rosemary Radford Ruether and Herman J. Ruether, *The Wrath of Jonah,* 2nd ed. (Minneapolis: Fortress, 2002), 89.

11. Abbas' denial of the Holocaust is in Mahmoud Abbas, "The Other Side: The Secret Relationship Between Nazism and the Leadership of the Zionist Movement," (Ph.D. diss., Moscow Oriental College, 1983), as cited in Yael Yehoshua, "Abu Mazen: A Political Profile," Middle East Media Research Institute, special report 15, April 29, 2003.

12. Raul Hilberg, *The Destruction of the European Jews* (New York: Holmes and Meier, 1985), 338–39.

13. Ateek, *Justice and Only Justice,* 116; cf. 104.

Chapter 12—Justice and Only Justice: The Case for Palestine

1. David Shipler, *Arab and Jew: Wounded Spirits in a Promised Land* (New York: Penguin, 2002), 150.
2. Ibid., 144.
3. Bernard Lewis as cited by Shipler, *Arab and Jew,* 143.
4. Naim Stifan Ateek, *Justice and Only Justice* (Maryknoll, NY: Orbis, 1989), 103.
5. The Problem of Palestine," political document, the Arab Office of Jerusalem, in Walter Laqueur and Barry Rubin, eds., *The Israel-Arab Reader,* 5th rev. ed. (New York: Penguin, 1995), 80.
6. Cited in "Palestinians and Jews Spar over Archaeological Claims," *Maranatha Christian Journal,* November 13, 2000, http://www.mcjonline.com/news/00b/20001113a.htm.
7. "Who Are the Palestinians?" http://www.dutchpal.com/pal/history-03.html.
8. Laqueur and Rubin, *The Israel-Arab Reader,* 15.
9. Edward Said, *The Question of Palestine* (New York: Vintage, 1992), 15–16.
10. Cecilia Toledo, "Israel: Five Decades of Pillage and Ethnic Cleansing," at the Marxism Alive web site, http://www.marxismalive.org/israelfive3.html.
11. Said, *The Question of Palestine,* 48.
12. Ateek, *Justice and Only Justice,* 122.
13. Yasser Arafat, "Address to the UN General Assembly," in Laqueur and Rubin, *The Israel-Arab Reader,* 331.
14. Ateek, *Justice and Only Justice,* 29.
15. Eric Reichenberger, spokesman for Students Allied for Freedom and Equality, quoted in Daniel Treiman, "Students Rap Israel at Divestment Parley," *The Forward,* October 18, 2002.
16. Yasir Arafat, "The Palestinian Vision of Peace," *New York Times,* February 3, 2002.
17. Daniel Pipes, "The Muslim Claim to Jerusalem," *Middle East Quarterly* (September 2001).
18. As cited in Pipes, "The Muslim Claim to Jerusalem" *Middle East Quarterly.*
19. Ibid.
20. Ibid.
21. Sura 5:20–21 reads, "And [remember] when Moses said to his people: 'O my people, call in remembrance the favour of God unto you, when he produced prophets among you, made kings, and gave to you what He had given to any other among the peoples. O my people, enter the Holy Land which God has assigned unto you, and turn not back ignominiously, for then will ye be overthrown, to your own ruin.'" Abdul Hadi Palazzi, "What the Qur'an Really Says," *Viewpoint* Winter, 1998.
22. Sura 17:104 reads, "And thereafter, We [Allah] said to the Children of Israel: 'Dwell securely in the Promised Land. And when the last warning will come to pass, we will gather you together in a mingled crowd.'" Palazzi, "What the Qur'an Really Says."
23. Issaev has said, "We Uzbeks rejoice that the Jewish people has returned to the land of Israel after 2,000 years of exile, in fulfillment of both biblical and Qur'anic prophecies." Quoted in Asher Eder, "Mauritania Not the Third Muslim Nation to Establish Diplomatic Relations with Israel," http://www.rb.org.il/Islam-Israel/commentary/islam21.htm.

24. S. D. Goitein, *Jews and Arabs: Their Contact Through the Ages* (New York: Schocken, 1964), 21. Cf. Shipler, *Arab and Jew,* 134.

25. This is the contention of Joan Peters' controversial book *From Time Immemorial,* which Norman G. Finkelstein has labeled a "fraud" [cf. *Blaming the Victims* ed. Edward Said and Christopher Hitchens (New York: Verso, 2001), 33–69]. While Daniel Pipes acknowledges Peters' tendentious style, questionable linguistics, and eccentric documentation, he also states that no "reviewer has so far succeeded in refuting" Peters' central thesis that "a substantial immigration of Arabs took place during the first half of the twentieth century." Daniel Pipes, "Response to Yehoshua Porath's 'Mrs. Peters's Palestine,'" *The New York Times Review of Books,* January 16, 1986: 21–22.

26. Thus, Arabs representing Palestine at the 1919 Paris Peace Conference adopted this resolution: "We consider Palestine as part of Arab Syria, as it has never been separated from it at any time. We are connected with it by national, religious, linguistic, natural, economic and geographical bonds." Mitchell G. Bard, *Myths and Facts: A Guide to the Arab-Israeli Conflict* (Chevy Chase, MD: AICE, 2001), 26.

27. Bard, *Myths and Facts,* 26.

28. As Benjamin Netanyahu wrote, "Spain never ceased to be the Spaniard's homeland—notwithstanding Moorish Arab attachment to the land and the creation of an impressive Arab civilization there. . . . What the Spanish achieved after eight centuries, the Jews achieved after twelve—but the principle is identical." Benjamin Netanyahu, *A Place Among the Nations* (New York: Bantam, 1993), 26.

29. Bard, *Myths and Facts,* 162. The total population at partition was 809,000, according to the armistice agreement of 1949, and the Israeli government set the Israeli Arab population at 160,000; thus the number of refugees could not have been more than 650,000.

30. The attack on the village of Deir Yassin (April 9, 1948), often presented as a massacre, was actually carried out by approximately one hundred radicals from Zionist splinter groups. Whatever actually happened there has been lost in myth. The residents of the town were able to inflict forty-one casualties upon the Jewish attackers. Numbers of Arab casualties vary widely, one hundred seven according to Bir Zeit University to two hundred according to the *New York Times* report on the incident. Regardless, the Jewish Agency repudiated the actions taken in the town, expressing its "horror and disgust." The Arab Higher Committee exaggerated the incident, wishing to shock the Arab nations into intervening but only succeeded in prompting further Arab exodus from Palestine.

31. "Is Israel Guilty of Ethnic Cleansing?" in "Refugees Forever," special insert, *Jerusalem Post,* February 21, 2003. For a more scholarly account of the Israeli attempts to have the Arabs of Haifa stay and of the Arab leaders' encouragement to flee, see Efraim Karsh, "Were the Palestinians Expelled? *Commentary* 110, no. 1 (July–August 2000): 29–35.

32. Laqueur and Rubin, *The Israel-Arab Reader,* 15.

33. As cited in Bard, *Myths and Facts,* 37.

34. Alan Dershowitz, *The Case for Israel* (Hoboken, NJ: Wiley and Sons, 2003), 86.

35. Efraim Karsh, "On the Right of Return," in Neal Kozoday, ed., *The Mideast Process* (San Francisco: Encounter, 2002), 128.

36. Bard, *Myths and Facts,* 186–87.

37. Ibid., 98.

38. A phrase used by then–Israeli Ambassador Abba Eban to describe "the crowded and pathetically narrow coastal strip in which so much of Israel's life and population is concentrated"; the strip existed from the 1949 armistice until June 5, 1967.

39. While recognizing the legality of the settlements, many Israelis question their wisdom. There is a broad consensus among Israelis that at least some of the settlements will need to be dismantled as part of a final agreement.

40. Bard, *Myths and Facts,* 45.

41. Dershowitz, *The Case for Israel,* 183.

42. Efraim Karsh, "What Occupation?" *Commentary* 114, no. 1 (July–August 2002): 49.

43. In a broadcast on Jordan television, Arafat told Palestinians immediately after the signing of the Oslo accords that this agreement was simply part of the continuing PLO "phased strategy."

44. Thomas Friedman, "Campus Hypocrisy," *New York Times,* October 16, 2002.

45. Dershowitz, *The Case for Israel,* 5.

Chapter 13—Islam in Prophecy: The Future Islamic Invasion of Israel

1. Yossi Klein Halevi, "The New Patriots," *Jerusalem Report,* November 5, 2001.

2. See Zola Levitt and Thomas McCall, *The Coming Russian Invasion of Israel* (Chicago: Moody, 1974).

3. This discussion is based on the excellent research in Charles H. Dyer, *World News and Bible Prophecy* (Wheaton, IL: Tyndale, 1993), 110–11.

4. Allen Paul Ross, *The Table of Nations in Genesis* (Th.D. diss., Dallas Theological Seminary, 1976), 203.

5. Ibid., 205.

6. Dyer, *World News and Bible Prophecy,* 111.

7. Also known as the Antichrist or the beast.

Chapter 14—The Arab States in Prophecy

1. These three categories are described in Arnold G. Fruchtenbaum, *The Footsteps of the Messiah* (Tustin, CA: Ariel, 1982), 345.

2. Charles H. Dyer, *World News and Bible Prophecy* (Wheaton, IL: Tyndale, 1993), 142.

3. An excellent commentary that maintains this view is John Walvoord's *The Revelation of Jesus Christ* (Chicago: Moody, 1966), 243–67.

4. Louis Goldberg, *Turbulence over the Middle East* (Neptune, NJ: Loizeaux Brothers, 1982), 107; Fruchtenbaum, *Footsteps of the Messiah,* 160–61. For the best technical defense of this view, see Charles H. Dyer, "The Identity of Babylon in Revelation 17–18 (Parts One and Two)," *Bibliotheca Sacra* 144, 145 (1987): 305–16; 433–49.

5. *Babel* is the same word as *Babylon* in the Hebrew.

6. Fruchtenbaum, *The Footsteps of the Messiah,* 354–55.

Chapter 15—Is Peace Possible?

1. Walter Laqueur and Barry Rubin, eds., *The Israel-Arab Reader,* 5th rev. ed. (New York: Penguin, 1995), 678.

2. Howard M. Sachar, *A History of Israel* (New York: Knopf, 1996), 121.

3. Laqueur and Rubin, *The Israel-Arab Reader,* 17.

4. Sachar, *A History of Israel,* 121.

5. Michael B. Oren, *Six Days of War* (New York: Oxford Univ. Press, 2002), 318–21.

6. Connor Cruise O'Brien, *The Siege* (New York: Simon & Schuster, 1986), 504–5.

7. Ibid., 509–10.

8. Ibid., 574.

9. Other principles of the initiative include (1) shared sovereignty of Jerusalem with neither side exercising sovereignty but rather guardianship over holy places; (2) a right of return for Palestinians to the new state of Palestine but not to Israel proper (with compensation from Israel, the International Community, and the Palestinian state); and (3) demilitarizing the Palestinian state.

10. Leslie Susser, "Something Needs to Change," *Jerusalem Report,* October 6, 2003, 14.

Appendix II—United States Policy Toward Israel

1. Benjamin Netanyahu, hearing of the U.S. House of Representatives Government Reform Committee, Washington, D.C., September 20, 2001. Web site of the Israel Ministry of Foreign Affairs, http://www.mfa.gov.il/mfa/go.asp?MFAH0ki30.

2. "Double Standards," *The Economist,* October 10, 2002.

About the Author

Dr. Michael Rydelnik has been Professor of Jewish studies at Moody Bible Institute since 1994. The son of Holocaust survivors, Michael was raised in an Orthodox Jewish home in Brooklyn, New York. He became a follower of Jesus the Messiah as a high school student and has been sharing his faith in the Jewish Messiah ever since then. He was the founding congregational leader of Olive Tree Congregation in Long Island, New York and also served for ten years in the leadership of Chosen People Ministries. Michael graduated with a diploma in Jewish Studies from the Moody Bible Institute, earned his bachelors degree from Azusa Pacific University in Biblical Literature, his Master of Theology from Dallas Theological Seminary in New Testament Literature and Exegesis, and his doctorate in Intercultural Studies from Trinity Evangelical Divinity School. Michael has lectured extensively on the messianic hope of the Hebrew Scriptures, the New Testament teaching regarding human responsibility and the death of Jesus, the Holocaust and the problem of evil, as well as the Arab-Israeli conflict. He has contributed to the Moody Publishers titles *Storm Clouds on the Horizon, Prophecy in Light of Today,* and *A Heart for the City.* Michael and his wife, Eva, live in Chicago, Illinois with their two sons, Zack and Seth, and their two collies, Feivel and Darby.

Since 1894, Moody Publishers has been dedicated to equip and motivate people to advance the cause of Christ by publishing evangelical Christian literature and other media for all ages, around the world. Because we are a ministry of the Moody Bible Institute of Chicago, a portion of the proceeds from the sale of this book go to train the next generation of Christian leaders.

If we may serve you in any way in your spiritual journey toward understanding Christ and the Christian life, please contact us at www.moodypublishers.com.

"All Scripture is God-breathed and is useful for teaching, rebuking, correcting and training in righteousness, so that the man of God may be thoroughly equipped for every good work."
—2 TIMOTHY 3:16, 17

MOODY
PUBLISHERS

THE NAME YOU CAN TRUST®

UNDERSTANDING THE ARAB-ISRAELI CONFLICT TEAM

ACQUIRING EDITOR
Greg Thornton

COPY EDITOR
Jim Vincent

BACK COVER COPY
Elizabeth Cody Newenhuyse

COVER DESIGN
Ragont Design

COVER PHOTOS
Reuters/Ahmed Jadallah,
Reuters/Ronen Lido,
Reuters/Havakuk Levison,
Michael Rydelnik

INTERIOR DESIGN
Ragont Design

PRINTING AND BINDING
Color House Graphics

The typeface for the text of this book is
Berkeley